Infant Feeding

Anatomy of a Controversy 1973–1984

Edited by John Dobbing

With a Foreword by Frank Falkner

Springer-Verlag
London Berlin Heidelberg New York
Paris Tokyo

John Dobbing, DSc, FRCP, FRCPath
Emeritus Professor of Child Growth and Development,
Department of Child Health, University of Manchester, Oxford
Road, Manchester M13 9PT, UK

ISBN 3–540–19514–9 Springer-Verlag Berlin Heidelberg New York
ISBN 0–387–19514–9 Springer-Verlag New York Berlin Heidelberg

British Library Cataloguing in Publication Data
Infant feeding: anatomy of a controversy
    1973–1984.
    1. Babies. Artificial food. Marketing
    I. Dobbing, John, *1922–*
    664′.62′0688
    ISBN 3–540–19514–9

Library of Congress Cataloguing-in-Publication Data
Infant feeding: anatomy of a controversy, 1972–1984 / John Dobbing.
    p.   cm.
    Bibliography: p.
    Includes index.
    ISBN 0–387–19514–9 (U.S.)
    1. Nestlé Alimentana Company.   2. Baby foods industry—Developing
countries.   3. Infants—Developing countries—Nutrition.   4. Infant
formulas—Health aspects.   I. Dobbing, John.
    HD9015.S93N448 1988
    338.7′66462′0917—dc19

Filmset by Wilmaset, Birkenhead, Wirral
Printed and bound in Great Britain at The Bath Press, Avon

2128/3916–543210

Foreword

This book is about a controversy which fascinated the medical and scientific world, as well as national and international health authorities, politicians, religious groups and consumer organisations, for more than 11 years. The controversy often disturbed public opinion, being concerned as it is with nothing less than the life and death of babies. It is a story which is full of confrontations, intrigue and passionately-held opinions, based nevertheless, on a sizeable body of medical science. After countless twists and turns it has some sort of "happy-ending". Yet a great deal remains to be said, as will be seen throughout the account which follows.

As is so often the case, great issues often go unrecognised in their early stages. This particular one began with an article *The Baby Food Tragedy* published in August 1973 in a little-known journal. It was pre-circulated to health professionals, soliciting comments from them so that a public campaign could be launched to draw attention to "a continuing scandal".

The infant food industry was directly accused of having caused a decline in breast-feeding through the inappropriate marketing of breast milk substitutes. The problem was said to be particularly acute in poor under-developed world communities, because illiterate mothers were unable to understand instructions for its use, water was often contaminated, and in order to "stretch" an admittedly expensive product, it was over-diluted. The inevitable result, said the critics of industry, was malnutrition, gastroenteritis and increased infant mortality.

These were very serious charges against companies which had until then been generally considered to provide an important contribution to medical progress and child health. One company was to be particularly singled out: Nestlé SA, the Swiss multinational, with its headquarters in the little lakeside town of Vevey where it was founded more than 120 years ago. Perhaps it became the target because it was the longest established, and served well as a symbol of the whole industry.

At first, the accusations levelled at the Company seemed absurd yet, at the same time, they were so potentially damaging for its reputation that they resulted in a law suit in a Swiss Court. Soon, however, it became apparent that matters were not that simple. This book gives an interesting account of the Bern trial, at which Nestlé sued Swiss activists for libel on the publication of a pamphlet entitled *Nestlé tötet Babys* ("Nestlé Kills Babies"). One of the fascinating features of the law suit was that although the Company won a legal victory, it was itself, rather than the defendants, who appeared to be on trial.

Later the issue was to escalate through a flood of publicity and happenings. Reports, statements, films, investigations, demonstrations, boycotts, followed in close succession. Congressional hearings in Washington, chaired by a well-known political leader, were followed by a series of international meetings under the auspices of the World Health Organization (WHO) and UNICEF, which led to the adoption by the World Health Assembly of an unprecedented international Code.

By this time the controversy had reached a point where even this important involvement of UN agencies failed to bring it to an end. The activists' attacks went on. They began listing a large number of alleged violations by Nestlé and others, and thereby kept the boycott alive. Faced with this inextricable situation, the Swiss Company made an innovative move in Spring 1982: it funded the creation of an independent Infant Formula Audit Commission, chaired by former US Secretary of State, Senator Edmund S. Muskie. The commission was to advise the Company on its procedures for implementing the WHO Code, and to investigate complaints raised by concerned groups or individuals related to its marketing activities in the infant feeding field. The impartial work of the Commission's distinguished members was probably more decisive than any other factor in bringing the conflict to its resolution.

This book does an excellent job of describing the long and eventual controversy. Having myself been an attentive observer throughout, I found in it the explanation for many hitherto unanswered questions, as well as plenty of food for thought. Two things remain foremost in my mind. First, that infant feeding is a highly complex, scientific subject with a mind-boggling mass of inter-related factors, especially when viewed in the multicultural context of the international arena. The book illustrates how vast the problems can become when seen from the particular vantage points of widely disparate interests such as industry, consumer advocates, churches, politicians and journalists. It highlights what strikes me as a remarkable and consistent lack of serious analysis by the activists throughout the controversy. Occasionally, the text implies that industry and Nestlé found themselves unfairly accused. I must say, however, that as a whole, the book appears to me to be restrained, based on historical and scientific facts, and to avoid polemics.

Secondly, I am staggered by the time and resources spent by so many people over these eleven years to achieve the end-result described in the last chapter: arguably the book's best. It is all the more astonishing when it is realised that basically there was never any disagreement on the essential point: every single party involved held the central tenet that breast-feeding is far superior to any other form of feeding during the first months of life.

At the same time, everyone knows that "wars" are extremely costly, and this one was no exception. Yet, I believe some good did come out of it all. The WHO International Code of Marketing of Breast Milk Substitutes gave and continues to give guidance to governments as to how health services, health professionals, industry and consumer groups can work together, in the context of its specific aim "to contribute to the provision of safe and adequate nutrition for infants". Few governments seem to have done very much to implement the code they approved, and some observers have therefore asked whether its formulation was not rather a lot of fuss about little. Such sceptics fail, however, to take into account the usefulness of the controversy as a precedent and the importance of the lessons which have been learned by all concerned.

First of all, Nestlé itself shows that it has gained a much deeper understanding of its role as a leading manufacturer in this sensitive area, having committed its operating companies to respect the aim and principles of the Code to the letter. In this way it has set an example for the entire industry, and this has come to be recognised by some of the Company's severest critics. It is hardly likely, however, that such a Code could have been conceived and born without the efforts of the critics of Industry. Nor should it be forgotten that the good which has come of the Code results from a coming together of the differing points of view of the parties concerned: industry and activists, scientists and government authorities. This could never have been the result had the original, somewhat negative, demands of the critics been accepted blindly.

These very important lessons have their application well beyond the field of infant feeding. They ought to serve as a model for resolving, at a lower cost in terms of energy, resources and emotions, the wider problems caused by poverty, poor nutrition and health care, and lack of hygiene, which threaten the life and future of children in the developing world and elsewhere.

In such a spirit of conciliation the controversy should not be seen as a wasteful experience, and this thought-provoking and honest attempt to describe the experience of industry, through the example of Nestlé, will hopefully contribute to better understanding in the interest of us all.

Berkeley, California   Frank Falkner, MD, FRCP
December 1987

Preface

Throughout a long career in medical scientific research I have constantly been motivated by an interest in the impact of medical science on the more widespread contemporary problems of human beings, as well as by a fascination with my own special scientific subjects. Thus my work on the growth and development of the fetus, of the baby and of the older child, and especially of the brain during this time, has mostly centred on the possible deleterious effects of developmental undernutrition, itself inseparable from the whole ecology of human poverty.

In all of this, and in addition to making one or two minor discoveries, I must confess to having often been temperamentally attracted by the task of trying to correct those whose similar interests have sometimes, in my view, led them away from reasonable scientific truth and proper social application. Thus I must admit to having frequently enjoyed denouncing, as well as creating. Examples have been my reviews, often somewhat polemical, of such diverse topics as the blood–brain barrier, maternal nutrition in pregnancy, early nutrition and later achievement, a cell number/cell size theory of tissue growth and development, and, latterly, of the very great importance (in which I passionately believe) of breast-feeding, in indigent society as elsewhere.

It is scarcely surprising, therefore, that in the last twenty years at least I have keenly followed both the developing scientific background as well as the wider social and commercial context of the "infant food" controversy which is the subject of this book, an interest first stimulated in me in 1966 by a sojourn in Kampala, Uganda. While there I was in close and admiring contact with Dr. Derrick Jelliffe, who was Professor of Paediatrics in Uganda at the time, and with Dr. Roger Whitehead, who was then deputy director of the Medical Research Council Unit next door, investigating infant malnutrition.

Since then the subject has embraced even wider issues still, leading to the famous World Health Organization meetings between 1979 and 1981, which produced the Code of Marketing of Breast Milk Substitutes, which I attended throughout, and which continue to occupy the energies of a wide range of activists, both my kind and those with even firmer roots in the social politics of both Third World and "First" World current affairs.

From what I have written it will now be quite readily appreciated why the subject appeals to me, both scientifically and temperamentally. Here is a topic in which the participants have argued long and loud, pulling no punches, and having recourse to a basis of scientific fact, and sometimes belief, in an area which I have adopted as one of my own.

Until the appearance of this book, almost everything which may be found on the library bookshelves has come from one side of the fence, a side which I have called "activist". I believe that is a misleading name, since I too am an activist, as must anyone be who feels strongly and takes action about something, as well as knowing some of the facts. I have long thought that the time has come when an attempt should be made to put the whole matter in a better perspective. It is one of the purposes of this book to do so, and for the record.

It has been my long-standing belief that the whole foundation of the controversy, commercial or political, is the medical science of the matter. Without that there would be no argument. I also believe that all sides have too often neglected this foundation in their quarrels, especially the lay militants who have so far written nearly all the books and pamphlets; but also, to some extent, the infant food industry itself, which has quite reasonably been more immediately concerned with the impact on their markets. That is why I have given pride of first place to the medical science in this book, and a few words should now be said on this.

Medical science is rarely exclusively factual, concerned as it eventually is with the impenetrable nature of life itself. This does not separate it from other kinds of science, which, at their frontiers, are equally speculative. In other words science must include opinion, but to be of any value that opinion must be based on an honest appraisal of the known "facts", and not on a distortion of them. Now it must be accepted that all scientists distort their facts, since all scientists worth their salt have motivation which guides them, and this applies to even the most "scientific" of endeavours. If science were simply a matter of ascertainable fact, then our task in setting out the medical science of our present subject would be easily accomplished, and would be decisive in the argument.

The best that can honestly be offered is a reasonable interpretation of the few "facts" which are available, and a collation of responsible opinion about them, in a form which the interested reader, whatever his background, can sufficiently assimilate for the purpose of making up his own mind.

Our book is not, however, exclusively an account of the physiology or sociology of infant feeding. It is mainly a history of a world-wide controversy, involving the infant food industry, medical scientists and certain activist movements. All the large manufacturers of breast milk substitutes (as they came to be called) were involved, and prominently the Nestlé Company, with whom I have had most contact. Several prominent medical scientists actively supported one side or another; while those very many people in many countries who followed the leading activists, and lent them support, were mainly ordinary, well-intentioned people. In enormous numbers they are daily appalled by the obscenity of world poverty and the ways in which children, especially, are afflicted by it. It is for them, as well as for paediatricians and other health professionals, including those responsible for organising the health services, that I decided to put this book together.

As I have said earlier, it begins with an account of the medical science, since it is this which is at the heart of the matter. Medical facts, as we shall see, have often been rearranged to serve the requirements of polemics. However, although I feel reasonably qualified to discuss the medical and scientific aspects, I was less confident when it came to things which concern the media, politics, international affairs and public attitudes. This is why I have been fortunate to benefit from the work of two specialists in the art of communication in producing the book. Both had independently studied the history of the controversy, each from their own viewpoint. Maggie McComas is an American business writer and public affairs analyst who first developed an interest in the controversy while conducting research for a study on Europe's consumer movement. Chapters 3 to 7 are based on a report she wrote in 1981. Gabriel Veraldi is a well-known French writer who has long been interested in what in 1958 he first called "l'humanisme technique". In this way the reader is presented with perspectives from the New, as well as the Old World, and this is quite appropriate to an affair which unfolded on both sides of the Atlantic.

My hope is that, as well as redressing the balance on the library shelves on which there is mainly a one-sided representation at present, our book may also interest newcomers to the subject, including those with a lay, as well as a professional, interest in the way a free society handles these sorts of problem, which surely concern us all.

I wish to thank my fellow contributors; my publishers; and the Nestlé Company, who have readily opened their doors, as well as their filing cabinets, to assist us in our task, even when they have occasionally not agreed with us.

St Julien de Cénac   John Dobbing
January 1988

Contents

Contributors

John Dobbing, DSc, FRCP, FRCPath, the editor, is Emeritus Professor of Child Growth and Development in the Department of Child Health, University of Manchester. As a practitioner and professional medical research worker in several fields of paediatric research, he has taken a special interest in the infant food controversy. He has published several books and many papers, and edited the leading reference work *Scientific Foundation of Paediatrics* (Heinemann, London, 1981).

Frank Falkner, MD, FRCP, who introduces the book, is Professor and Program Head, Maternal and Child Health Program, University of California, Berkeley. He was elected senior member of the Institute of Medicine of the National Academy of Sciences in 1985 in recognition of his distinguished work in the study of human biology and international child health.

Maggie McComas is an American business writer and public affairs analyst. She first developed an interest in the infant food controversy whilst working on the study, *Europe's Consumer Movement: Key Issues and Corporate Responses* (Business International, Geneva, 1981). She is a former associate editor of *Fortune* magazine and is now a free-lance writer based in New York City.

Gabriel Veraldi is a French novelist and investigative journalist who has had a long-standing interest in the relationship between industry and society (*L'humanisme technique*, 1958), as well as in development issues. He was once a close associate of Josué de Castro, a former Director General of the UN Food and Agriculture Organisation (FAO). He has been studying the infant feeding controversy since 1981, in the context of a book to appear shortly, *L'industrie, l'information et les mythologies modernes*.

Chapter 1
The Charges
G. Veraldi

In July 1973 a number of paediatricians, public health workers, and specialists in Third World development questions received a letter from a Mr. Hugh Geach, writing on behalf of the *New Internationalist*, a monthly magazine launched earlier that year by two British charity organisations, Oxfam and Christian Aid. The letter enclosed a copy of an article to be featured in the August edition of *New Internationalist* under the title *The Baby Food Tragedy*. The recipients were invited to send a letter or short article to be featured in the letter pages of the September and October editions, and were told:

We need some replies by Aug. 3 to keep the pot boiling. We hope to use your comments as a base to launch a public campaign to draw attention to this continuing scandal.

So began a controversy which has attracted international attention ever since. It led to a vigorous boycott campaign against Nestlé, particularly in North America; to the formation of action groups throughout the world; to a flood of publications on the benefits of breast-feeding and the risks of using substitutes; and not least, to the unprecedented development by a United Nations agency of an international Code to regulate the marketing of breast milk substitutes.

With the exception of a handful of medical specialists and activists, developments during the early stages of the controversy met with reactions ranging from indifference to general incredulity. It took a long time before the infant food industry, the news media, and public opinion, perceived the gravity of the charges laid at the door of a company widely regarded as a model, both for the quality of its products as well as for responsible business practice. After all, what could be more beneficial to the community at large than to supply milk for babies? We must therefore begin by examining the accusations which sparked off a campaign which was unique, not only for its longevity and geographical extension, but also for the passions it aroused and the regulatory precedents it created.

"Breast is Best"

The preamble to the World Health Organization's International Code of Marketing of Breast Milk Substitutes [1] gives a clear and concise statement on the superiority of breast-feeding:

Breast-feeding is an unequalled way of providing ideal food for the healthy growth and development of infants; it forms a unique biological and emotional basis for the health of both mother and child; the anti-infective properties of breast milk help to protect infants against disease; and there is an important relationship between breast-feeding and child-spacing.

The same message, but in a rather more direct style, has been repeated by critics of Industry[1] throughout the controversy. Breast milk is "better, cheaper and safer" than anything a mother could buy in a tin, said the *New Internationalist* [2]. "Breast milk is the original convenience food. No mixing, warming or sterilising needed; no dirty pots and bottles to wash afterwards; always on tap from its specially designed unbreakable containers. And it is genuinely the most nutritious wholesome product on the market. A copy-writer's dream", was the description given by the British charity, War on Want [3].

Few, and certainly not the infant food industry, would argue with such statements or attempt to dispute the fact that breast milk has evolved over aeons of time to meet the specific needs of the human baby, just as the milk of the cow, the sheep, the camel, the whale, and other mammalian species is exactly suited to the calf, lamb and so on. It is hardly surprising, therefore, that widespread and deep-seated concern was expressed when evidence was produced seeming to support the allegation that Nestlé and other manufacturers were dissuading mothers from breast-feeding, thereby creating an artificial need for commercial breast milk substitutes.

Decline in Breast-Feeding

In spite of its universally recognised benefits, much evidence has been produced to show that the number of women who breast-feed their baby from birth has declined substantially, not only in the industrialised Western countries but also in the rapidly growing urban areas of the Third World. Moreover, babies are being weaned from the breast earlier and earlier. As a leading critic of Industry put it recently:

A vast upheaval in infant feeding habits has occurred in little more than 100 years. For nearly two million years infants have been successfully breastfed. However, by the middle of the twentieth century, more and more infants were being switched to the bottle, filled with specially formulated powdered skim milk preparations [4].

Statistics published in the early 1970s spoke of dramatic declines in breast-feeding in different countries such as Chile, where it was reported that in 1960 over 90% of infants were breast-fed, whereas just 8 years later the figure was lower than 10% [5]. Similar patterns have been reported in Mexico: more than 95% of infants breast-fed at the age of 6 months in 1960, declining to about 40% in 1966; and in Singapore, where some 80% of 3-month-old infants were breast-fed in 1951, falling to only 5% in 1971 [5]. Evidence suggesting a similar rapid transition was reported in many other countries [6]. Activist groups and some professional authorities singled out the aggressive marketing and advertising campaigns of

---

[1] Throughout the book, the term Industry is used for companies which produce and market infant formula.

infant formula[1] manufacturers as the factor mainly responsible for the reported decline in breast-feeding [7,8,9].

The charge is all the more serious when it is considered in the context of assertions that the vast majority of mothers do not need to use breast milk substitutes, and that the health, even the chances of survival, of infants fed on substitutes may be severely compromised.

Although at first glance many people would tend to dismiss such assertions on the grounds that the great menace in most countries today is galloping over-population, due very largely to *improved* infant and young child survival, we must nevertheless examine the assertions closely since they underly the whole campaign against Industry.

The Vast Majority of Mothers can Breast-Feed

If it is true that the vast majority of mothers are able to breast-feed, and that breast-feeding provides the best possible start in life for babies, then the legitimate market for breast milk substitutes must be very small.

UNICEF states that at least 98% of mothers can breast-feed [10], while a recent editorial in a leading medical journal stated that "at least 95% of mothers are able, if they wish, to breast-feed their infants for 4–6 months and can provide enough milk over this period to allow their babies to grow to their full potential" [11].

In a report prepared for the 39th World Health Assembly [12], it is stated that unless there are signs of severe maternal malnutrition or other physiological or psychological reasons for reduced levels of mother's milk, breast milk alone satisfies the energy requirements of the infant for at least the first 4 months of life, and frequently up to 6 months.

Even in poorly nourished women the volume and composition of human milk is considered surprisingly good [13]. This implies that unless the mother is very severely malnourished, she is capable of satisfying her baby's needs from the breast alone for at least the first 4 months of life. Many authorities and organisations subscribe to this view [14,15,16].

Health Hazards of Feeding Breast Milk Substitutes

Numerous studies reached the conclusion that the infant mortality rates of breast-fed babies are significantly lower than those of bottle-fed babies. Very early in the public controversy, critics of Industry drew public attention to research conducted in Chile, which showed that babies who were "bottle-fed" during the first months of their life suffered three times the mortality rate of their brothers and sisters who were exclusively breast-fed [3,17]. A review paper prepared by WHO and UNICEF for the meeting, Infant and Young Child Feeding, held in October

---

[1] Infant formula is an industrially produced breast milk substitute which meets international FAO/WHO Codex standards of composition and quality.

1979, which they sponsored, highlighted the problem of survival of artificially-fed infants in difficult environments. Referring to a longitudinal study carried out in Punjabi villages in the 1950s, it was pointed out that among the 20 infants in the study population who were not breast-fed from birth, only one survived past 6 months of age.

Frequent reference is made to the striking results reported when changes were made in early (neo-natal) feeding practices at the Baguio General Hospital and Medical Centre in the Philippines. The number of mothers who breast-fed while in hospital increased from 40% to 87% and this resulted in a nearly ninefold decrease in the number of cases of clinical infection, a twentyfold decrease in deaths from clinical infection, and a sixteenfold decrease in cases of diarrhoea. Overall, deaths were reduced by 47% and morbidity by 50% [18].

Dramatic estimates have been made to demonstrate the world-wide impact on infant health of the decline in breast-feeding and the concomitant widespread introduction of breast milk substitutes at an ever earlier age. For example, Professor Derrick Jelliffe, coauthor with his wife of many publications on breast-feeding and one of the most forceful critics of the infant food industry, testified as follows at a Senate Hearing held in Washington:

We have calculated that if breast-feeding could be reinstituted in developing countries, very probably – and this, of course, is based on available figures, but partly a guesstimate – some 10 million babies would be saved from diarrhea disease and marasmus each year [19].

In a written statement submitted for the Senate record, the Jelliffes identified inadequate bottle-feeding as one of the causes for the 10 million cases of marasmus and diarrhoea occurring annually in infants in developing countries [20]. UNICEF believes that 1 million infant lives a year could be saved within a decade from now if the campaign to halt and reverse "the disastrous trend from breast to bottle feeding" were comprehensive enough to change medical attitudes and hospital practices, to control irresponsible promotion and marketing of artificial infant formulae, and to help mothers both to improve their own nutrition and to be reassured that breast-feeding is best [21].

On the basis of their estimates of the number of cases of marasmus and diarrhoea associated with bottle-feeding, the Jelliffes go even further and postulate that 3 million lives a year could be saved [22]. Speaking of the decline in breast-feeding in the peri-urban slums and shanty town areas of the developing countries, Jelliffe [7] stated that marasmus and diarrhoeal disease have come to predominate in the first year of life, as mothers who attempt to bottle-feed their babies are only able to afford inadequate amounts of formula, and very low levels of environmental home hygiene make contaminated feeds unavoidable. He described promotion of formulae by commercial concerns as unethical in communities where there is *no possibility* (his emphasis) of such formulae being purchasable in adequate quantities or used in a cleanly fashion, and/or where breast-feeding is still the norm.

By May 1978 public interest in the controversy was such in the United States that it became the subject of Senate Hearings on the Marketing and Promotion of Infant Formula in the Developing Nations. In opening the Hearings, Senator Edward Kennedy posed the following rhetorical question:

Can a product which requires clean water, good sanitation, adequate family income, and a literate parent to follow printed indications be properly and safely used in areas where water is contaminated, sewage runs in the streets, poverty is severe and illiteracy is high? [23]

The problems facing mothers in poor environments who have to bottle-feed their babies indeed seem insuperable. From the very beginning of the campaign against Industry, critics were quick to point out that most Third World mothers were illiterate, even in their native language [3]; that the cost of feeding an infant on infant formula absorbed between 10% and 80% of the average wage [24]; that most Third World mothers did not have adequate cooking facilities [3] and could not afford the fuel necessary to boil water and feeding utensils [25]; that few mothers enjoyed the luxury of having a refrigerator so that prepared foods could not be kept safely [26]. The result is not difficult to predict: over-diluted, contaminated feeds given to the baby from a filthy feeding bottle, instead of the nutritious and hygienic breast milk nature intended, leads almost inevitably to diarrhoea, malnutrition, and often death. Little wonder, said the critics, that infant mortality in bottle-fed babies was so much higher than in breast-fed babies. Little wonder too that the question was asked whether the developing countries could afford to have breast milk substitutes on the open market [3]. The Jelliffes put the cost of treating babies afflicted by marasmus and diarrhoea due to inadequate feeding practices at 1 billion US dollars per year [22], and that was not the only economic consequence.

Infant Formula a Drain on National Resources

According to one estimate made in 1977 [27], total world production of human breast milk may be 12 billion litres short of production potential. This "loss" in monetary terms was calculated to be in the order of 6 billion US dollars. Such estimates are obtained by extrapolating statistics on the decline in breast-feeding at the national level. For example, based on the figures quoted for Chile [6], it was estimated that potential breast milk production in that country in 1950 was 57 700 tons of which only 2900 tons were realised. By 1970, according to Berg, 78 600 tons of the 93 200 potential tons were unrealised. The milk of 32 000 cows would be required to compensate for the loss.

Added to these costs are those of importing breast milk substitutes, resulting in a loss to the country of foreign exchange. Estimates of the total world market for commercial infant formula as high as 4 billion US dollars have been advanced, with annual growth at 15–20%, and sales in the developing countries accounting for about half the total [28,29].

Yet another significant impact on national resources is said to be caused by the costs of additional births due to a decline in breast-feeding, and the resulting loss of contraceptive protection which breast-feeding confers [6,7,10,25].

Infant Formula Marketing

In the face of such serious charges, it is hardly surprising that the methods used by the Industry to promote substitutes for breast milk should have attracted particular criticism. Nestlé, the company particularly singled out by the activists, was accused of dissuading mothers from breast-feeding through aggressive and unscrupulous promotion which suggested that its infant formula brands were superior to breast milk and were the "modern way" to feed babies.

Media advertising, including the use of radio spots with catchy jingles, was used in some African and Asian countries and reached a very wide cross-section of the population. Even when, in response to criticism, the superiority of breast-feeding was emphasised in the message, the very mention of an *alternative* was considered to undermine the confidence of mothers in their ability to meet their babies' needs exclusively from the breast. A Western, modern and healthy image of bottle-feeding, was conveyed by featuring chubby caucasian babies on labels, in attractively illustrated mother books, and on posters and calendars. According to many observers, bottle-feeding came to be perceived by poor mothers as a status symbol, and they would even express their own milk into the gutter because they believed that by using "powdered milk" instead, their babies would grow up as healthy as the one on the label.

Perhaps the single most-criticised activity of Industry was the employment of "Milk Nurses". In some cases, according to critics, these so-called nurses were nothing more than sales-girls dressed in white uniforms to convey the impression that they were qualified health workers, and their job was simply to promote the sales of infant formula. By masquerading as real nurses they were able to gain the confidence of mothers and convince them that their babies would thrive better on the bottle than on the breast. Jelliffe described this practice as one of the most insidious forms of advertising and promotion [7]. Last, but by no means least, the promotion of bottle-feeding to and through doctors and other health workers was severely criticised.

Jelliffe coined the phrases "manipulation by assistance" and "endorsement by association" [7] to describe the promotional nature of the relationship between Industry and the health professions. According to these concepts, donations to institutions and professional associations (in money and kind), entertainment, travel grants, gifts to individual health workers, and contributions towards the costs of medical and scientific meetings all ensured a commitment on the part of the institution or individual concerned to promote the company's products, to the detriment of breast-feeding. The use of a company's products in a leading institution or the display of company-sponsored educational material, posters or equipment where it could be seen by the public conferred that institution's "seal of approval" on the company, and so on.

Apart from the employment of "milk nurses", the sampling and supply of infant formula to individual health workers and hospitals was considered the most prejudicial to breast-feeding. Not only was this activity viewed as "endorsement by association", but maternity ward procedures became orientated towards bottle-feeding as the routine, since it required fewer staff to feed babies artificially than to help and encourage mothers to breast-feed. Worse still, it was pointed out that once the baby was "hooked" on the bottle, the mother's breast milk would dry up within a few days and it would then be difficult, if not impossible, for her to begin breast-feeding again [30]. The analogy with drug addiction was graphically portrayed by the cover of the February 1982 *New Internationalist*. Over the title, "Stop the Babymilk pushers . . ." milk powder, measuring scoop, feeding bottles, a cleaning brush, and an aluminium sachet had been arranged to suggest the preparations for a junkie's trip. All it lacked was the needle.

To summarise, Nestlé and other companies were accused of aggressively promoting infant formula, thereby dissuading mothers from breast-feeding. According to the critics, this led to unnecessary use of unaffordable substitutes in poor communities where mothers had neither the education nor the facilities required for the safe preparation of bottle-feeds. As a result it was claimed that mothers "stretched" the formula to make it last longer, and their babies were given a contaminated over-diluted feed. Diarrhoea, malnutrition and death, in most cases preventable, were inevitable under these circumstances and occurred on a massive scale. Up to 10 million babies a year suffered the consequences, according to critics of Industry.

Based on the apparently overwhelming evidence, and seeming to be backed by authoritative opinion, the lurid title of War on Want's 1974 pamphlet, *The Baby Killer* [3] gave the appearance of being fully justified.

References

1 World Health Organization (1981) International code of marketing of breast milk substitutes. WHO, Geneva
2 Anonymous (1973) Action now on baby foods. New Internationalist Aug: 1
3 Muller M (1974) The baby killer. War on Want, London
4 Chetley A (1986) The politics of baby foods. Frances Pinter, London
5 Latham MC (1977) Infant feeding in national and international perspective: an examination of the decline in human lactation, and the modern crisis in infant and young child feeding practices. Ann NY Acad Sci 300: 197–209
6 Berg A (1973) The nutrition factor: its role in national development. The Brookings Institution, Washington DC
7 Jelliffe DB (1975) Advertising and infant feeding. J Trop Pediatr 21: 161–162
8 Latham MC (1973) Innovative techniques in consumer economics. Seminar workshop on nutrition of the pre-school child, Honolulu, Hawaii. The Food Institute, East-West Center, University of Hawaii: 1–6 (Evidence submitted by Arbeitsgruppe Dritte Welt at the Bern libel suit, 1974–76)
9 Infant Formula Action Coalition (INFACT) (1977) Baby bottle disease – there's big money in it. Mother Jones, Aug. (Advertisement prepared by Public Media Center, San Francisco. Distributed separately as handout)
10 Anonymous (1981) Questions and answers on infant feeding. UNICEF Information, UNICEF, New York
11 Editorial (1986) Infant feeding today. Lancet i: 17–18
12 Béhar M (1986) Physiological development of the infant and its implications for complementary feeding. World Health Organization Document WHO/MCH/NUT/86.2, WHO, Geneva, pp 1–20
13 Jelliffe DB, Jelliffe EFP (1978) The volume and composition of human milk in poorly nourished communities: a review. Am J Clin Nutr 31: 492–515
14 Dellums RV (1979) The infant nutrition act. Congressional Record: 125 (62), May 16, 2pp
15 Oxford Committee for Famine Relief (Oxfam) (1981) The baby milk campaign. Some questions answered. Oxfam, Oxford
16 Belavady B, Gopalan C (1959) Chemical composition of human milk in poor Indian women. Indian J Med Res 47: 234–245
17 Plank SJ, Milanesi ML (1973) Infant feeding and infant mortality in rural Chile. Bull WHO 48: 203–210
18 Clavano NR (1982) Mode of feeding and its effect on infant mortality and morbidity. J Trop Pediatr 28: 287–293
19 Jelliffe DB (1978) Statement. In: Marketing and promotion of infant formula in the developing nations, 1978. Hearing before the subcommittee on health and scientific research of the

committee on human resources. US Government Printing Office, Washington DC, pp 42–43 (United States Senate 23 May 1978)

20 Jelliffe DB, Jelliffe EFP (1978) Feeding young infants in developing countries. In: Marketing and promotion of infant formula in the developing nations, 1978. Hearing before the subcommittee on health and scientific research of the committee on human resources. US Government Printing Office, Washington DC pp 71–80 (United States Senate 23 May 1978)

21 Grant JP (1982) The state of the world's children 1982–83. UNICEF, New York, pp 1–42

22 Jelliffe DB, Jelliffe EFP (1978) Human milk in the modern world. Oxford University Press, Oxford, p 298

23 Kennedy E (1978) Opening statement of Senator Kennedy. In: Marketing and promotion of infant formula in the developing nations, 1978. Hearing before the subcommittee on health and scientific research of the committee on human resources. US Government Printing Office, Washington DC, pp 1–2 (United States Senate 23 May 1978)

24 International Babyfood Action Network (IBFAN) (1983) Action pack "A dangerous trend"

25 Chetley A (1981) The crisis in infant feeding. War on Want, London

26 Lappé FM, McCallie E (1978) On the bottle from birth. Food Monitor Sept/Oct: 13–14

27 Latham MC (1977) Introduction. In: Greiner T (ed) Regulation and education: strategies for solving the bottle feeding problem. Cornell University, Ithaca NY, I–XIV (Cornell International Nutrition Monograph Series, No 4)

28 Baer E (1982) Babies means business. New Internationalist February: 22–23

29 Post JE (1985) Assessing the Nestlé boycott: corporate accountability and human rights. California Management Review 27:113–131

30 Ebrahim GJ (1976) Audienz des Gerichtspräsidenten VIII von Bern. Forsetzung der Hauptverhandlung wegen Ehrverletzung, 22–24 Juni 1976. (Libel Proceedings, Verbatim Record, Bern, 1976)

Chapter 2

Medical and Scientific Commentary on Charges made against the Infant Food Industry

J. Dobbing

Introduction

An attempt will be made in this chapter to set out a balanced and factual account of some of the medical and scientific and socio-cultural issues which are central to the charges made against Nestlé and other companies in relation to their marketing and other practices, especially in developing countries. It is not its purpose to justify those activities of Industry which may have been mistaken in the past, but it will seek to point out the errors, mainly of oversimplification, in the tactics of Industry's critics when recruiting the sympathies of ordinary, concerned and well-intentioned citizens to their crusade.

Indeed it is necessary to stress from the outset the considerable complexity of the issues, the difficulties inherent in collecting and interpreting data, and the relative scarcity of satisfactory evidence, which was especially true in the early seventies when the controversy began to be extensively publicised, and is still so today.

Let us look at some important general matters.

Oversimplification of the issues has led to damaging and often unnecessary polarisation. For example the slogan "Breast is better than bottle" which we shall examine in more detail later, implies a simple either/or choice. In fact feeding patterns differ very considerably from country to country and from region to region. They include not only an extraordinary range of foods which are given as substitutes for breast milk, but also a very wide range of methods for administering them. These methods are by no means confined to the feeding bottle depicted in the activist literature. Many of the feeding methods used have existed for centuries; certainly long before the advent of modern Industry. It is significant that such traditional methods should have been so largely ignored.

Secondly, there is now a popular fervour for *naturalism* in matters of health. "Naturalism" is a term for the worship of all things natural, but more particularly for the condemnation of everything man-made, or civilised, whether perpetrated by the medical profession or by industry. We all to some extent yearn for the "natural" way, often forgetting that it is "nature" which permits a degree of maternal and childhood death and disease in traditional, "unspoilt" communities which all of us would find unacceptable in our own. The proper business of doctors, and of civilisation, that is to say of all of us, is often and properly to *defeat* some of the forces of "nature".

Much of the confusion in this complex subject has been generated by various lay activist groups who rely heavily on the quoted opinions of people we may describe as "expatriate doctors". It is almost as if just because a doctor with many years of experience in the tropics says something is so, then that is enough evidence. The implication is that expatriate doctors who laudably devote their lives to practise in underprivileged parts of the world and who do such wonderful work there in the relief of suffering, are also accomplished and experienced research scientists. A combination in the same person of good medicine and personal dedication with scientific competence, is in reality only given to a very select few, and these are the ones who make enormously important, historic discoveries.

Terminology

Another major source of confusion has been the misuse of terminology, and a discussion of this is now necessary.

The term "breast milk substitute", as we have seen, refers to any food used to replace breast milk, regardless of whether or not it is appropriate for the purpose. "Infant formula" is a breast milk substitute which conforms to internationally recognised standards of composition and quality [1]. An infant formula must be "nutritionally adequate to promote normal growth and development when used in accordance with its directions for use". A recent WHO paper points out that generally speaking commercially produced infant formulae are a considerable improvement on most traditional substitutes, particularly for the very young infant [2].

In their enthusiasm to promote their cause the critics of Industry have avoided, or neglected, the use of clearly-defined terms in their accusations.

The design of infant formula is still improving, just as much as that of cameras and computers, the product being a cleverly adapted one, sometimes based on the milk of other species, and sometimes containing no animal milk whatever. Therefore to speak of it as "dried milk powder", and of the manufacturers of it as "dried milk companies" is a misnomer, to say the least. Mothers in many parts of the world feed quite unsuitable substitutes to their children, including various types of processed milks, as well as raw cow's or buffalo's or goat's milk, or variants of the many gruels. These other substances do not meet the baby's nutritional needs and are usually dangerous, both nutritionally and bacteriologically. These substitutes are often fed from *bottles*. It is therefore misleading and scientifically inaccurate to speak of formula feeding as "bottle-feeding", as if the contents of the bottle were of no importance. It is scientifically essential, whenever talking of "bottle-feeding" to be careful to specify what the bottle contains. This is surprisingly often not stated, even in scientific papers, yet it provides convincing support for the activist case to have an "expert" demonstrate the "dangers" of the "bottle", even when its contents may be material which Industry would never market as an infant formula and which is neither designed nor suitable for babies.

One journalist has carefully contrived a definition of "infant formula" which is in an inconspicuous note at the beginning of a recently published book. This definition is worth quoting in full:

> *Infant formula*: **Although a very specific product** (*sic*), the term has been used in a more generic sense throughout the book to include products which are *used* to feed infants, **even though they may not have been designed specifically to do so**. The term is used in preference to *breastmilk substitutes* in order to avoid the possible assumption that there is an interchangeable and complete equivalent substitute for breast milk. Other terms that may occur include *powdered baby milks, infant milks/ foods* [3] (original italics, but bold print added).

It is usual in such literature for these terms not to be properly defined, and, intentionally or not, this has led to confusion which has often seemed to support the activists in their criticism. It is by no means clear how pap, or bush tea, which are both "used" could ever be mistaken for a "complete equivalent substitute for breast milk"!

The Charges

The substance of the medical and scientific charge, as we have seen in Chapter 1, is that Nestlé has diverted mothers away from the successful breast-feeding of their babies towards a reliance on manufactured infant formula, in circumstances in which the formula constitutes a threat to the welfare, and even to the life of those babies. These circumstances include a lack of hygienic facilities, a lack of literacy in the mothers, a lack of the means to buy the product, and the product's failure to match the manifest advantages of breast-feeding, which the mothers in the overwhelming majority are said to be able to do successfully, even when they are malnourished.

Points of Agreement

First let us set out two of the more important points about which there is no disagreement. These centre on the clear advantages of breast-feeding, a normal process which is the product of aeons of evolutionary time. No sensible person would pretend that any alternative devised by man could completely match the excellence of what is, after all, a normal physiological function. As we have seen, the purpose of good preventive, as well as curative medicine is to assist, and sometimes improve upon the body's responses to pathological situations; but it would be a vain doctor who would pretend to improve on naturally occurring, evolutionary developed normal physiology. Paediatricians have sometimes got themselves into scientific or logical difficulties by insisting unnecessarily on the superiority of breast-feeding when this has never been in dispute [4].

Another matter on which all sides agree, and which is sometimes forgotten amidst the strife, is that we all deplore the widespread poverty in which most of our fellow human beings live, and which is really the root cause of the problems we are now discussing. Poverty, on the scale we none of us have any right these days to be ignorant of or to ignore, is an obscenity: something which persists to our individual and collective shame, and which should, and does, give rise to deep-seated feelings of guilt in all right-minded people. A few of us can still not imagine what it is really like for those whose lot it is to experience it, but in recent times awareness of poverty is less and less confined to missionary doctors. Large numbers of the world's more fortunate citizens have at last been shown the spectacle, but not the smells, of poverty by the media, and have been driven by natural compassion to find ways of helping, by contributing to one or another appeal.

Breast is Best (with Few Exceptions)

As we have noted earlier, everyone agrees with the basic premise that "breast is best", but it would be wrong, in a medical and scientific context, to ignore certain limitations of human milk from a nutritional point of view, or the problems that can be caused, for example, by the presence of harmful pharmaceutical or other contaminants [5].

Of course there is a long list of special circumstances in which breast-feeding is either impossible or not as beneficial as an alternative, but the list is almost longer than the number of cases involved. Nor must it be forgotten that it is unfortunately not uncommon for babies in poverty to find themselves without mothers, either because of death or delinquency; and there are a number of medical conditions in which breast-feeding is even dangerous, or the mother may be too ill; but no-one should pretend that these constitute more than a small fraction of the whole population.

The superiority of breast milk, however, does not necessarily imply that all mothers who are able to, do breast-feed their babies. There have always been mothers who have regarded breast-feeding with distaste and have delegated the responsibility to wet nurses. Their counterparts today turn to modern infant formulae which, when used correctly, give perfectly satisfactory results. Few advocates of breast-feeding suggest that a mother be denied the basic freedom to choose how she feeds her baby. What the critics do insist on, quite properly, is that the mother be given all the information necessary to make her choice, bearing in mind all the advantages and disadvantages of the alternative solutions for herself and her baby.

It is important to realise, however, that the great majority of Third World mothers have no such freedom. Their feeding practices are dictated by health, environmental and economic conditions over which they have no control. To extol the undeniable advantages of prolonged breast-feeding without recognising the constraints on the mother's ability to live up to this ideal, without, in many cases, serious harm to herself and her baby, has been one of the most disturbing aspects of the campaign against the infant food industry.

Immune Properties of Breast Milk

Related to the question of the dangers of poor hygiene in the management of artificial feeding is the fact that breast milk contains antibodies which protect the very susceptible baby against infection. This, by common consent, is perhaps the single most important property of breast milk which cannot be imitated by its substitutes. Even so, perhaps stemming from a desire to cover up other weaknesses in their scientific case, activists are often prone to be rather uncritical about this anti-infective role of breast-milk antibodies. It is quite true that these can be shown in the laboratory to be present in breast milk, and it is certain that they do also have these protective functions in real life. However, laboratory demonstrations that constituents are naturally present do not always imply that they have the purpose attributed to them by scientists, and their presence may just as much be for the protection of the mother against relatively common mastitis and breast abscess, as for the baby. It must be accepted that their usefulness in protecting the baby is often derived from theoretical reasoning rather than from direct demonstration. This view is supported in a recent review which suggested that breast-feeding had, at most, a minimal protective effect in developed countries [6]. It is clearly a matter which deserves much more investigation, especially the question of the protective role of breast-milk antibodies in real-life conditions in developing countries.

Hazards of Feeding Breast Milk Substitutes

It must be accepted that the administration of any food other than breast milk is a hazardous undertaking in poor communities. It is this fact that has led to the central activist theme, that Nestlé, or manufactured infant formula, kills babies; and that it does this largely because of the greater risks of infection, mostly gastrointestinal, in impoverished conditions, as well as by starvation due to the mothers not being able to afford adequate quantities.

The author of *The Baby Killer* report built up his case against a background of the "three-stone" kitchen [7][1], so let us examine how mothers who do not feed a manufactured product give breast milk substitutes and supplements to their babies in traditional communities.

Traditional supplementary feeds are almost invariably nutritionally inadequate as well as contaminated, and this has been the case throughout recorded history [8]. In our day, as in the past, such feeds vary according to culture [9], and include rice cooked in broth or mixed with bananas, or rice previously chewed by the mother and fed directly from her mouth into the baby's (Thailand and Bangladesh [10,11]), sugar, sweet beverages or raw milk (Zaire [12]), and bush tea (Jamaica [13]), as well as home-made paps in many parts of the world, and gruels made from local grain, for example in parts of West Africa.

Because the traditional supplementary foods are of low nutritional value, they are, in most cases, quite inadequate for proper growth. In addition, they are necessarily made up in the same dangerous conditions as would be the manufac-

---

[1] According to its author, the vast majority of West African mothers cook in a "three-stone" kitchen. The three stones support a pot above a wood fire.

tured product. In other words the water is just as filthy and contaminated, the receptacles just as dirty, the flies which buzz around just the same, and so forth.

It is not unusual for the supplementary gruel in traditional villages to be made up in old tins, not boiled because that makes it like glue and impossible to handle, for a day or more's supply to be made up at one time, and for the remainder to stand around on the dirt floor with the flies settling on it, and this for hours at a time at an ambient tropical temperature which might have been expressly designed for bacterial multiplication. It is interesting how this description of normal, traditional conditions is similar to the one the activists supply to describe the making up of the manufactured product, as if the companies were actually responsible for the conditions as well as the product.

The main differences between the manufactured and the traditional product are the very high nutritional quality and suitability of the infant formula compared with the traditional alternative; and, unfortunately, its high cost in relation to the family income.

It is worth noting, in passing, that breast-feeding in such communities is not without its hazards either. Dirty, unwashed nipples with flies on them are mentioned as a cause of widespread infection in a recent paper from Southern Sudan [14] and we have already noted the hazards of traditional supplementary feeding.

This sketchy account of traditional practices also casts an interesting light on the frequent call for a product based on cheap, locally available materials. Cost is certainly a major problem, but so are the problems of hygiene and the equally important question of nutritional value. The root problem is, of course, poverty, but this is not much mentioned by critics of Industry, perhaps because it is rather harder to solve.

Returning to the question of the relative hazards of artificial feeding, it would be surprising if the exclusively breast-fed baby of a healthy mother did not have a better chance than the baby fed with diluted goat's milk administered by soaking a filthy rag in the milk and placing it in the baby's mouth so that the milk is extracted by a combination of sucking and chewing on the rag. Lest this seem an exaggeration, it should be pointed out that the study quoted in Chapter 1 [15], comparing the mortality rates of breast-fed with "artificially fed" babies, which reflects just this sort of situation, has been widely quoted in support of the case against infant formula.

However, it takes more than a demonstration that more dying babies are "bottle-fed" than are breast-fed to show that the relationship is *causal* [16]. Modern, sophisticated techniques of epidemiology, of the kind that have shown beyond doubt a causal relationship between, for example, cigarette smoking and a host of lethal diseases, have not depended on such a simplistic demonstration of a mere association between the two variables, although they may have begun that way. Recognition of the many confounding variables which have to be allowed for is now mandatory in such studies. Confounding variables must be either eliminated, for example by using the techniques of the randomised controlled trial, or at least quantified in relation to each other and to the main proposed variable. The author blushes to have to point this out to an intelligent readership. That it is necessary is illustrated by the facility with which the ordinary rules of epidemiology have been ignored in numerous studies purporting to show the association of infant death and morbidity with "bottle-feeding", leaving aside the caveats elaborated above such as considerations of what is *in* the bottle.

Scientific sins, such as non-random sampling, no proper selection of controls, failure to employ multivariate analysis when there are many confounding variables, or failure even to define either breast-feeding, or the outcome measure such as diarrhoea, in other words failure to define criteria for identifying variables and so forth, abound in these studies [6]; as do such things as failure to appreciate that non-breast-feeding babies are, to a large extent, self-selected on the basis of their already having medical and other problems which led them selectively to join that population which is at a greater risk anyway. In this connection it is worth quoting the American Academy of Pediatrics:

Any change in the method of feeding will almost always occur in the direction away from breast-feeding, i.e. infants who begin breast-feeding will change to bottle-feeding at a subsequent period, whereas the reverse is extremely rare. This one-way flow effectively nullifies the ideal of obtaining two groups of infants who are exclusively breast-fed or exclusively bottle-fed from birth and remain in their respective feeding groups for prospectively determined intervals regardless of whether their progress is good or bad. This is so because, if a breast-fed infant is not doing well, the infant is likely to be switched to partial or complete bottle-feeding. This factor is of great importance in assessing the superiority of breast-feeding over bottle feeding in such matters as infectious morbidity because it has the effects of keeping the breast-fed group healthy and adding "non-healthy" infants to the bottle-fed group. Even if the infants lost from breast-feeding were not added to the bottle-fed group, the selective removal of non-thriving infants from the breast-fed group would tend to maintain the selectivity for healthy infants [17].

It has even more recently been pointed out [18,19] that most studies of feeding methods and infection, even in industrialised countries, can be similarly flawed and come to unreliable conclusions. Also "One of the major reasons for these conflicting results is the impossibility of conducting randomized controlled trials in which infants are randomly assigned to be fed either formula or breast milk" [6].

All that said, a very recent and reputable judgement is that there does exist some causal connection between non-breast-feeding and poorer outcome, even when the confounding variables have been taken into account, although breast-feeding "cannot be concluded to be the sole, or even primary, factor in infant survival" [20]. This balanced conclusion is quite different from the activist case. They relied on older scientific literature which was known even at the time to be flawed.

The key point being made by the critics of Industry, however, was that babies were being subjected to avoidable risks, either because the mother had been dissuaded from breast-feeding or because she had introduced supplementary feeding unnecessarily. In presenting studies showing considerably higher infant mortality among those babies who were "bottle-fed" or "artificially fed" (terminology interchanged at will) the activists failed to address the vital question: was the baby at risk because it was artificially fed, or was it artificially fed because it was at risk? This is evident from the reasoning used to estimate a figure of 10 million babies who could be saved from diarrhoea and marasmus [21], which was later to be turned by the activists into the statement: "ten million babies suffer because of the heartless, money-hungry activities of powerful multinational companies". (See Chap 8).

Breast-Feeding, Lactational Infertility, and Demography

Another important claim in favour of the "Breast is Best" argument is that breast-feeding has an important contraceptive effect, and that to discourage it leads to a heavy child-bearing and child-rearing burden on the mother and to overcrowding of the population. Before accepting the scientific premise, let us pause to reflect that traditional society is not particularly noted for curtailment of the population explosion, except by unacceptable methods like disease and war or unreasonable restrictions on liberty, and its village streets are disproportionately filled with young children in spite of the contraceptive effect of lactation; and that the conception of the next child occurs in an unpredictable manner *during* prolonged lactation, illustrating the incompleteness and unreliability of lactational protection.

Lactation, provided it follows the right pattern of suckling interval and suckling strength and so forth, does of course inhibit ovulation and hence protect against conception [22], so presumably matters would be even worse if breast-feeding were to stop. An unexpected and very interesting fact has, however, quite recently emerged in this regard.

Briefly the story is as follows. In an attempt to improve lactation in a population of poor village women in West Africa, a research team planned to give quite massive food supplements to lactating women [23,24]. It was this project which showed that such measures ("feeding the mother") were without any effect on the quantity of milk produced, and had only marginal effects on quality. However the team was also interested in the topic of lactational infertility, and discovered, quite unexpectedly, that the period of infertility in these women, which was known to be extended by prolonged lactation, became considerably shortened when they were properly fed. For many other reasons which are too voluminous to go into here, the awful conclusion was reached that a good deal, but by no means all, of the protection afforded by breast-feeding against conception seemed to depend on the poor nutritional state of the mothers. The conclusion that most of us reached [22] was that alternative contraceptive measures should be offered and reliance on lactation for this purpose should be curtailed. Even so, and for the record, the role of nutrition in lactational infertility is disputed in some of the older scientific papers. In any case lactation is a most unreliable contraceptive for the individual woman, who is much more interested in the impact of the arrival of more babies on her own life-style, however useful it may be in controlling a population explosion [25].

Mother-Infant Interrelationships

It is quite reasonably claimed that breast-feeding promotes a closer emotional bond between mother and child than "bottle" feeding. The Jelliffes, while acknowledging that "not all breast-fed babies grow up to be saints, nor all bottle-fed babies to be sinners", extend this proposal by speculating whether breast-feeding may be one remediable factor for the present-day increase in "senseless, destructive, vindictive purposeless violence, including child abuse in the Western World" [26]. Others have pointed out that the further back in history one goes, the lower the level of child care, the more likely children were to be killed, abandoned, beaten, terrorised and sexually abused: but the further back in history we go, the more likely children were to have been breast-fed [27,28].

At best this is an area which is extremely difficult to research, and such evidence as exists does not justify the use of this argument to imply that the mother, who does not breast-feed for any reason, is necessarily any less loving than her breast-feeding peers.

To summarise this section, it is indeed strange that the benefits of breast-feeding, which are so manifestly obvious, should have been subject to such exaggeration, and its limitations, which are few, but none-the-less important for the health worker to know about, have been down-played or even ignored. Clearly the World Health Organization's recommendation to restrict information to "scientific and factual matters" (WHO Code, Article 7.2) should apply to all infant feeding issues, and not only to the promotion of breast milk substitutes.

Decline in Breast-Feeding

Since all are agreed on the importance of protecting and promoting breast-feeding, it is naturally a matter of great concern when we are told that more and more mothers are turning from the breast to the bottle, and that this is largely the result of the aggressive marketing campaigns by Industry.

There can be little doubt that the incidence and duration of breast-feeding has declined in many developing communities, just as it has in industrial countries. Whether or not credit for the current reversal of this trend in some Western countries will be claimed by those who have campaigned against Industry remains to be seen. The underlying reasons for this encouraging trend are no doubt as complex as those which led to the earlier decline. However the same critics of Industry have left no stone unturned in their efforts to cast Industry promotion of infant formula as the principal villain responsible for the decline.

The truth is that the causes for the decline are so multifactorial, interdependent and complex that no meaningful analysis, even by the intricate techniques of modern epidemiology, can take us very far. The many factors which motivate a mother in her decision to breast-feed or not, and the equally numerous environmental pressures by which she is surrounded, can be enumerated; but they will remain a list of impressions rather than facts, and an analysis of their relative weights will be illusory, however persuasively displayed. It follows that neither "side" in the argument can validly claim its own explanation to be true, and for that reason there will be no attempt here to offer an alternative one to that of the activists. It would not be logical to denounce their "explanations" for the above reasons of complexity etc., and at the same time counter with another set which would be equally invalid for the same reasons.

The actual extent of the decline in breast-feeding in most countries of the Third World is difficult to evaluate, in part due to a lack of useful historical data on feeding patterns. Recent analysis of data by WHO [29] is very circumspect, and does not give the impression of a massive world-wide decline in breast-feeding which has been so widely promoted by the critics. For example the WHO report states that "nearly all the 21 million infants born in Africa are breast-fed, usually for a protracted period of time". Similarly in Middle and Western South Asia (38 million births), "breast-feeding is almost universal", although feeding patterns in Eastern South Asia and East Asia (34 million births) "are more diverse", with high prevalence in all rural areas, but lower frequency and duration in some urban areas. In Latin America (12 million births) initial prevalence is generally high, but the average duration "varies considerably", with longest durations amongst rural populations, but not as long as is found in Africa and Asia. Similar findings are reported elsewhere [30].

Although it can hardly be denied that inappropriate promotion of breast milk substitutes may indeed have been a contributing factor to the decline reported in some countries, it does not seem reasonable to lay the major portion of the blame on the manufacturers. Certainly they cannot be held responsible for the declines in countries where there is no commercial activity for profit, for example in communist countries [31], including the People's Republic of China, where, according to the Chinese delegate to the 1982 World Health Assembly, in some major cities the percentage of breast-feeding mothers had dropped to 20% or 30%. He explained this decline by the fact that most women in the urban sector held jobs which interfered with breast-feeding [32].

Supplements, Complements and Weaning

Breast or Bottle: a Non-Choice

Throughout the controversy, Industry's critics have promoted the idea that breast-feeding and artificial feeding are mutually exclusive, the former being the safe, "natural" way, and the latter its perversion for profit. Put in its crudest forms, it became known as the "breast vs. bottle" controversy. In fact, except for a relatively short period of time, it is a gross misconception to pretend that most babies are usually exclusively on the breast. We must now carefully examine this misconception.

Throughout the developmental period of life, beginning at conception and continuing throughout babyhood, childhood and adolescence, the individual is constantly changing, anatomically, physiologically, and, hence, in his nutritional needs. The fetus and the baby and the child are not miniature adults, simply getting bigger. They are different creatures from one age to the next; and there are no sudden jumps, except for the incident of birth. Even birth, which dramatically and suddenly revolutionises the mechanisms for breathing and circulation of the blood, does not interrupt the steady development of most other features of growth and development, including nutritional need. Similarly nutritional needs as the individual grows are not simply for *more*, but for a changing *quality* of food, adapted to the changing kinds of metabolic demand made by the growing child.

Thus nutritional needs do not advance in sudden leaps either, but gradually. In the same way, in natural, normal circumstances, the transition from breast-feeding to more adult, grown-up foods must also be gradual, and for this reason the best methods of feeding babies, devised by evolution, have never included a sudden stopping of exclusive breast-feeding and an equally sudden starting of non-equivalent alternatives. Wherever this happens, as it occasionally does in traditional society, where a breast-fed baby is suddenly rejected on the arrival of the next child, a very serious threat to proper growth and even survival results. In some parts of Africa such a sudden "weaning" is the main cause of kwashiorkor.

However there does come a time, an age or a stage of development, even under optimum conditions, when breast milk is inadequate, both in quantity and quality, to support the proper growth of the increasingly larger and more developed and demanding child. At this stage, as can be seen in all traditional communities, the mother traditionally adopts the practice of supplementing the baby's diet with other foods: at first liquid or semi-solid, then gradually more solid, until, over the course of many months and even years, a more adult diet, like that of the rest of the family. The change from breast milk to an older age diet is therefore not an *event*, but a process which should and usually does gradually occur over quite a long period of time. In other words the end of breast-feeding should not be sudden either, but should tail off over a long period as alternative foods are gradually introduced.

It can easily be seen from this how mistaken it is to speak of "breast or not". This is not a problem a mother normally faces. Her problem is rather to decide when, and with what, her breast milk should be supplemented.

Supplementation in Traditional Society

Few people realise, and the activists do not emphasise the fact, that in traditional communities supplementation is practised quite early [33]. The custom in many countries is to feed artificially, even in the very first days of life, immediately after birth, due to a cultural taboo against colostrum. It is common in these first days to give extra water, sugar water or jaggery water [34], or even raw cow's or goat's milk [33, 35], sometimes soaked in cotton cloth, and usually contaminated.

Even where this is not the case, it is quite usual and normal to supplement the supply of breast milk quite early in lactation, sometimes in the first month, and certainly in the first 2–3 months [36]. WHO studies in a number of Third World countries (Ethiopia, Nigeria, Zaire, Chile, Philippines) have shown, for example, that over 30% of breast-feeding mothers in rural traditional communities give regular supplements at 2–3 months [37]. Indeed there is now evidence that exclusive breast-feeding is relatively rare [38]. Perhaps the mother begins to sense the need for more than she can herself produce, probably taking her cue from a changing behaviour in the baby, who may be more hungry or thirsty, or suck harder, or show other signs of being dissatisfied.

It has been suggested that under such circumstances the introduction of a supplement has a negative effect on breast-feeding, and even "dries up" the supply of breast milk [39]. But if it is true that the baby is hungry because the supply of breast milk is beginning to be inadequate, then it is unlikely that the introduction of a supplement will reduce the baby's desire to suckle [40] as it has been shown to do in well-heeled society [41]. In the latter, where the baby is already almost satiated, supplementation may satiate completely, or over-satiate, thus reducing his desire to suckle, and this can be harmful to continuing breast-feeding. Studies in some developing countries, on the other hand, have shown that mixed breast- and bottle-feeding can and does continue for many months [12,38,42,43,44].

Can the Great Majority of Mothers Breast-Feed Successfully?

We now come to the key question. We have agreed that "Breast is Best" and that there has indeed been a decline in breast-feeding, although we may have some doubts as to its extent, and the degree of Industry's responsibility for the situation. We now need to examine whether the introduction of drastic marketing reforms will really lead to a situation where 98% of mothers could successfully breast-feed their babies. In doing so we must also attempt to analyse exactly what the critics of Industry mean when they say that 98% of women *can* breast-feed successfully.

The Adequacy of Exclusive Breast-Feeding

Let us see what objective criteria there are to determine the age at which breast-feeding alone becomes inadequate.

It has been explained above that weaning is a gradual process which may be said to begin in traditional society when supplementary food is first commenced in response to an apparently developing inadequacy of breast milk as a sole source of sustenance. A topic which has recently begun to be hotly debated in serious medico-scientific circles is the age at which this inadequacy of breast milk begins [45], and there are many points of view.

Firstly we must define what we mean by "adequate". If the age when inadequacy of exclusive breast-feeding begins is calculated from theoretical considerations, the answer, in *healthy, well-off mothers* is about 3–4 months [9]. Another way of arriving at an answer is to follow directly the growth of babies who are exclusively breast-fed, and to notice when growth begins to "falter" without supplementation. Some of the snags with this method, which is in many ways more appealing because it is a more direct "outcome" measure, are that babies are individuals who grow at differing and changing rates, and it is not always easy to know what would have been the normal growth trajectory in one who may be faltering; and also that faltering, when it occurs, is not a sharply defined event, but the beginning of a gradual process which is therefore difficult to detect precisely. By this method of reckoning, however, exclusive breast-feeding becomes inadequate for normal growth at about 6 months in optimum conditions.

The age of faltering is a relevant topic, since it is an important question whether a lactating mother in poverty can sustain the proper growth of her baby as effectively as her more fortunate sister. Activist campaigns have always pretended that she can, but most informed people, including some critics of Industry [46,47], are now agreed that she cannot if she is not well-nourished. It is accepted that the normal process of faltering may occur in her baby at anything from about 2 months of age onwards, sometimes even before. Now if this be so it is to the baby's benefit that the mother should be supplementing from at least this age. As we have seen, in practice in traditional society this is exactly what actually happens without the mother being told to, but in many cases it is without the desired effect because of the nutritional inadequacies and poor hygienic qualities of local traditional foods mentioned above.

The main reasons for the earlier onset of inadequacy of the mother's lactation and the consequent faltering in the growth of her baby are thought to be her chronic undernutrition and her low metabolic reserves, which are partly the consequence of her repeated and too-closely-spaced pregnancies and lactations, as well as the enormous amount of energy she often expends, and which is therefore lost to her metabolism, in her traditional role as the main manual labourer in the fields. She is usually responsible for the cultivation and gathering and preparation of the whole family's food. Most of us in privileged society simply do not realise that the usual life-history of such a woman is to conceive soon after puberty; to have two or even three babies before she herself is maturely adult, i.e. before the usual age in developed society; for each pregnancy to be followed by a prolonged period of lactation lasting 18 months to 2 years, a process which itself is very hard metabolic work; to be immediately followed, often without a return of menstruation, by the next pregnancy; and so on, throughout her reproductive life; and for this to be continuously accompanied by actual hard manual labour in the fields or in the grinding and preparation of food. It is small wonder that her life expectancy is low, that she ages prematurely and dies before her more fortunate sisters in other countries are beset with the problems of the menopause. It is these considerations of the mother which make it necessary to include the mother's own well-being in any proper definition of "successful breast-feeding" (see below).

Perhaps some paediatricians have been too exclusively concerned with the baby. This is an illogical stance, since the same paediatricians correctly emphasise the importance of caring for the whole mother–infant "dyad", the welfare of the baby being intimately bound up with that of the mother. It is surprising that the American Academy of Pediatrics, in an otherwise excellent and balanced account of infant feeding practices and infant health [48], specifically [16] ignores maternal welfare.

The ideal solution to these problems would of course consist of a complete reorganisation of society in developing countries, the near impossibility of which will be clear on serious reflection. The task should, none-the-less, be attempted.

Lactation in Malnourished Mothers

The theory of there being a "minimal need for breast milk substitutes", which is the very foundation stone for the infant formula "demarketing" concept which will be described later (Chap. 8), is accompanied by the frequent assertion that mothers can lactate successfully even when they are quite seriously malnourished. It is conceded on all sides that in extremely severe malnutrition such as occurs in certain special regions and circumstances, lactation is necessarily inadequate; but, distressing as these are, they are probably not sufficiently widespread even in the present-day world to be a basis for general policy, except in the relief of severe famine. However, the proposition is that the commoner forms of chronic malnutrition from which the majority of women in the world suffer do not interfere with successful lactation, and this is easily flawed.

We have already discussed the main reasons for inadequacy of lactation in chronically undernourished mothers (p. 20) and our analysis corresponds closely with that of the Jelliffes [49]. In their discussion of the evidence concerning the ability of undernourished mothers to breast-feed [50], they quote studies applicable to a variety of poor countries, some reporting "excellent growth for about the first 5–6 months of life", on "breast-feeding with little or no supplementation"; others reporting "comparable weight curves to those of Western standards of reference only up to about 4 months of age", and still others which found that weight gain "in some babies" was inadequate after only 3 months. Their conclusion from these findings was: "It seems possible, then, that decreasing lengths of satisfactory lactation are becoming evident in poorer communities in some less developed countries, perhaps especially in slum areas".

It is perhaps rather surprising that they give no indication of the possible extent of the problem, in view of their imaginative calculations as to the number of babies whose health could be protected by the "re-institution of breast-feeding" [51]. Indeed it is difficult to find any reference in the literature to the extent of the problem of inadequate lactation in chronically undernourished women. An exception is a comprehensive study of infant feeding practices carried out in Bombay, Calcutta and Madras by the Nutrition Foundation of India and funded by UNICEF [52]. This study found that where women in the *high socio-economic group* breast-fed their infants exclusively, the growth status of those infants was "distinctly superior" to that of exclusively breast-fed infants of the poorer groups. Of the different groups studied, in those which were poor and in which there was a high incidence of exclusive breast-feeding, between 25% and 64% of the babies younger than six months were *below the third centile of the Harvard scale*, which is considered to be the lowest limit of the normal standard range of growth, and must therefore have faltered seriously in their growth at a very early stage, despite being breast-fed.

In considering the proposition that "the majority of women can breast-feed successfully", everything, therefore, will depend on the definition of "successful lactation". If one simply means that all mothers, including such malnourished women can produce milk, then the statement is incontrovertible. However, in humanitarian, as well as in strict scientific terms the best definition of successful lactation has to be: **"that which provides for the proper growth of the child, without detriment to the health of the mother"**.

It is unlikely that one would find much opposition for this definition amongst most of those well-intentioned people who lend their support to the campaigns against Industry, and certainly not amongst those with a normal concern for the welfare of mothers and their babies, or for a more equitable place for women in society, but, *when looked at in this more reasonable light*, it would be more accurate to say that *very few* impoverished women can lactate successfully, since their babies do *not* grow properly, and they may themselves be dragged down into a lower state of health, as described above.

Those who promote the idea that there is only a minimal need for breast milk substitutes do so on the basis of the argument so explicitly set out in the *Lancet* [53] that "at least 95% of mothers are able, if they wish, to breast-feed their infants for 4–6 months and can provide enough milk over this period to allow their babies to grow to their full potential". We can see just how false and how potentially dangerous this statement is.

Feed the Mother

A seemingly more practical solution would be to improve the nutrition of the mother, as a more economical and less hazardous procedure than supplementing breast milk from an early age.

Unfortunately, apart from the almost insuperable economic and political and cultural difficulties of this proposition, it does not work physiologically. There is now evidence (e.g. [54]) that even the fullest possible supplementation of the poor mother during her lactation has no effect on the quantity of her milk, and only marginal effects on its quality or on the growth of her baby, the reasons for which are becoming better understood. Without going into detail, the metabolic physiology of both pregnancy and successful lactation is such that success depends on there being preparatory metabolic stores in the mother, sometimes even from before the conception of her baby and certainly from early in pregnancy, whose purpose is to be devoted later to the very high, subsequent metabolic cost of reproduction [55]. The only nutritional solution to the problem is therefore to have ample time between the end of lactation and the beginning of the next pregnancy, for her to be adequately fed during this interval as well as later, and to be protected from hard labour, undernutrition and debilitating disease throughout her reproductive life.

Does Faltering Matter?

Another aspect of "faltering", which is only now being considered, because it is only now reaching the consciousness of scientists is to do with whether it *matters* if there is some faltering of growth in babies due to environmentally induced inadequacies of lactation? After all, a person's achievement is not to be measured in terms of bodily size or growth attainment in the way that it is for farm livestock, and, besides, faltering does not kill. It is perhaps for this reason that it has been suggested that it is preferable to expose the child to a period of moderate undernutrition at the breast rather than run the risk of infections and diarrhoeal diseases following administration of formula [56].

The answer to this important question is still speculative, but if it has any substance it may yet turn out to be amongst the most important aspects of this whole problem for humans. A possible answer concerns the growth and development of the brain. It is known that the brain passes through a growth spurt just like that in other organs, but earlier. It lasts approximately from the beginning of the last third of pregnancy until about the second birthday, although it has slackened its pace somewhat by about 18 months. It therefore mostly coincides with lactation. It is also known that growth restriction, in particular nutritional growth restriction, timed to coincide with this brain-growth spurt period in young babies, results in permanent deficits and distortions of the brain's architecture, which are often not recoverable even if there is energetic nutritional rehabilitation [57]. The brain, unlike most other organs of the body, has only one opportunity to grow properly, and if that is not accomplished in good conditions the opportunity to grow a whole, healthy brain is lost. It is well-established that children who are malnourished in the last part of gestation and in the first 2 years suffer detectable deficits of achievement in later life. However it must be conceded, in the interests of scientific accuracy, that there are many other features of a poverty-stricken environment which may account for the later behavioural and intellectual deficits, and it is by no means certain how much, if at all, they are due to the well-established deleterious effects of growth restriction on the physical development of the brain. Ordinary clinical prudence, however, in the present state of knowledge, should lead us to want to promote the very best physical growth of the human brain, and this is not likely to be possible in the presence of growth faltering during the brain-growth spurt, which occurs in untold numbers of the world's poorer children. Thus any "ideal" solution must include the promotion of proper bodily growth, by all possible means, during this very vulnerable period for the brain, and this means optimum nutrition.

The Working Mother

All our discussion on the ability of mothers to breast-feed has centred on the physiological aspects. But what of the socio-economic factors which may prevent mothers from breast-feeding exclusively (or at all) for the first six months of their babies' life?

According to Jelliffe [58] the percentage of mothers in developing countries who work away from home and whose babies may require a bottle-feed "varies considerably, but is often rather small". Latham quotes a review of 11 studies showing that employment was given as the reason for weaning by an average of only 6% of mothers [59]. Many authorities, however, point to the increasing economic role of women in the developing countries as a major constraint on breast-feeding [60,61,62,63]. This is easy to understand when it is realised that in many Third World countries statutory maternity leave, where it exists at all, is limited to a very short time. Few, if any, day nurseries are available near the place of work, and even if they did exist, how many Third World employers would allow mothers time off to breast-feed? It has to be pointed out that even where adequate maternity leave is provided, mothers are often reluctant to take full advantage of it for fear of losing their jobs. These problems, as well as the additional pressures on women's time caused by the distances between home and place of work, and the difficulties of urban transport, are well described in the WHO publication *Women and Breast Feeding* [61].

None of the physiological and socio-economic constraints on breast-feeding described above are new discoveries. It was precisely the recognition of these constraints which led the UN Protein Advisory Group to speak of the dilemma for governments and Industry: the need to promote breast-feeding, yet at the same time making formulas and foods, and instructions for their correct use, available to mothers [60].

No matter how important it is to encourage and protect breast-feeding, its dogmatic promotion to the exclusion of all else may well be counterproductive in the quest for improved infant nutrition in the Third World.

Concluding Note

Nothing in this chapter should be construed as either an attack on breast-feeding, nor even as a promotion of it. That was not its purpose. Breast-feeding is so self-evidently the best way of feeding babies that it would be ridiculous to attack it. Its promotion is clearly required in many parts of the world to avoid its being unnecessarily and harmfully abandoned by many women in many countries, both impoverished and rich.

However, this chapter also illustrates how some of the biological truths of infant feeding have been dressed up in false clothes and used to attack an industrial, and sometimes a political target. Such a tactic can rarely be practised without doing harm, however good the cause.

No-one questions the real and serious hazards to which a baby born in impoverished circumstances, whether in the Third World or not, is subject. Nor is there any question that the unnecessary use of breast milk substitutes, whether the indigenous variety or the commercial infant formula, should be discouraged, but all mothers need help in ensuring the safe and adequate nutrition of their babies under the conditions in which they live. Those who live in impoverished circumstances are all going to have to cope with the problem of unsafe water supplies, poor sanitation, inadequate cooking facilities, lack of education, and inadequate financial resources as soon as breast-feeding has to be supplemented or replaced. It is a monumental disservice to those mothers to ignore this need, as many of those promoting the infant feeding controversy have done.

Most women can be taught the importance of boiling water and cleaning feeding utensils. Nor is illiteracy a reason to abandon efforts to inform and instruct, but rather a challenge to the creativity and ingenuity of all concerned, as can be seen, for example in the fields of oral rehydration solutions and family planning.

Even the problem of cost can be tackled if there is a genuine spirit of cooperation between the public and the private sector. No wonder one writer, commenting on the years of campaigning leading to the adoption of the WHO Code in 1981 said "Let us hope that the people who organised this campaign to condemn the baby food companies will now turn their attention to actually doing something about the major causes of infant mortality" [64].

The harm done to countless individual women in inhibiting their personal choice on the road to successful development, and to babies who have been unreasonably excluded from a proper consideration of their need for optimum nutrition in a modern world, is something the activists and their medical advisers will have to live with, just as will the Industry with those examples of inappropriate practices which have undoubtedly occurred, and inevitably so during a period of rapid social and political change.

We will now examine the history and chronology of the charges made against the infant food industry and of the events to which they gave rise.

References

1   FAO/WHO (1981) Food standards programme, recommended international standard for foods for infants and children. Codex Alimentarius Commission 72
2   Thirty-ninth World Health Assembly (1986) Guidelines concerning the main health and socioeconomic circumstances in which infants have to be fed on breast milk substitutes. Document A 38/8 Add. 1, 10 April
3   Chetley A (1986) The politics of baby foods. Frances Pinter, London
4   Dobbing J (1984) Breast is best, isn't it? In: Freed DLJ (ed) Health hazards of milk. Baillière Tindall, London, pp 60–74
5   Miller SA, Chopra JG (1984) Problems with human milk and infant formulas. Pediatrics 74: 639–647
6   Bauchner H, Leventhal JM, Shapiro ED (1986) Studies of breast-feeding and infections: How good is the evidence? JAMA 256: 887–892
7   Muller M (1974) The baby killer. War on Want, London

8   Fildes V (1986) Breasts, bottles and babies. Edinburgh University Press, Edinburgh
9   Seward JF, Serdula MK (1984) Infant feeding and infant growth. Pediatrics 74: 728–762
10 Knodel J, Kamnuansilpa P, Chamratrithirong A (1982) Breast-feeding in Thailand: data from the
    1981 Contraceptive Prevalence Survey. Stud Fam Plann 13: 307–315
11 Brown KH, Black RE, Becker S et al. (1982) Consumption of foods and nutrients by weanlings in
    rural Bangladesh. Am J Clin Nutr 36: 878–889
12 Franklin RR, Bertrand WE, Mock NB et al. (1985) Feeding patterns of infants and young
    children in Kinshasa, Zaire. J Trop Pediatr 29: 255–259
13 Almroth S, Latham MC (1982) Breast feeding practices in rural Jamaica. J Trop Pediatr 28: 103–
    109
14 Woodruff AW, Adamson EA, Suni AE et al. (1984) Infants in Juba, Southern Sudan: the first six
    months of life, Lancet ii 262–264
15 Gordon JE, Chitkara ID, Wyon JB (1963) Weanling diarrhoea. Am J Med Sci 245: 345–377
16 Kovar MG, Serdula MK, Marks JS et al. (1984) Review of the epidemiologic evidence for an
    association between infant feeding and infant health. Pediatrics 74: 615–638
17 American Academy of Pediatrics (1982) The promotion of breast feeding. Pediatrics 69: 654–661
18 Leventhal JM, Shapiro ED, Aten CB, Berg AT, Egerter SA (1986) Does breast-feeding protect
    against infections in infants less than three months of age? Pediatrics 78: 896–903
19 Barros FC, Victora CG, Vaughan JP, Smith PG (1986) Birth weight and duration of breast-
    feeding: are the beneficial effects of human milk being overestimated? Pediatrics 78: 656–661
20 Jaso JM, Nieburg P, Marks JS (1984) Mortality and infectious disease associated with infant-
    feeding practices in developing countries. Pediatrics 74: 702–727
21 Jelliffe DB, Jelliffe EFP (1978) Human milk in the modern world: psychosocial, nutritional and
    economic significance. Oxford University Press, Oxford, p 298
22 Dobbing J (ed) (1985) Maternal nutrition and lactational infertility. Raven Press, New York
23 Lunn PG, Prentice AM, Austin S et al. (1980) Influence of maternal diet on plasma prolactin
    levels during lactation. Lancet i 623–625
24 Lunn PG, Watkinson M, Prentice AM et al. (1981) Maternal nutrition and lactational
    amenorrhoea. Lancet i: 1428–1429
25 Cameron M, Hofvander Y (1976) PAG manual on feeding infants and young children. 2nd edn.
    United Nations, New York
26 Jelliffe DB, Jelliffe EFP (1978) Human milk in the modern world. Oxford University Press,
    Oxford, p 159
27 de Mause L (1976) The history of childhood. Souvenir Press
28 Gomm R (1976) Breast – best or bestial. Midwife, Health Visitor and Community Nurst 12: 317–
    321
29 World Health Statistics (1982) Prevalence and duration of breast-feeding. 35: No 2
30 Popkin BM, Bilsborrow RE, Akin JS (1982) Breastfeeding patterns in low income countries.
    Science 218: 1088–1093
31 WHO/UNICEF (1979) Meeting on infant and young child feeding, background paper. October:
    19
32 Zhang Jing (1983) 36th World Health Assembly: verbatim records; Document WHA 36/1983/
    REC/3. WHO, Geneva (Committee B, 6th Session)
33 Notzon F (1984) Trends in infant feeding in developing countries. Pediatrics 74: 648–666
34 Wijga A, Vyas U, Vyas A et al. (1983) Feeding, illness and nutritional status in young children in
    rural Gujarat. Hum Nutr Clin Nutr 376: 255–269
35 Dev K, Agarwal KN, Agarwal IC et al. (1982) Breast feeding practices in urban slum and rural
    areas of Varanasi. J Trop Pediatr 28: 89–92
36 Lozoff B (1983) Birth and "bonding" in non-industrial societies. Dev Med Child Neurol 25: 595–
    600
37 WHO (1981) Contemporary patterns of breast feeding. WHO, Geneva
38 Dimond HJ, Ashworth A (1987) Infant feeding practices in Kenya, Mexico and Malaysia – the
    rarity of the exclusively breast-fed infant. Hum Nutr Appl Nutr 41A: 51–64
39 Ebrahim GJ (1976) Audienz des Gerichtspräsidenten VIII von Bern. Forsetzung der Hauptver-
    handlung wegen Ehrverletzung, 22–24 Juni 1976. (Libel Proceedings, Verbatim Record, Bern,
    1976)
40 Gray EH (1981) Effect of supplementary food on suckling patterns and ovarian activity during
    lactation. Br Med J 283: 1547
41 Howie PW, McNeilly AS, Houston MJ et al. (1981) Effect of supplementary food on suckling
    patterns and ovarian activity during lactation. Br Med J 283: 757–759
42 Orwell S, Murray J (1974) Infant feeding and health in Ibadan. Environ Child Health 20: 205–219

43 Orwell S, Clayton D, Dugdale AE (1984) Infant feeding in Nigeria. Ecol Food Nutr 15: 129–141
44 Clayton D, Orwell S, Dugdale AE (1984) Infant feeding in the Ivory Coast. Food Nutr Bull 6: 2–6
45 Waterlow JC, Thomson AM (1979) Observations on the adequacy of breastfeeding. Lancet ii: 238–242
46 Ebrahim GJ Practical mother and child health in developing countries. East African Literature Bureau, Nairobi
47 Helsing E, King FS (1982) Breast feeding in practice. Oxford University Press, Oxford
48 American Academy of Pediatrics (1984) Report of the task force on the assessment of the scientific evidence relating to infant feeding practices and infant health. Pediatrics 74: 579–762
49 Jelliffe DB, Jelliffe EFP (1978) Human milk in the modern world: psychosocial, nutritional and economic significance. Oxford University Press, Oxford, pp 79–80
50 Jelliffe DB, Jelliffe EFP (1978) Human milk in the modern world: psychosocial, nutritional and economic significance. Oxford University Press, Oxford, p 78
51 Jelliffe DB (1978) Statement. In: Marketing and promotion of infant formula in the developing nations, 1978. Hearing before the subcommittee on health and scientific research of the committee on human resources. US Government Printing Office, Washington DC, p 42 (United States Senate May 23, 1978)
52 Gopujkar PV, Chaudhuri SN, Ramaswami MA et al. (1984) Infant feeding practices, with special reference to the use of commercial infant foods. Nutrition Foundation of India, Scientific Report No 4, New Delhi
53 Leading Article (1986) Infant feeding today. Lancet i: 17–18
54 Prentice AM, Roberts SB, Prentice A, et al. (1983) Dietary supplementation of lactating women. I. Effect on breast milk volume and quality. Hum Nutr Clin Nutr 37C: 53–64
55 Dobbing J (ed) (1981) Maternal nutrition in pregnancy. Academic Press, London
56 A Swedish code of ethics for marketing . . . (1977) Acta Paed Scand 66: 129–132
57 Dobbing J (1981) The later development of the brain and its vulnerability. In: Davis JA, Dobbing J (eds) Scientific Foundations of paediatrics, 2nd edn. Heinemann, London, pp 744–759
58 Jelliffe DB (1975) Advertising and infant feeding. J Trop Pediatr 21: 161–162
59 Latham MC (1977) Introduction. In: Greiner T (1977) Regulation and education: strategies for solving the bottle feeding problem. Cornell International Nutrition Monograph Series No 4, 1977, Ithaca, NY
60 Protein advisory group of the United Nations System (PAG) Introduction. Promotion of special foods (infant formula and processed protein foods) for vulnerable groups. PAG statement No. 23, 18 July 1972; revised 28 November 1973
61 World Health Organization (1983) Women and breast feeding. WHO, Geneva
62 UNICEF (1983) News about breast feeding: Sri Lanka survey. UNICEF News, No 1 UNICEF, New York
63 Human Lactation Center (1977) Mothers in poverty. Lactation Review 2: No 3
64 Lucey JF (1981) Does a vote of 118 to 1 mean the USA was wrong? Pediatrics 68: 431

Chapter 3

Origins of the Controversy

Maggie McComas

It has been agreed in the previous chapter that the superiority of breast-feeding and human milk over possible substitutes has never been in dispute. In addition to high nutritive value, breast-feeding involves none of the hazards inherent in preparing substitutes especially in settings where babies are particularly vulnerable to disease.

In spite of these advantages, alternative feeding methods have been used since the beginnings of recorded history. The consequences of using breast milk substitutes have long been documented. Thus the origins of the controversy were in evidence long before the development of the infant formula industry that was at the centre of this debate.

The unmodified substitutes of two centuries ago probably had little more nutritive value than the starchy gruels that many Third World mothers give their babies today, and the sanitary conditions of eighteenth century urban areas were not very different from the villages of today's developing countries. One medical observer estimated that attempts to bring up children "by hand" in Dickensian London resulted in the death of seven out of every eight [1].

The feeding bottle itself is not a recent invention. Glass feeding bottles were in evidence some 200 years ago, products of the Industrial Revolution. But these were no more than improvements on earlier, cruder instruments used for artificial feeding in ancient Egypt and during the Graeco-Roman era. While the bottle unquestionably made easier the administration of breast milk substitutes, doubts over their nutritive value and suspicions about the hygienic hazards of artificial feeding remained. Partly because of the obvious dangers in administering breast milk substitutes, wet nurses were for a long time the preferred alternative for middle- and upper-class mothers who could not, or chose not to breast-feed their own children.

Thus, until the twentieth century, human milk, whether administered by a child's own mother or a surrogate, was the primary form of nutrition during an infant's earliest months of life. The great majority of babies who could not be breast-fed, died [2].

That pattern began to shift in the late nineteenth century with the advent of commercially prepared breast milk substitutes; sweetened condensed milk and other precursors of more nutritionally-adequate infant formulae. The parallel decline of the wet nurse was not necessarily a trend to be mourned, for many physicians of that era had recognised the financial, physiological and moral obstacles of this form of feeding as a replacement for the breast of a baby's own mother [3]. The availability of safe breast milk substitutes was the factor that made these other disincentives to use wet nurses all the more valid.

Third World Context

In today's version of the controversy over artificial feeding, the nutritional adequacy of most commercial infant formula is not questioned. Rather, critics of Industry seek to curb the promotion of commercial formula to consumers who cannot duplicate the conditions required for safe preparation and administration of these products, and for whom, the advocates insist, the product is not necessary, and one they cannot afford.

Changing patterns of infant feeding, particularly in the Third World, and the role of Industry in those changes might have continued to be merely the object of the occasional academic study or survey had not the entry of UN agencies into the discussion given it some new life and greater coherence. The catalytic agent in the infant formula controversy proved to be the UN's Protein Advisory Group (PAG), later to become the Protein-Calorie Advisory Group, whose job it was to assure coordination of research projects and aid programmes concerning nutrition. It came under the purview of such UN bodies as WHO (World Health Organization), FAO (Food and Agriculture Organization) and UNICEF (UN Children's Fund). Throughout the 1960s, a PAG working group had conducted an evaluation of nutrition among young children, the preschool age group. Late in the decade, the working group decided to extend this work, to investigate problems of nutrition *in utero*, i.e. in the unborn child, and also during the first few months of life.

Feed the Mother

One PAG recommendation was that pregnant women and mothers be properly advised on nutritionally appropriate diets. Adequate nourishment for the mother, PAG experts knew, was almost a precondition for successful breast-feeding. While implementation of this informal directive was not considered the responsibility of the infant food industry, these companies certainly had no reason to argue against better maternal health.

However, promoting better maternal nutrition requires more than encouraging messages. Food subsidy programmes must be provided for the very needy and, as far as the developing countries are concerned, better maternal nutrition essentially means better nutrition for most of the adult female population.

Some nutritionists and lay critics have argued that the provision of nutritional supplements to pregnant women and new mothers is a cost-effective way of assuring that infants get a healthy start in life. They would attempt to correct the nutritional deficiencies of those adults whose improved health would directly affect that of the next generation. The result, they say, would be healthier newborns and mothers better equipped to produce adequate breast milk for a longer period of time.

Others doubt that adult nutrition programmes can catch potential mothers in their net early enough. As we have seen in Chapter 2, they would need to be effective at least throughout pregnancy and lactation to have much impact on infant health. There would still be babies born "at risk": underweight, weak, susceptible to disease and consequently in need of food supplements.

Industry Participation

In December 1969, the PAG working group drew up a preliminary action programme addressed not only to UN member governments and health professionals, but also to the infant formula industry, whose representatives were to become regular participants in the group's subsequent activities. The first formal joint meeting on the subject of infant nutrition took place at a two-day conference in November 1970. The group could not all at once hope to examine the global problem of malnutrition. Despite the many common attributes of developing countries, the Third World is anything but homogeneous, and good nutritionists appreciate the dangers of extrapolating "findings from a rural Asian community to a plantation in Guatemala" [4]. Thus it was appropriate for this first discussion to examine a particular region, which also became the meeting site: Bogotá, Colombia. Participants were selected from academia, government health services and Industry and represented a considerable body of experience in dealing with the nutrition problems of particular relevance to Latin America and the Caribbean.

Four general objectives were set out in advance:

- Emphasis of the importance of prolonged breast feeding
- Tentative guidelines for the promotion of infant foods
- Discussions on the development of low-cost protein-rich weaning foods
- Possibilities for public health and Industry "joint action"

Companies were fully aware that their marketing practices were an important enough factor in nutrition to be prominent on the agenda, but the ensuing discussion was more harshly critical than expected, and that was only a prelude to what was to come later when the debate went beyond the circle of health professionals.

The most outspoken of the conference participants was Dr. Derrick B. Jelliffe, a PAG consultant who was at that time Director of the Caribbean Food and Nutrition Institute. This was the first time that a health professional in such a forum had emphasised a connection between infant mortality trends and the promotion and use of infant formula. Jelliffe did so in dramatic fashion, offering few reservations and no apologies: commercial formulae were significantly linked to infant disease and death, he said.

His claim evoked lively debate and highlighted differences of opinion. A more reserved view was expressed by several others, who contended that the decline of breast-feeding was caused by factors largely independent of the promotion of commercial infant formulae. Addressing the serious charge linking the products to disease and death, they suggested that infant mortality be examined in the context of a wide range of other environmental and socio-economic factors [5].

Jelliffe's challenge could not be fully answered in the course of a two-day conference. The closing plenary session noted diplomatically that "no constructive purpose would be served at this time in relating the world-wide decline of breast-feeding to any single factor including processed infant foods. Research is urgently needed on current patterns and social dynamics of breast-feeding in order to obtain information on which to base actions" [6].

Despite this stated need for better information on the actual state of infant nutrition, the recommendations for action in the meeting's conclusions focussed on Industry:

- Product labels were to be made "as clear as possible" to prevent misuse
- Companies were to employ only personnel "adequately trained . . . in all matters concerning infant foods . . ."
- Industry was "to *continue* (emphasis added) to instruct all personnel not to discourage breast-feeding"
- Industry was "to design labels and literature to foster an education campaign of sanitation" (use of boiled water, etc)
- Industry was to encourage breast-feeding "through all of its skills and *communications to mothers* (emphasis added) as appropriate"
- "Modern processed infant foods" which were nutritionally complete were to be made "widely available"

On the face of it, Industry was not so much being lectured to as encouraged. Those "proposals for action" were largely prescriptive rather than proscriptive in nature, reflecting the positive contribution that the promotion of commercial products could make to safe infant nutrition. Health professionals and the international agencies seemed ready to treat Industry as an equal partner in the effort to solve problems of nutrition in the Third World. There was no mention of restrictions on advertising or other promotion: those were to come later.

The conference thus ended on an upbeat note, despite the acrimonious debate that had occurred. The participants departed with the intention of meeting at a later date to produce a more formal action programme with more clearly specified objectives and commitments.

Not everyone was satisfied, however. Jelliffe, Industry's most severe and most persistent critic within the health profession, was one who was not. At the time, he expressed mixed feelings on the issue. Shortly after the conference, for example, he issued an appeal for a "dialogue" between Industry and paediatric nutritionists [7] that implied a recognition of the Industry as a partner in the larger nutrition issue. Yet in the same breath he began hammering away at the notions he had outlined in Bogotà, namely that commercial formula products had had a "disruptive effect" on the pattern of breast-feeding, that their purchase posed an economic hardship on consumers in developing countries, and that children in the

Third World were suffering from "commerciogenic malnutrition" caused by the "thoughtless promotion" of infant milks [7]. The attempt to link Industry's promotional practices to infant disease and death had been made. In this basic form, and frequently in Jelliffe's own language, the charge was to resurface when advocacy groups in Europe and the US picked up the campaign banner.

PAG Statement No. 23

Nevertheless the dialogue continued, with the PAG working group convening next in June 1972 in Paris. This time the experts posed questions on infant nutrition and the role of Industry against the background of conditions in African and Asian countries. From that session came an even firmer set of recommendations, scrutinised and revised after yet another meeting a year later in New York, then finally released as a policy document in November 1973.

Although this document, *PAG Statement No. 23* [8], was the product of a long process of negotiation and consensus-making, it was not as innocuous as such compromise documents so frequently turn out to be. On the contrary, it spelled out in firm tones the obligations and responsibilities of the three relevant parties, national governments and UN agencies, nutritionists and physicians, and the infant formula and food industries, in promoting better infant nutrition in the Third World. The expressed attitude towards Industry was still basically positive, and its role recognised as legitimate. The statement urged, for example, that in countries lacking suitable breast milk substitutes, commercial infant formulas be "developed and introduced to satisfy the special needs of infants who are not breast-fed".

The statement did outline in fairly stark terms the risks posed where infant formula was employed by consumers in the lower socio-economic groups and administered in unsanitary conditions. Marketing practices might be altered to protect particularly vulnerable babies, yet if those same infants really needed a breast milk substitute in the form of a commercial formula, such products should be provided. Well thought out as *Statement No. 23* was, it was unavoidably presented on the horns of the classic moral dilemma, as its authors themselves acknowledged: "It is clearly important to avoid any action that would accelerate the trend away from breast-feeding, at the same time, it is essential to make formulae, foods and instructions available to those mothers who do not breast feed *for various reasons*" (emphasis added).

Governments were called upon to:

– Encourage industrial investment for the development of highly nutritious foods
– Reduce fiscal burdens on processed infant formulae and weaning foods
– Consider subsidy programmes (including free distribution) to provide nutritious infant formulae and weaning foods to the poorest groups
– Stimulate the use of mass media channels for both education and responsible product promotion

Paediatricians and other physicians, for their part, were urged to:

- Keep themselves informed of developments in infant and child feeding,
  including the promotion of breast-feeding but also the use of processed foods
  and home-prepared weaning foods
- Meet with representatives of the food industry to discuss progress in child
  nutrition, with particular emphasis on the needs of low-income populations

Industry was asked to:

- Ensure that breast-feeding be stressed in its own employee training programmes and that sales and promotional methods discouraging appropriate
  breast-feeding be avoided
- Avoid direct promotion to new mothers, recognising that the hospital nursery
  was not appropriate for any promotion of infant foods directed at other than
  professional personnel
- Develop "unambiguous" standard directions for the preparation of commercial formulae, taking into account the needs of illiterate persons
- Use product labels and literature as a means of encouraging better hygiene
  practices in infant food preparation

Industry was thus directly charged with eliminating unethical marketing
practices and developing what amounted to a programme of education in proper
feeding methods. What stood out even more prominently in the statement's list of
action points, however, was the message to governments to encourage the
development and use of commercial formulae and the message to health
professionals that Industry representatives were to be welcomed as partners in
cooperative efforts to improve infant nutrition.

ICIFI: Formalising Industry Cooperation

Taking their cue from this policy statement, companies began to take individual
and collective action. On the occasion of the next PAG-sponsored regional
meeting of government representatives, health professionals and Industry executives, held in Singapore in November 1974, company representatives first
discussed the notion of forming an Industry Council. The first informal meeting of
that group in spring 1975 drew the participation of nine companies accounting for
a substantial proportion of the infant formula business world-wide: two US-based
firms, Wyeth (a subsidiary of American Home Products) and Ross-Abbott (of
Abbott Laboratories), Dumex (a Danish firm), Cow & Gate (the major UK
producer), four Japanese companies (Meiji, Morinaga, Snow and Wakodo) and
Nestlé.
    The first item on the agenda was concerned with organisational formalities, a
constitution was to be drafted and objectives outlined. It was apparent from the
outset that this group, to be called the International Council of Infant Food
Industries (ICIFI), was to be no ordinary industry association. Its justification
was to be found in the ability to address itself specifically to the growing
controversy over the marketing and use of infant foods in developing countries.
The companies' hope was that the Council could contribute to the study of infant

nutrition in the Third World and, in line with the PAG recommendations, help to develop feeding methods and instruction for product preparation and use appropriate to developing countries, designed to prevent the misuse of infant formula.

Initially, however, some brush fires would have to be fought. Members of ICIFI saw that the group would need to respond not only to the general problems of infant nutrition in the Third World but also to the specific allegations that various critics had levelled at Industry concerning the promotion of its products.

The Council immediately set to work formulating a code of marketing practices that would reflect the principles of *PAG Statement No. 23*. Late in 1975, ICIFI (minus Ross-Abbott, which by then had decided to pursue its own route in dealing with the issue) was formally constituted. Many of PAG's recommendations were never to be realised, however. The "continuing efforts of cooperation between industry, nutritionists and pediatricians" eventually faded out, and the suggested "permanent group" representing those interests was never formed. One reason was the sheer weight of bureaucracy involved and the consequent lack of momentum. Each new PAG conference had required a considerable effort of organisation, and maintenance of a permanent working group would have been even more of a problem. In addition, PAG itself was to be disbanded in 1977, partly as the result of the UN's reorganisation of such coordinating units.

In retrospect, however, ICIFI was also at fault in its slowness to capitalise on the effective stamp of legitimisation that this UN group had given Industry the role in Third World infant nutrition programmes and, in particular, marketing strategies for those countries. As a result, Industry was to lose the first round in what was to become a fully fledged campaign against infant formula marketing. All the best intentions of PAG were soon overtaken by events.

The Debate Goes Public

Dr. Jelliffe, who had emerged from the PAG discussions as the most outspoken critic of Industry, did not hesitate to make his dissent known. In July 1973, even as *Statement No. 23* was undergoing its last round of refinement, he spoke in despairing terms of PAG's three-year effort to "obtain some sort of overlap between nutritional adequacy, modest profit [for the industry] and a mass market". Implementation of *Statement No. 23* would not, he thought, do the job. "I don't think we shall get far with this", he told an audience of health professionals, "and some other group may have to take a more aggressive, Nader-like[1] stance in this regard" [9].

It did not take long for the "Nader-like" stance to manifest itself, and it did so within advocacy organisations composed of laymen, not professionals, as far as nutrition was concerned. These were quintessential advocates, speaking on behalf of others, the others in this case being continents away. They ushered the debate into a new phase quite different in character from what had gone before, as cooperation gave way to confrontation.

---

[1] Ralph Nader, a prominent American consumerist.

The *New Internationalist* Report

The subject of Third World malnutrition and infant formula marketing appealed particularly to the new wave of investigative journalists, and it was in their magazines and other media that the critics fired the first round.

As is related in Chapter 1, the *New Internationalist*, a British periodical concerned with Third World issues, first described the hazards of infant formula misuse in terms that the layman could easily grasp [10]. *The Baby Food Tragedy* based on interviews with Dr. David Morley, and Dr. Ralph Hendrickse, two child health specialists with extensive experience in the Third World, sowed some seeds of doubt about Nestlé's marketing of infant formula. The report was even more harshly critical than Jelliffe had been, although the careful reader could see that the Company's practices were almost as often commended as condemned. For example, according to Dr. Hendrickse:

Nestlé did in fact modify its advertising policies [in Nigeria] and you'll find that right up to the present time an advert for, let's say, Nestlé's milk over the Nigerian radio will start with the quote, "You should always breast feed your baby, but if you cannot then use . . . such and such". *I think this is a very reasonable approach* (emphasis added).

However, when he was asked whether "this responsible advertising" policy was followed in other African countries, Hendrickse replied that to the best of his knowledge the Company had not instituted the same policy elsewhere. In fact, this was not correct, since Nestlé policies in other African markets had followed much the same pattern.

In another specific reference to Nestlé, Dr. Morley cited his experience in seeing a Nestlé sample and feeding bottle stamped with the company logo at a new mother's hospital bedside. "In Bangkok I was told these are given to all mothers before they leave hospital", he said. (Nestlé was later to end unsolicited distribution of formula samples and to eliminate gifts of bottles altogether).

Most of the report, however, referred to Industry in general. Many damaging assertions were made:

– The typical Third World user of infant formula really could not afford it and thus was invariably tempted to over-dilute the product in preparation
– Companies in the infant food industry attempted to maximise sales "at almost any cost"
– Infant formula was sometimes imported into developing countries and sold past its expiry date, with quality no longer guaranteed
– Infant formula producers had not made the effort to develop simplified preparation and feeding instructions for Third World mothers
– Infant formula producers employed local nurses "to go into government clinics to sell baby milk". (This was hardly an accurate description of Nestlé practice since the company-employed nurses had no responsibilities for actual product sales – see Chap. 8)

The blame for the trend away from breast-feeding was not laid entirely with Industry. Dr. Hendrickse cited a number of other factors aside from the "seduction of advertisement", among them the tendency of young married women to continue their education or to work away from home.

Moreover, he cited the need for improved employment policies taking into account the needs of the growing number of working women in developing countries. "When they build factories that are going to accommodate women, let provision be made . . . for a crèche for the babies and let the women breast-feed them and do their job . . . We can't put the clock back and say women must return to the home".

The medical profession also came in for its share of criticism, with the teaching of infant feeding in most medical schools being described as "appallingly bad". Perhaps the most positive element in an otherwise critical report was the recognition of the need for an "international consensus" on advertising and promotion.

The suggestion that international bodies such as WHO, as well as the governments of developing countries, should share responsibility for the development and enforcement of such guidelines was a notion that Nestlé could readily accept, and in fact did so when such a code became a reality eight years later.

The overall impression left by the interviews was very negative for Industry, however. The errors were obvious only to those familiar with the actual situations described, but even the uninitiated exposed to the issue for the first time should have been able to tell, from the way in which the article was presented, that it was intended to be more than straightforward reporting. The interviews appeared on the journal's pages set aside each month for a "campaign" on Third World issues, and the title called for *Action Now on Baby Foods*. Then there was the magazine's cover photograph: an infant's grave on which had been placed an empty feeding bottle and a crumpled container of Lactogen, a Nestlé product.

The *New Internationalist* editor's procedure in sending out prepublication photocopies of the article to health professionals and others presumed to have an interest in the subject had its desired effect. It prompted letters both from paediatricians who unequivocally criticised Industry practices, and those more willing to recognise the complexity of factors involved in infant-feeding problems. Nestlé, by contrast, heard from the *New Internationalist* only *after* the article was published, when its editor wrote to Management, offering (with some irony, as Nestlé saw it) "fair representation of your views on this distressing matter" [11]. The editor's letter continued in a tone which left the impression that "fair representation" would inevitably be equated with an admission of guilt. He went on to say "If the facts quoted . . . are correct, the causes of the diseases and consequent deaths should be rectified as soon as possible". Nestlé fully agreed with his concern, but that important "if" needed answering. It was difficult to know just where to begin, but Management took the opportunity to respond with a short reply suitable for publication.

Part of that response did appear in the magazine, but the editor chose to omit those of the Company's comments which refuted the article's report of two particular sins of the infant food industry, one of commission and the other of omission. First, Nestlé Management pointed out that no observer in the field had reported that "substandard goods", i.e. goods delivered to export markets past the expiry date guaranteeing their quality, were being "offloaded" in the Third World. Second, it was not true, as claimed, that "no milk company had troubled" to develop simplified mixing instructions for its branded products. Nestlé, for one, had done just that.

There was yet more to be rebutted or explained. The Company had long ago instituted a policy of recruiting and retaining only qualified nurses, midwives or nutrition professionals to communicate product and feeding information to mothers and health workers. The observation that Nestlé was not emphasising the superiority of breast-feeding in its marketing efforts throughout Africa was also inaccurate: this was both policy and practice in the Company's African markets.

There was still more to take issue with, but the difficulty went beyond the Company's having been wronged in print. If what Management then considered to be a progressive policy on infant feeding and formula promotion was misinterpreted by credible professionals who had hitherto not spoken out and had no apparent axe to grind, and if such people quite sincerely could not see Company policy for what it was, then something was very wrong. The *New Internationalist* had said that Nestlé's product promotion was very effective. But at the same time, it had implied that the educational messages accompanying such promotion, specifically, the recommendation to breast-feed, were ineffective. If professionals such as those interviewed could not see that the company had taken pains to recommend breast-feeding and ensure that its products were used appropriately and correctly, how could the public at large be expected to get the message?

It was going to take more than a Letter to the Editor to correct this perception. As a start, Nestlé Management invited the editor to their headquarters in Switzerland in order to pursue the broad-ranging discussion that was obviously needed to provide the "fair representation" that the editor himself had suggested. The *New Internationalist* responded with a disparaging editorial [12] that dismissed not only Nestlé's efforts but also those of the paediatricians who had been cooperating with Industry under the UN umbrella. The editor considered, for example, that Nestlé's reference to the "immense socio-economic complexities" of the issue was a red herring, yet it was PAG which had first taken account of that reality back in 1970 in Bogotá. The editorial went on publicly to refuse Nestlé's invitation for a headquarters briefing, objecting as much to the symbolism as to the substance. The editor noted that "the answers to the questions we raised are not to be found on the banks of Lake Geneva" (incidentally, the site of WHO headquarters, too). This biting commentary concluded with an appeal for a stepped-up campaign, which was not long in coming.

The Baby Killer

One particular irony of the infant formula campaign's concentration on Nestlé was that Management, represented by specialists in the Infant and Dietetic Products Department at headquarters in Switzerland, was readily accessible from the outset as a source of information, even to outsiders who might have had no professional background in nutrition but only an expressed interest in this particular aspect of infant nutrition in the Third World. In practice, Nestlé simply did not deserve its public image of corporate impenetrability. Such openness was to contribute to the Company's vulnerability, however. Explaining the complexity of the issue was not synonymous with giving industry a suitable defence. Once certain hazards of using commercial formula were admitted, it seemed that the "interested parties" proved considerably less interested in hearing of Industry's efforts to eliminate those risks.

If the *New Internationalist* was not interested in pursuing the discussion on Nestlé's home territory, others were. The Company was visited late in 1973 by Mike Muller, a free-lance journalist on assignment for War on Want, a British charity organisation whose principal activities of disaster relief and medical aid programme were complemented by "research at home and observation in the field". Muller surmised that the issue was more complex than the *New Internationalist* interviews had indicated, as Nestlé had always said. The journalist, who also interviewed Cow & Gate, a UK-based infant formula producer, spent two days with Nestlé company managers responsible for infant formula, pursuing a constructive, if often tough, line of questioning. After several follow-up letters in which additional information was provided and points in the previous discussions clarified, Nestlé awaited the advance proof copy of the article which Muller had promised. It did not arrive. The Company next heard from War on Want at the same time as the public at large, when the report was released with the flourish of a London press conference which befitted its sensational title, *The Baby Killer* [13]. The stated objective of the tract: "To make known to a wider public the dangers that follow from the promotion of powdered baby-milks in communities that cannot use them properly".

The report was constructed in a skilful, thrust-and-parry style giving Industry some credit for good intentions at the same time as the result was being disparaged. An introductory disclaimer pointed out that "the object of this report is not to prove that baby milks kill babies . . . not to prove that the baby food industry is exclusively responsible for this trend [away from breast-feeding]". Part of the appeal of Muller's report lay in its very positive pitch for breast-feeding as the panacea for problems of infant nutrition in developing countries. Socio-economic constraints on breast-feeding were glossed over, the report suggesting that mothers' milk was being displaced particularly by commercial infant formula, as put so bluntly in a headline, *Breast Versus Bottle*. Following a brief recitation of familiar statistics noting the decline in breast-feeding in a handful of countries, the report focussed on anecdotes concerning mothers' expressed beliefs about the value of bottle-feeding. Then came the conclusion of cause and effect: Company marketing practices were responsible for a dramatic upsurge in artificial feeding in an environment where malnutrition and death were the all-too-common result.

Nestlé managers could not really complain that they had been misquoted. They had, rather, been caught in what journalists admit are the fly traps of the editorial process: the quote taken out of context, the crucial (at least from the interviewee's standpoint) sentences that are never printed. If the Company had thought Industry's case would be helped by telling all, it was mistaken in assuming that all that was told would actually be printed.

Nestlé managers felt that among the omissions from the published report were their painstaking explanations of the need for different types of formula products, particularly in the markets of the Third World. The value of acidified milks, products less susceptible to bacterial contamination in tropical areas, which the Company had carefully explained, was not mentioned at all, for example.

Considerably more damaging than this failure to provide what the Company felt was the full picture of its product policy was the recitation of "unethical and immoral" promotion practices, such as the use of "unqualified sales girls dressed in nurses uniforms" and, on the other hand, the use of "qualified nurses paid on a sales-related basis". It was Nestlé that had described the practices of some competitors to Muller. But as these reports were attributed to an unidentified "industry man", it was all too easy to get the impression that Nestlé had been guilty of this practice, and activist leaders did nothing to discourage that belief.

Although War on Want's proposed solution to the problem of infant formula misuse included directives to governments and the medical profession, its most pointed suggestions were, predictably, aimed at Industry. These were:

– Elimination of "all consumer promotion of breast milk substitutes in high risk communities"

– Abandonment of promotion to the medical profession "which may perform the miseducation function of suggesting that particular brands of milk can overcome the problems of misuse"

– "Constructive cooperation" with international organisations working on the problems of infant and child nutrition in the developing countries.

While the first two suggestions were obviously the most dramatic in terms of their implications for company policy, management could see that they were based on assumptions, by then a plank in the critics' platform, of how promotion influenced consumers. Nestlé disagreed profoundly with those assumptions. As for the suggestion concerning cooperation with the international agencies, what was three years' worth of work within PAG, if not "constructive cooperation"? Added to these recommendations was a call to potentially like-minded campaigners, and a warning flag to Industry. War on Want suggested that a "more broadly based campaign involving many national organisations" could have an effect on "intransigent" corporate policies.

Policy Review

Nestlé felt that the curbs on marketing suggested by War on Want were so extreme, and the follow-up letters from the organisation's general secretary so dictatorial in tone, that it would have a hard time continuing a dialogue with War on Want. As long as the suspicions about infant formula's link to disease and malnutrition could not be definitively cast aside, Nestlé would need to give even greater assurance that its promotional campaign provided truly useful information and did not discourage mothers from breast-feeding. So, after an internal review of Nestlé marketing practices which was then being pursued in all the developing countries where the Company had a market, Management introduced more stringent controls on the distribution of samples to health professionals. Direct contact between Company representatives and mothers was to be strictly avoided where such a policy was suggested by local authorities, and advertising not meeting with the approval of health officials was suspended. Meanwhile an extensive review of the body of scientific evidence about infant malnutrition and feeding patterns in developing countries was undertaken in order to determine the extent to which Muller's version of infant nutrition in these countries was actually true. Even as Nestlé was in the process of this policy review, however, the Company found itself faced with another challenge, this one to result in a legal battle much nearer home, the legal instruments being brought out as weapons of last resort.

War on Want had made *The Baby Killer* widely available for translation into other languages and dissemination by similar groups elsewhere. One organisation taking advantage of the offer was a Swiss group based in Bern, the Arbeitsgruppe Dritte Welt (Third World Working Group). When its German-language translation appeared in Switzerland, it sparked considerable public interest and attention in the media. A company that was a household word to Swiss consumers, a prominent employer and an important financial concern with thousands of shareholders, was prominently featured. But in this version there were greater problems than the out-of-context quote or omitted explanation. The allegations of too-aggressive promotion, and the unproven thesis that commercial formula contributed to malnutrition and disease, now became frankly libellous in the book's title: *Nestlé Kills Babies*.

References

1   Duncum BM (1947) Some notes on the history of lactation. Br Med Bull V: 1141
2   Fildes V (1986) Breasts, bottles and babies – a history of infant feeding. Edinburgh University Press, Edinburgh
3   Apple RD (1980) "To be used only under the direction of a physician": Commercial infant feeding and medical practice, 1870–1940. Bull Hist Med 54: 402–417
4   Pelto GH (1981) Perspectives on infant feeding: decision-making and ecology. Food Nutr Bull 3: 16–29
5   Cox DO (1978) Summary statement of Abbott Laboratories on the role of prepared infant formulas in the third world. In: Marketing and promotion of infant formula in the developing nations, 1978. Hearing before the subcommittee on health and scientific research of the committee on human resources. US Government Printing Office, Washington, DC. (United States Senate May 23, 1978) pp 198–203
6   Internal Report (1970) PAHO/WHO-UNICEF Conference of pediatricians and representatives of the food industry on infant feeding in Latin America and the Caribbean, Bogotà, Columbia, Nov 5–6
7   Jelliffe DB (1971) Commerciogenic malnutrition? Time for a dialogue. Food Technol 15(Feb): 55–56
8   Protein advisory group of the United Nations System (PAG) (1973) Introduction. Promotion of special foods (infant formula and processed protein foods) for vulnerable groups. (PAG statement No. 23, 18 July 1972, revised 28 November 1973)
9   Jelliffe DB, Jelliffe EFP (1974) Food supplies for physiologically vulnerable groups. In: Elliott K, Knight J (Eds) Human rights in health. Amsterdam: Elsevier, 1974: 133–151 (Ciba Foundation Symposium 23).
10 Geach H (1973) The baby food tragedy. New Internationalist Aug: 8–12, 23
11 Peter Adamson (1973) Editor, New Internationalist, letter to Nestlé. Aug 16
12 Anonymous (1973) Milk and murder. New Internationalist Oct: 1
13 Muller M (1974) The baby killer. War on Want, London

Chapter 4

Focus on Nestlé: the Bern Trial

Maggie McComas

Later in the controversy, other major manufacturers of infant formula were to come under the scrutiny of the activists. American companies, for example, became the object of a newly discovered pressure-group weapon, the shareholder resolution, which was used to transform the Annual General Meeting into a debating arena on this specific issue of public policy. But it was perhaps from the moment that the War on Want publication was translated into German and given its new libellous title by a Swiss activist group that Nestlé became the company most specifically, prominently, and consistently associated with allegations linking the use of infant formula to malnutrition and disease in developing countries.

The original version of *The Baby Killer* itself constituted a hard-hitting challenge to Nestlé's policies. That report had interpreted a few selected scientific and field studies to support the basic case against infant formula marketing in the Third World. Although War on Want insisted its objective was not to attribute disease and malnutrition in those countries "solely" to the use of infant formula, it was easy for the reader to draw the conclusion that commercial products were indeed a major factor in this adverse nutritional chain, more often contributing to the problem than solving it. Nestlé and one competing company had been interviewed, and had provided substantial source material on corporate marketing practices, and their contribution had been acknowledged. Yet the manner in which the report was built upon examples of aggressive promotion left the reader to determine whether this was a narrative or a confession.

Nestlé had been disillusioned by the results of its efforts to open its doors to outside enquiry. Management had participated in two days of interviews based on what it assumed was mutual trust; but Muller had not kept his promise to let the Company review his draft manuscript. As a consequence, Nestlé had no opportunity to question or discuss his misrepresentations of Company marketing practices. Although the booklet claimed that problems of infant nutrition were its main concern, Nestlé began to find it difficult to believe that the motivation was quite so high-minded. Given the appearance of the final product, it looked as though War on Want had probably always intended to mount an all-out attack on the infant formula industry. However, *The Baby Killer* had raised some important issues concerning infant nutrition, and had posed some delicate questions about marketing practices that needed answering. Accordingly Management undertook to review all the data and field studies referred to in the report and to make sure that what headquarters had stated as policy was actually being practised in the field, with adjustments where necessary.

Naming Nestlé

The Swiss activists' translation of the report had the effect of turning a rather defective literary creature into a monster which management decided to confront with the appropriate legal weapon. The title itself, *Nestlé tötet Babys* (*Nestlé Kills Babies*), left nothing to the imagination. Not only was the alleged link between infant formula and death from malnutrition restated as a matter of cause and effect, but the title also seemed to cast Nestlé as the sole perpetrator of this heinous crime. This version omitted the crucial introductory disclaimer that had appeared in the English version, the statement that "the object . . . is not to prove that baby milks kill babies" and that it was "not the object to prove that the baby food industry is exclusively responsible for this trend [away from breast-feeding]". Seen against the new title, such a disclaimer would have been obviously contradictory. In its stead, the Swiss version appeared with a new introduction that contained a double misrepresentation.

The Baby Killer in its original English version had attributed "unethical and immoral" practices to unnamed companies, without making it clear whether Nestlé was among them. The Swiss version eliminated this confusion not only by specifying Nestlé as the culprit, but also misrepresenting the original publication. It claimed that "the English study described the conduct of Nestlé and other companies as unethical and immoral". The War on Want report had done no such thing. The Swiss translation then elaborated on the point, saying that Nestlé and Cow & Gate, the UK company interviewed, were "accused of being responsible for the death or permanent mental and physical damage of thousands of children", and this again was untrue. *The Baby Killer* had indeed suggested that such ill-effects arose from the use of infant formula, but the two companies had not been singled out. Finally the translated version omitted the credit given to the two firms' executives for their collaboration in the report. The resulting impression was that War on Want had on its own somehow exposed "unethical and immoral" practices as carried on by these two companies specifically.

The Swiss Activists

Nestlé had no warning of the publication of *Nestlé tötet Babys*, which first came to the Company's notice when it was released to the press and general public in early June 1974. This time there was no opportunity to pursue a rebuttal through a Letter to the Editor. Nor could the Company simply turn a deaf ear to the accusations. Nestlé's employees and shareholders were, in effect, being slandered, and they, as well as the wider public, deserved a response that matched the challenge. Cleverly muddled allegations were one thing, but the published lie was something else, and quite literally an injustice. Management was confident of its ability to show that the accusations had no foundation and had no qualms in filing a libel suit against the publishers and authors. Nestlé speculated that the outcome would put the allegations to rest once and for all, or, at the very least, alter the tone and direction of the controversy.

Later events were to show that Nestlé's optimism was misplaced. Determining whether libel had been committed was to require a detailed examination of the statements in question in the courtroom, statements that dwelt on Nestlé's marketing practices. The judicial process itself was to have the effect of widening that examination into an even broader discussion of the use and marketing of infant formula.

An even more important obstacle to settlement of the controversy at this time was the transformation of the legal challenge into a media event. This was partly the result of the intriguing nature of the case. It was not usual for a staid Swiss company to go running off to the judiciary to have its virtue defended. But the Swiss activists seized this opening and played their role to the hilt, staging press conferences and organising letter-writing campaigns timed to coincide with each stage of the trial. They seemed to sense that the verdict of public opinion would have much more impact than the judge's decision.

Identifying the Activists

Almost as disconcerting as the title and content of the report was the fact that this new challenge was being made on the Company's home territory by a group of critics hitherto unknown to Nestlé. The publishers of the booklet were identified only as the Arbeitsgruppe Dritte Welt (Third World Working Group-ADW), the report itself being credited to War on Want and another Swiss group, Schweizerische Arbeitsgruppen für Entwicklungspolitik (Swiss Working Groups for Development Policy-SAFEP). Naturally, the Company wanted to know who these people were.

However, Management was not going to delay action waiting for that answer. The Company moved quickly, retaining an outside law firm and filing its suit in Bern District Court less than a month after the publication's first appearance. The original charge was something of a shot in the dark, naming "persons yet unknown" as having libelled the company on four counts:

– The title, *Nestlé Kills Babies*
– The introductory statement that Nestlé's practices were "unethical and immoral"
– The allegation, also contained in the introduction, that the Company was responsible for the deaths of thousands of babies
– The accusation that Nestlé employed "sales girls dressed in nurses' uniforms" for marketing purposes

It took several weeks to discover some of the background of ADW and SAFEP and to identify the individuals responsible for the booklet's translation and publication. As it turned out, the groups were not so much clandestine as obscure. Formed in 1970, ADW, by mid-summer 1974, still only had 17 formally enrolled members. Most of them were university students. SAFEP was essentially an overlapping group; its two members to be named in the suit also belonged to ADW. Although that organisation's activities were not nearly as wide-ranging as those of War on Want, the group espoused a philosophy very similar to that of the British organisation in regard to what they saw as the West's exploitation of the Third World. And, like their British counterparts, the members of ADW and other Swiss activists involved with the dissemination of *Nestlé tötet Babys* considered themselves quite capable of turning back the encroachment of Western commercialisation and cultural values on the developing countries. Their political orientation was reflected, for example, in an editorial accompanying one student journal's publication of extracts from the libellous tract:

Those who want to intervene in order to improve the quality of life for the poor masses of the Third World must understand that the most useful development aid is to struggle against economic structures which promote underdevelopment. According to the circumstances, more lives can be saved by controlling or preventing the activities of multinationals than by financing aid projects or distributing food products in the traditional way [1].

Suggested Settlement

The first meeting of the adversaries before the Bern District Court, on 9 October 1974, might have been the last, for the judge followed what is considered standard procedure in such cases, suggesting a settlement. But Rudolf Strahm, who later became a prominent member of the Swiss Socialist Party and the ADW leader who was to act as the group's chief spokesman throughout the affair, answered with a categorical "no" to the settlement terms outlined by Nestlé: destruction of the undistributed copies of the document (3000 had been printed), publishing a notice of the settlement in journals of Nestlé's choosing (at the activists' expense), and, finally, the requirement that the critics contribute a specific sum to Third World charities. Such a settlement, it appeared, would not serve the purposes of the defendants, who had publicly welcomed the court action. Their avowed objective was to bring Nestlé's practices under close public scrutiny, and the trial would do just that.

Defendant's Public Relations Strategy

As the proceedings unfolded, the contrasting behaviour of the adversaries mirrored their very different objectives. Nestlé, following what it saw as the only route to vindication of its position, was concerned solely with the courtroom proceedings, at least at the outset. The defendants, on the other hand, appeared to believe that their cause would be more effectively promoted through sympathetic public opinion than by courtroom victory, the prospects for a court judgment in their favour being slim in any event. Thus ADW and SAFEP issued private appeals and held press conferences to draw attention to their cause. Some of this activity clearly flouted generally-recognised judicial standards for conduct in such cases. When ADW in March 1975 sent a circular letter to solicit support from members of the Swiss medical profession, for example, a civil court in Bern issued a temporary injunction, backed by the threat of a SwF 5000 fine or a one-year prison sentence, to stop such campaigning.

By contrast, Nestlé, on the advice of its lawyers, kept a low profile at the beginning. This approach reflected the Company's determination to observe the accepted standards of conduct by not trying its case in the media.

The judicial wheels began to grind in a predictably slow fashion, and the first hearing in the case was not scheduled until November 1975, nearly a year and a half after the charges had been filed. In the meantime, debate on the issue and, more specifically, speculation on the outcome of the case had ebbed and flowed more than once. Both plaintiff and defendant hastened to submit written evidence to the court where the case was to be decided by a single judge, as is standard procedure for libel cases in Bern canton. Each side also prepared to take the stand. For Nestlé this meant selecting the appropriate in-house experts on both the marketing and scientific aspects of the issue. The task was not difficult, the logical choice being those who had been involved with the issue at the time it was first discussed by the working group of the UN's Protein Advisory Group (PAG) and, later, when the Company had received the War on Want journalist.

Finally, the adversaries combed the field for third-party witnesses to appear in court, persons whose credibility depended on both their degree of expertise in the subject and their presumed impartiality. That field would turn out to be narrower than expected, for the controversy had by then grown to such proportions that even the qualified and presumably impartial expert who knew the issue well enough to have developed some tentative conclusions of his own would, by definition, be seen to have taken sides.

And which side was more attractive, after all? The activists had already succeeded in having themselves identified with the interests of mothers and babies. It was easy enough to muster supporters for that particular cause and to produce testimony that relied more on emotion than on examination of the facts that would verify or refute the allegations against Nestlé. The Company, on the other hand, found that its hitherto benign image, developed in large measure from the contribution of its specialised products to infant nutrition, was being challenged. How could both the adversaries in this legal conflict be considered legitimate defenders of infant health in the Third World?

Reduced Charges

As the first court session opened, Nestlé and its legal counsel had to wrestle with emerging technical difficulties in the string of charges that made up the suit. There seemed to be no problem with the first charge. The Company was confident that the defendants could produce no evidence to back up the claim of the booklet's title. Similarly, Nestlé was sure that the related charges dealing with the text's conclusion that the Company was responsible for the deaths of thousands of babies, could not be substantiated.

As to the charge that the Company employed "sales girls dressed as nurses", Nestlé personnel engaged in marketing support were all qualified nurses, nutritionists or midwives. There was, none-the-less, the problem of drawing the distinction between their educational and marketing functions and demonstrating that these employees did not fall prey to conflicts of interest that might prove detrimental to the very mothers and babies they were supposed to assist.

The most amorphous charge was the one concerning the claims of "unethical and immoral" conduct. The very subjectivity of those terms meant that the court might have to get involved in establishing appropriate criteria for judgment of what was "ethical" or "moral". That could take literally years of testimony, extending beyond the statute of limitations, four years in the case of libel, almost half of which had already slipped away since the suit was filed. So when hearings opened, Nestlé's counsel announced that the suit would only focus on the publication's title, with the other charges to be treated as "support". This announcement provoked no comment at the time.

Other features of the legal action's structure were to pose difficulties for Nestlé. For example, the Company did not have "equal time" in the courtroom during the first round of hearings. The fact that 17 defendants had been named meant that the defence had 17 opportunities to try to show that the alleged libel was a valid statement. Nestlé, as the only plaintiff, could not match that testimony in volume. Only two Company representatives appeared, one a member of the legal department, the other the head of scientific information for infant foods. That the representation would be so unbalanced should have been neither surprising nor, at least at the outset, alarming to the Company. After all, each of the defendants was entitled by law to establish his defence and to respond in full to the charges. But as the hearings progressed, the testimony of the defendants began to sound less like a defence of their own actions than an oral version of *Nestlé tötet Babys*. The media reports of the hearings, in turn, made it seem as if Nestlé were on trial.

From the start, ADW and other defendants were outspoken, waging their defence in public as well as in the courtroom. In a press conference two weeks before the November 1975 hearings opened, for example, ADW described the coming hearings as a precedent for the Swiss courts, whose task would be, in the words of the critics, to "examine the activities of a Swiss multinational in developing countries". Strictly speaking, the court was charged with examining the defendants' actions, not those of Nestlé, but ADW's public announcement was a self-fulfilling prophecy.

The Swiss activists also took care to line up witnesses to speak on their behalf outside the courtroom as well as within. Scheduled to appear at their initial press conference, for example, was Mike Muller, author of *The Baby Killer*, along with a representative of the World Council of Churches, whose support foreshadowed the later involvement of the clergy when the campaign moved on to the US.

Courtroom Testimony

The Company's courtroom presentation was straightforward and concise, as befitted the legal and scientific backgrounds of the two spokesmen. They reviewed Nestlé's marketing policies in developing countries, concentrating on the contentious elements of the libellous publication. The Company employed qualified nurses and midwives, it was explained. These employees' work in product and marketing support included giving advice on how to use infant formula. They did not receive sales bonuses. The spokesmen also reviewed scientific evidence supporting the need for breast milk substitutes, citing examples of a lower infant mortality coinciding with increased use of commercial formula. Finally the Company representatives introduced samples of the Company's promotional and educational materials, tangible evidence that Nestlé did not discourage breast-feeding and did make the effort to ensure correct preparation and use of the product.

The defendants' courtroom statements were as dramatically different in style as they were in content. Each in turn contributed what was in effect a chapter in the saga of misuses of infant formula in the Third World, told for the most part through anecdotes and frequently in quite emotional tones. The fact that some of them had been eye-witnesses to what they claimed were misuses of commercial products and what they saw as aggressive promotion, only added to the appeal of their defence. One of the more vivid recitals, though told second-hand, recalled the death of a "Nestlé baby" and was later to be repeated many times over, eventually becoming a sort of keynote in the US campaign. As the story was told, two Nestlé representatives in Kenya, calling on a hospital staff paediatrician, by chance witnessed the death of an infant in the hospital's emergency ward. This scene, tragic enough in any circumstances, was doubly disconcerting to the Company men, for the young mother had in her possession what the activists considered material evidence of their claims against Industry; a tin of Nestlé infant formula.

The courtroom raconteur did not say that the mother was only 15–16 years old, unmarried, and had probably resorted to artificial feeding out of necessity because she was employed outside the home. Nor could it be determined just how long the baby had been ill or when infant formula was first administered. Nestlé had good reason to believe that this was one example of a baby who was at serious risk from the outset, the odds being against him perhaps from the day of his birth. Administering infant formula to such an infant may have been a case of too little, too late. But those factors were not explained in the courtroom.

Nestlé Press Conference

After two intensive days, the hearings were temporarily adjourned. Written statements and oral testimony from third parties were still to come. Yet, as the Company emerged from this first round of the proceedings, it was obvious that the discretion it had maintained during the pre-trial period and the two days of hearings would not serve to strengthen its case. Nestlé therefore decided that a more visible stance might help its position. The Company would have nothing to lose, particularly if going public would not be construed as prejudicing the decision. In addition, Nestlé Management had by then realised that public opinion was likely to be just as important as the judge's decision in quelling what had become an acrimonious debate on the topic of infant formula marketing.

For this reason Nestlé decided to hold a press conference immediately following the two-day hearing. The timing seemed propitious, for the Company had by then completed its review and analysis of the body of literature on trends in infant mortality and feeding patterns in developing countries, including those studies from which extracts had been used to build the case against Industry in *The Baby Killer*. The results looked encouraging. Nestlé felt it had a good case to make, and this appeared to be the time and place to do it.

Managing Director Dr. Arthur Fürer, Head of Research Prof. Jean Mauron and the infant foods expert who had presented courtroom testimony, Dr. Hans Müller, delivered to the media audience a long-overdue defence of the product in developing countries, at the same time refuting many of the claims that had by then become a standard feature in the outpourings from the critics. Among the points made by Nestlé in the session were:

- The study conducted in Chile, showing a mortality rate three times higher among bottle-fed infants when compared with breast-fed babies [2], a favourite bit of fuel for the critics' fire, told only part of the story of infant nutrition in that country. Although Company spokesmen took due note of the other frequently-quoted statistic concerning Chile, the claim that breast-feeding had declined dramatically from a rate of 95% to 16% at one year of age, over a 30-year period [3], what the critics did not mention was the accompanying decline in infant mortality rate, from about 140 to approximately 70 per 1000 live births. Over the longer term, then, there was no evidence to show that artificial feeding was incompatible with better infant health, despite the hygienic risks that seemed to accompany bottle-feeding
- Data from a variety of sources showed that the output of breast milk by mothers in Third World areas such as Nigeria, the South Pacific Islands and India, fell far short of the daily requirements determined by the World Health Organization (WHO). The need for a supplementary product at the early stages of the infant's development was evident, Nestlé said

The Company spokesmen also produced evidence that more directly refuted the correlation between artificial feeding and infant mortality, yet Nestlé was still stuck in a defensive mode. The critics had a few dramatic statistics to offer, backed by vivid and emotionally appealing anecdotes that seemed to prove their case. Nestlé's rebuttal consisted of the more esoteric task of showing the faulty logic in the critics' conclusions, and sometimes in those of the experts themselves, drawn from field research. Furthermore, Nestlé offered even more data, rather than anecdotes, to back its side of the argument. The layman and the media interlocutor were clearly burdened with more information and analysis than they could absorb. Nestlé felt that the presentation had been effective, but media reports showed otherwise.

Written Testimony

Nestlé had other support, to be sure. The Company was counting heavily on the support of written testimony that recognised experts were prepared to supply.

The statement by Dr. Wallace Aykroyd, for example, a former head of the Food and Agriculture Organization's nutrition division and author of what even *The Baby Killer* report had described as "one of the definitive works on malnutrition", rejected outright the notion that the availability and promotion of commercial breast milk substitutes were directly responsible for the decline in breast-feeding. He argued against the prohibitions on importing commercial formula into developing countries (although the critics themselves had not gone as far as to make that particular demand), despite continued risk of misuse. "The effect of eliminating the artificial foods would be to raise the proportion of malnourished infants in the population and the infant mortality", he wrote. "It would not increase the number of infants satisfactorily fed at the breast." He further suggested that the withdrawal of Nestlé products and other high-quality infant formula from the market would result in a "flood" of less satisfactory products [4].

Another statement on the Company's behalf, made by a Nigerian paediatrician, rejected one premise that had been crucial to the critics' argument, but which had proved too awkward a point for the companies themselves to pursue: that poor hygienic conditions were an accepted fixture of both rural and urban life in the Third World. Dr. Adeoye Adeniyi, a senior consultant in paediatrics at University College Hospital in Ibadan, Nigeria, said: "It is assumed that Africans as a whole are incapable of attaining standards of hygiene which have made artificial feeding acceptable and practised in all parts of the world . . . one can hope this is not an attempt to insult the intelligence of Africans generally!" [5]. It was the kind of comment that an African professional, but not a Swiss corporate manager, could deliver with credibility.

Dr. Adeniyi also rejected the critics' claim that physical separation of baby and mother was a phenomenon only of industrialised countries. "The economic development of Nigeria has produced the working mother" he noted. "The Nigerian woman of today is at work . . . it will be criminal to deprive her of the only sensible means of feeding her baby while she is at work."

Back to the Courtroom

The next round of hearings, tentatively scheduled for June 1976, was to be devoted to the testimony of independent witnesses, two for each side. Appearing for the defence would be Dr. Jelliffe, who had by this time moved to an academic post at the University of California, Los Angeles. Dr. Jelliffe came within a hair's breadth of not appearing at all: while the judge recognised his professional credentials in the field of nutrition, he pointed out that "witnesses" were supposed to be literally that, people who had personal experience with Nestlé's marketing practices. Dr. Jelliffe was finally deemed to meet that requirement, for Nestlé's products were prominent in the market during his stay in Jamaica, where he had been director of the Caribbean Food and Nutrition Institute.

Nestlé's search for a similarly suitable witness proved more difficult. It was not that the Company could not find general support among qualified health professionals for use of infant formula in developing countries. Nutritionists, paediatricians and researchers who were in a position to dispute the conclusions the critics had drawn concerning the link between use of infant formula and infant mortality were not necessarily people who were familiar with Nestlé's marketing and promotional practices. Health and nutrition, rather than corporate marketing practices *per se*, were, after all, the main concern of such professionals. By the same token, mere observers of Nestlé's activities in the field might not be the best people to answer questions on the larger scientific issues of infant nutrition, should the occasion arise in the course of their testimony. Added to that was the growing impression that Nestlé's image as conveyed through the media was now heavily weighted against them. Thus a witness called to testify on the Company's behalf might be putting his professional standing in jeopardy. Indeed, this has been a major source of difficulty for Industry throughout the controversy. Any medical or scientific authority whose work or opinion questioned the case being promoted by the critics, or who could be quoted in support of the Industry position, was immediately accused of acting as a paid Industry stooge. So sensitive did the matter become that an official disclaimer was issued by the UK delegation to the 34th World Health Assembly when an Industry publication [6], quite legitimately, quoted a statement made by the Chief Medical Officer of the Department of Health and Social Security in the United Kingdom [7], to the effect that "alternatives to human milk must be available for those mothers who do not breast-feed".

Finally, two witnesses were proposed, one a missionary with 18 years' experience in Uganda, the other a Nigerian professor of paediatrics, implicitly a representative of the Third World. Less than a month before the hearing's date, however, the professor backed out, apparently under pressure from his colleagues in academia. Nestlé's pessimism about finding a qualified professional to speak in the Company's defence had been justified. Someone else acceptable to the court was found, another missionary to Africa. But the Company had lost its "balanced ticket". It would have to do without a supporter from scientific/professional circles. That proved to be a distinct disadvantage, considering the testimony of Dr. Jelliffe and the other witness for the defence.

Dr. Jelliffe's Testimony

As Dr. Jelliffe could conveniently participate in the proceedings only *en route* from Africa back to his home in the US, a special session for his testimony alone was scheduled for February 1976, with the second witness for the defence and Nestlé's two witnesses to appear later. On the stand, Dr. Jelliffe quickly got to the point, although his testimony actually seemed rather innocuous compared to the defendants' impassioned arguments during the earlier courtroom session. First of all, he did not give direct support to the claim of the booklet's controversial title. Nor was he ready to indict Industry as a whole as a "killer". Instead he re-iterated what had for some time been his primary thesis, equally disputable in Nestlé's view, that the heavy promotion of commercial infant formula had led to a decline in breast-feeding in the developing countries. Like *The Baby Killer* and his own published critiques, he accepted that there were other factors contributing to this decline: urbanisation and general modernisation of Third World societies, the consequent employment of mothers outside the home and the inability of health professionals to provide mothers with the assistance necessary for successful "natural" feeding.

He also gave Nestlé the benefit of the doubt on the question of "milk nurses", confirming that these Company employees did not actually "sell" in the sense of collecting money for delivery of the product. He went on, however, to describe a convincing picture of the Nestlé nurses' ability to persuade mothers to give up the breast for the bottle, specifically for the Nestlé brand. One of the more interesting aspects of his testimony was the evidence of inconsistency in his own beliefs and actions. Earlier he had coined phrases describing the medical and health professions' involvement with the Industry, "endorsement by association" and "manipulation by assistance", that were to prove so useful to lay critics. Yet during the hearing, Dr. Jelliffe acknowledged that Nestlé's financial support for research when he was head of the paediatrics department in an East African institute was considered at that time not only useful but proper. Moreover, he had solicited and received research funding from Nestlé even while he was in Jamaica.

Final Hearings

The final round of hearings opened on a sour note and led to another advantage point for the defendants brought about by confusion over procedures. Although the Company had told the judge the preceding November that the case would be pressed on the count of the libellous title alone (see p. 48), he still requested confirmation about the status of the three other charges. Therefore Nestlé formally confirmed that the three subsidiary charges had been withdrawn, a fact that had been part of the Company's own thinking and the preparation of its case since November. However clarification of this point provided a bonus for the defendants, with ADW announcing in a press conference as "news" what had, of course, been announced months earlier. It was the opportunity for the activists to claim a moral victory of sorts, even though the formal verdict was not in. In later accounts, it was claimed repeatedly that Nestlé withdrew the subsidiary charges because it feared losing on one or more of them.

The courtroom testimony of the two Nestlé witnesses was rather an anticlimax. Though they provided sincere support for the Company's arguments regarding the need for commercially produced breast milk substitutes, their testimony lacked the professional astuteness of the witnesses on the other side. Nor could they deliver first-hand confirmation that the Company's conduct in marketing practices was quite different from that alleged by the defendants. At this juncture more was needed than mere expression of faith in Nestlé's intended policy and stated practice.

The defendants' final witness was Dr. G. J. Ebrahim, an East African-born British citizen with several years of experience in Tanzania and, at the time of his testimony, a member of the staff of the Institute of Child Health in London, in charge of WHO/UNICEF-sponsored courses for health workers in developing countries. Dr. Ebrahim expressed himself in even harsher terms than Dr. Jelliffe on bottle feeding, naming the bottle as a "killer". Considerably more damaging than this generalisation were his claims to have observed specific instances of the unethical and immoral practices attributed to Nestlé. The Company had placed advertising in hospital wards, he said. He introduced as evidence what he said were photographs of "sales girls dressed in nurses' uniforms" and specimens of aggressive advertising for formula were presented to the court. It was powerful, provocative stuff against which the testimony of the Nestlé witnesses paled.

Summing Up

The summing-up proceedings gave each side the opportunity to restate its case. But for Nestlé, this formal last word did not correct the many wrong impressions that had been created partly as a result of the idiosyncrasies of courtroom procedures. For example, on-the-spot translation of statements by those who did not speak German slowed the proceedings. More important, the Company's ability to undermine the credibility of the critics had been frustrated by the fact that cross-examination of witnesses is not admitted in Swiss courts. Questionable statements had gone unchallenged, and vague references that could have been re-emphasised by Nestlé representatives to support the Company's case had sunk under the weight of more melodramatic statements by the defendants.

One example of this was the display of aggressive advertising introduced as evidence by Dr. Ebrahim. Nearly all of these were promotional pieces from competitors. The one that was clearly Nestlé was for powdered milk, not infant formula.

In the case of Dr. Jelliffe's written testimony, he had emphasised the "unethical promotion" of infant formula, yet failed to mention Nestlé by name. Nor did Nestlé have the opportunity to point out the inconsistencies between Dr. Jelliffe's statements to the court and his other expressions of attitude on the issue. He had called the use of "milk nurses" one of the most "insidious" forms of advertising and promotion. Yet while he was head of the Caribbean Food and Nutrition Institute in Jamaica, the Institute had participated in the training of Nestlé nurses. His testimony had also depended on generalisations about mothers' ability to breast-feed, noting in court that with "certain exceptions" mothers were able to provide adequate nourishment for the first 6 months of life. Yet only a few months previously he had outlined to the *British Medical Journal* the problem of determining the adequacy of human milk in various populations. "We really know rather little" he had acknowledged [8].

The Judgment

The judge's decision was a technical victory for Nestlé, but the manner in which it was delivered left the impression that the Company would continue to be on trial. The title *Nestlé tötet Babys* was indeed libellous, said the judge. It implied a deliberate intention to kill, or culpable negligence, as opposed to a general moral responsibility. The judge accepted the evidence of product misuse as a direct cause of disease, but noted that the Company could not be held legally responsible for it. The ADW defendants were declared guilty, fined (only SwF300 each), and ordered to pay part of Nestlé's legal costs.

Had this pronouncement ended the proceedings, the controversy might have subsided immediately, with Nestlé withdrawing to concentrate on monitoring its marketing practices to ensure their conformity with the code drawn up by the recently formed International Council of Infant Food Industries (see Chap. 3). But the judge had further observations to make on the larger issue and a severe admonishment to Management. Having confirmed that Nestlé was not subject to legal responsibility for the misuse of its products, he nevertheless questioned whether product labels and instructional material were effective enough in warning the consumer of possible hazards. He also observed that Nestlé's promotion in the developing countries, posters, colour brochures on feeding, the presence of mothercraft personnel and free sampling, was much more extensive than its marketing support activities carried out in Europe. That was a point Nestlé would not have even tried to refute, for Third World promotion included a wide range of educational activities aimed at preventing the product-misuse complained of by the critics.

The judge's observations, while not legally binding, amounted to some sort of legitimisation for future demands by other activist groups

It follows that the Nestlé company must fundamentally rethink its methods of promotion for infant milks in the developing countries, since its practices can transform a life-saving product into a dangerous, life-threatening product. If the Company wishes to avoid the charge of immoral and unethical behaviour in the future it must change its promotional practices.

Nestlé's decision to pursue legal action against ADW was probably the most significant defensive gesture the Company was to make during the infant formula controversy. Occurring early in the campaign as it did, this action to some extent set the tone for Nestlé's subsequent encounters with its critics as the campaign spread to other countries. The Company had won its case, at least technically. ADW immediately lodged an appeal against the verdict, but later withdrew, presumably because they had achieved their objective and the fact that they had indeed slandered Nestlé could be brushed aside as "the end justifying the means". They had seen to it that the court proceedings would be well publicised and that the public opinion that was finally to result would owe little to the formal decision. One reason was that the judge, even while validating Nestlé's claim of having been libelled, strongly sermonised on the Company's marketing practices. This was to affect the Company substantially. Nestlé later undertook a review of its policies as suggested by the judge, and as a result modified some of its marketing practices. Although Management had traditionally maintained a policy of adjusting policy even in the absence of controversy, any observer of the court proceedings was naturally left to wonder whether Nestlé could have made such significant marketing policy changes, and so quickly, in the absence of the judge's advice?

Hindsight compels the observer of Nestlé's actions to question the decision to pursue legal action in the first place. Drawn-out over two years, the court proceedings undoubtedly had provided a new sort of public platform for a number of critics, some of them health professionals who until then had confined their opinions primarily to published commentary. The Company was also mistaken to assume that legal redress would be effective against a new breed of critics, who were themselves obviously not very concerned with legal niceties and who were prepared to risk all, even to go outside the boundaries of law, for what was to be gained in terms of public opinion. This much was obvious at the outset when the leaders of ADW publicly expressed their delight at the prospect of being brought to court as defendants. Their behaviour stood in stark contrast to Nestlé's concern to observe the rules.

In the wake of the court decision, the Swiss activists ceased to hold the spotlight in the campaign against industry marketing practices. The transatlantic migration of the controversy had already begun. Painful though it had been for Nestlé to defend its name through legal action on its own home territory, the Company had been involved in no more than a war of words. The US activists opened a new chapter in the controversy, however, concentrating on a campaign of action that was to prove considerably more troublesome than the most libellous of tracts.

References

1   Focus (Zurich) (1974) July/August
2   Plank SJ, Milanesi, ML (1973) Infant feeding and infant mortality in rural Chile", WHO Bull, 48, 203–210
3   Monckeberg, FB (1973) Infant feeding and weaning practice; the problem as it exists in developing countries. Aust Paediatr J 9: [Suppl. No. 2] 48–63
4   Aykroyd WR (1976) Note on aspects of artificial infant feeding. (Testimony submitted to the Bern cantonal court, May 1976)
5   Adeniyi A (1976) The place of artificial feeding in Africa. (Testimony submitted to the Bern cantonal court, May 1976)
6   International Council of Infant Food Industries (ICIFI) Charter, for the provision of safe and adequate nutrition for infants. April 1981.
7   DHSS Report on Health and Social Subjects No. 18 (1981) Her Majesty's Stationery Office, London
8   Jelliffe DB (1975) Br Med J iv: 464

Chapter 5

The US Campaign

Maggie McComas

For Nestlé, the Bern trial and the attendant publicity during 1974–76 were practically all-absorbing insofar as the infant formula controversy was concerned. Following the formation of the International Council of Infant Food Industries (ICIFI) in 1975, Nestlé committed itself to working with its ICIFI colleagues to implement the recommendations of the Protein Advisory Group (PAG) (See Chap. 3), especially with regard to the development of "unambiguous and standard directions . . ." for infant feeding. But the greater part of the Company's attention was turned to the court challenge.

Other producers of infant formula, in particular the US companies, had already begun to understand that Nestlé's role as a lightning rod in the controversy was more apparent than real. These companies, too, would soon face similar allegations concerning the impact of their marketing in developing countries and consequent demands that they alter their marketing practices. By 1975, the debating forum had in effect been transplanted from Europe to the US, and the American activists who carried on the campaign were to prove even more persistent than their European counterparts.

The seeds of protest in the US were sown in part through widespread dissemination of the article in the *New Internationalist* and the original version of *The Baby Killer*, both of which, in turn, had gained greater currency through their use as evidence in the Bern trial. While the self-appointed advocates who took up the cause in the US had much the same orientation as their British and Swiss counterparts, advocacy on behalf of Third World consumers, several other factors gave the US campaign a rather different flavour and produced more dramatic results.

Religious Groups' Support

The first factor was the nature of the critic groups themselves. The endorsement by organised religion, for example, was a prominent feature of the US movement. This was to prove crucial to drawing out the grass-roots support of church-going middle Americans not normally found even on the fringes of social activism. For them the clergy's stance on the issue seemed to confirm the campaign's claim to be concerned with a moral issue. Companies would begin to hear from individual consumers that the endorsement of the anti-Industry campaign by church and other opinion leaders, both at the local and the national level, was an important factor in their decision. Apart from convincing members of their congregations that the cause was not only just but one that demanded a commitment, religious leaders were able to exercise their power even more directly, and effectively, against companies. Many of these religious orders and church organisations were institutional investors, holding blocks of shares in the American companies concerned. This financial passport to the exercise of moral power was to prove even more effective than mere preaching from the pulpit.

The second major factor shaping the campaign was the nature of the target itself: a large, relatively homogeneous consumer audience, geographically widespread but united by a common language, highly receptive to the media and to direct mail appeals, the same tools that commercial enterprises use so effectively. The earlier call for a "Nader-like" campaign had been prophetic (see page 35). The infant formula industry became the target right in the home territory of Ralph Nader, who was to fire a barrage or two of his own during the campaign.

It was not a religious group, however, but that most secular of organisations, the highly-respected Consumers Union (CU), which launched the first volley in the US campaign. Although the organisation was not to play a very prominent role as the movement advanced, its writing on the subject at the outset provided a particular air of legitimacy. This organisation speaks mainly on behalf of consumers in the US, so it was something of a departure for it to take up the issue of infant formula use and marketing in developing countries in an editorial published in September 1974. Interestingly, CU's report on the subject [1], while largely devoid of much of the polemic that characterised the *New Internationalist* article and *The Baby Killer*, drew heavily upon these two sources, as well as upon studies produced by Jelliffe.

Shareholder Resolutions

Action soon followed. In December 1974, Bristol-Myers, a US company whose production and marketing of infant formula is part of a diverse pharmaceutical and toiletries business, became the target of an Ohio-based Roman Catholic order, the Sisters of the Precious Blood, and other religious groups holding significant blocks of shares in the company. Guided by the Interfaith Center on Corporate Responsibility (ICCR), a corporate watchdog group affiliated with the National Council of Churches (NCC) and supported by numerous Protestant denominations and Roman Catholic orders, the Sisters lodged, in the form of a shareholder resolution, what looked like a simple request for information on the company's infant formula business in developing countries. Shortly thereafter the religious groups were joined in this request by other well known institutional investors: the Ford and Rockefeller Foundations.

Bristol-Myers, although obliged under US law governing companies listed on stock exchanges to reply to the request through a "proxy statement" issued to all shareholders, was reluctant to reveal what it considered proprietary information that could hurt its business, once in the hands, as it presumably would be, of competitors. Thus in 1975 the company issued only a short statement, effectively denying that its products were marketed where they might be misused or produce harmful effects. The company hoped this would be enough to answer the question the Sisters had raised. The shareholder groups were not satisfied, however, so they introduced another, similar resolution early in 1976, again requesting information and also calling upon the company to correct the "inaccuracies" of its original statement.

Shareholders Go to Court

When this tactic failed to produce the desired results for the second time, the shareholder groups, becoming increasingly sophisticated about how to have their rightful say in company affairs, filed suit in federal court. To support their case in what they suspected might develop into as long and drawn-out an affair as the Bern trial, they sent an investigator (the author of *The Baby Killer*) to developing-country markets to gather first-hand evidence of the misuse of infant formula and the aggressive promotional techniques they suspected the company of employing.

This corporate brush with the law ended much more quickly than had Nestlé's. The suit was dismissed by the court as invalid, for the shareholders had failed to show, as the law required, that their financial interests were damaged. When the decision was immediately appealed, however, the company began to see just how persistent these critics could be. Finally both parties agreed to an out-of-court settlement in order to avoid prolonged, costly, legal proceedings. Bristol-Myers negotiated directly with the shareholder groups and, as a consequence, altered some of its marketing practices.

This brief involvement of a US court seemed to put Bristol-Myers in much the same position as Nestlé found itself following its libel suit. Nestlé's legal victory, and the court's refusal to rule on the complaint in the case of Bristol-Myers, did little to support either company's position in the infant formula controversy. Experience now showed that the critics had nothing to lose in such challenges, while the companies had little to win. The fact or mere threat of a court battle brought the companies very much into the public eye on terms that were inherently unfavourable to them.

Meanwhile, other US firms such as Borden, whose sales in developing countries consisted of powdered milks and limited quantities of infant formula, along with Ross-Abbott, the market leader for infant formula in the US (but with a relatively small business in the Third World) had also become the objects of shareholder resolutions. Faced with some evidence of what could indeed be described as over-aggressive promotion, these two firms, like Bristol-Myers, decided to negotiate with their critics. Borden agreed with the critics that its powdered milk products were in some instances being promoted as suitable for infants. Such promotion was to be ended. Ross-Abbott, for its part, responded to the demand to scale down personal promotion by requiring its employees calling on health professionals and mothers to abandon the nurse's white uniform. Finally, Bristol-Myers, having undergone perhaps the harshest scrutiny, agreed by mid-1978 to eliminate its mothercraft activities and ordered company employees to abandon all contacts with mothers, whether in their homes or in hospital wards.

A precedent of sorts had been set. Companies had negotiated directly with their critics, groups with no professional credentials in the field of infant nutrition, to set boundaries on marketing practices in developing countries. It was a precedent that would later give the more vocal critics a wedge when accusing Nestlé of what they saw as particular "intransigence" on the subject of marketing infant formula. The difference in Nestlé's case was that the US critics were to ask much more, and their demands were to be backed by measures much more intimidating than shareholder resolutions: a nation-wide consumer boycott.

Nestlé in the US

At the very earliest stages of the US campaign, Nestlé's activities seemed to be of little concern to the activists, even though they were aware of the Company's significance in Third World markets and of the European campaign against the Company and the resulting libel case. Nor did Nestlé's US presence go unnoticed, despite the fact that most of its products there were much more strongly identified under their own brand names than by any particular association with the name "Nestlé".

However, Nestlé is not a US-based company, its operations there being wholly owned by the Swiss parent firm. The Company is not listed on any stock exchange in the US, so there was no potential for the introduction of the type of shareholder resolution that had plagued the American companies producing infant formula. Moreover Nestlé had not for many years produced infant formula in the United States, either for the American market or for export. Thus it made little sense for the critics to attempt to discuss the infant formula issue with Nestlé's American managers who had nothing to do with the product, and it appeared impractical to wage a campaign against a company whose headquarters and infant formula business were based elsewhere. Later, however, this "logic" was to be turned on its head, and the very factors which had at first seemed to make Nestlé immune to pressure from US activists proved, in the end, to constitute its vulnerability.

Management of The Nestlé Company Inc., in White Plains, NY had kept an eye on developments in the US campaign from the start, reporting these to headquarters in Switzerland. Nestlé managers responsible for infant food policy were therefore able to keep in touch with the US Industry's response to the issues. Nestlé still did not seem to get much attention from the US activists, busily pursuing their shareholder resolutions, except in the context of the Bern trial, which had become an anecdote in activist literature. By spring 1975, however, enquiries began to trickle into the White Plains office from consumers who had heard or seen the Company's name mentioned in connection with what was by then a growing public issue. As Nestlé White Plains could neither answer the questions on infant formula marketing nor speak to the larger issue of infant nutrition in developing countries, these queries were forwarded to Company headquarters in Switzerland for response.

Suddenly, however, Nestlé's name became considerably more prominent as activist groups began to attract public audiences to screenings of a documentary film, *Bottle Babies*, shot primarily in Kenya. This was a strong indictment of the infant formula industry's marketing practices, and Nestlé's in particular (see Chap. 8).

Formation of INFACT

The other factor which directed the US campaign toward Nestlé was the formation of a new group, INFACT, The Infant Formula Action Coalition. This group drew upon existing organisations and individuals already committed to curbing infant formula marketing, but turned out to be much more radical than would have been expected from the simple sum of its parts. Nestlé management in Switzerland first learned of this group not from White Plains, but from an article in the *New Internationalist*, early in 1977 [2]. This new organisation had plans "to educate the US public about the role of Nestlé and develop strategies along with their European counterparts to pressure that giant".

The White Plains company was immediately asked for some information about INFACT, and it was found that the group had indeed sprung up virtually overnight, its origin in part traced to student-backed "food activist groups". The formal organisation of INFACT was primarily the work of the Interfaith Center on Corporate Responsibility (ICCR) and the University of Minnesota's Third World Institute, whose Minneapolis offices served as INFACT's national headquarters.

The fact that they were a coalition was strategically significant to the US campaign and to Nestlé. INFACT's leaders, who were to come from its founding groups, became single-minded in their work and were prepared to devote themselves to no other cause. In addition, the coalition structure invited participation from a wide spectrum of organisations and individuals ranging from politically oriented, professional social activists to apolitical "concerned citizens". Expansion of the loosely defined coalition and intensification of the campaign against Nestlé was achieved by soliciting "modest" financial contributions from the public, obtaining endorsement of INFACT's aims by prominent public figures and the support of community organisations' memberships to participate in INFACT's activities.

Launch of the Boycott

Finally, on 4 July 1977, INFACT announced the launch of a consumer boycott of Nestlé products sold in the US. Having accused the Company of placing a higher value on corporate profits than on infant health, the activists apparently decided that public pronouncements would not get them very far and that the only message the Company would ever really understand was one that would threaten it financially.

This strategy had potential for considerable impact, as INFACT no doubt appreciated: Nestlé's total US sales accounted for some 20% of annual world sales at the time. And while the Company's US subsidiary had rightly disclaimed any responsibility for the marketing of infant formula, INFACT considered White Plains the conduit to otherwise unreachable Swiss management. In its announcement of the boycott, INFACT requested White Plains to inform Switzerland of the new action and to "work within your company to rectify this situation by transferring this list of demands:

- Stop all promotion of infant formula
- Stop mass media advertising of formula
- Stop distribution of free samples to hospitals, clinics and homes
- Discontinue service of milk nurses
- Stop promotion to the medical profession
- Assure that infant formula does not reach 'people who do not have the means or facilities to use it safely' "

As a postscript, INFACT also pressed for an immediate response to these demands, to be delivered from Headquarters management through White Plains.

The activists seemed to realise that for the boycott to be effective, a brief educational campaign on tactics would be required. The difficulty was that the boycott could not be directed at the sale of infant formula. Nestlé did not market these products in the US. In addition, most of the products making up the bulk of Nestlé's US business, instant coffee and tea, chocolate, prepared and frozen foods, were well-known brands but did not bear Nestlé's name prominently. So INFACT's boycott literature invariably included a quick-reference "antishoppers" guide listing Nestlé products. The objective was to persuade consumers to switch to competing brands on the grocery shelf.

Nestlé was hoping that there would be some refusals among the identified INFACT adherents, individuals and groups who, although they had seriously questioned Industry's practices, would not go so far as to endorse the boycott. In addressing various supporters of INFACT, White Plains referred to what the Company regarded as the favourable Swiss court decision, and concentrated on the point that the boycott as structured was quite literally misdirected, threatening as it did the livelihood of the 13 000 employees of Nestlé's US operations.

That approach prompted a long-overdue communcication directly from an INFACT leader instrumental in organising the boycott, but it was hardly the sympathetic response that Nestlé was looking for. In a seven-page letter to the President of the Nestlé Company, Inc., Douglas Johnson of the Third World Institute (later to become national chairman of INFACT), outlined in some detail the motivation for using that particular strategy. He rejected out of hand White Plains management's protestations that the boycott was misdirected. Johnson and his INFACT colleagues recognised that the US Company was not involved with the marketing of infant formula, but for the purposes of the campaign White Plains was seen as a "hand" of the transnational "body", the crucial link to the corporate "head" in Switzerland. As for the threat to Nestlé's US business and consequently to its employees' jobs, this was acknowledged as an inevitable side-effect. Those jobs would be protected, Johnson suggested coyly, if headquarters were only to alter its marketing policies along the lines of the INFACT demands.

He also cited changes in marketing practices already implemented by other US-based companies (mostly as a result of shareholder resolutions) as examples of what he considered an appropriate response to INFACT demands. Ross-Abbott had curbed mass media advertising and had taken its milk nurses out of uniform, restricting their activites. Borden had revised its promotion for milk products not modified for infant feeding. With these examples of good faith at hand, which were evidence that changes could be "honestly negotiated" with the activists, Nestlé seemed to be dragging its feet. Johnson's communication was a curious mixture of challenge and cordiality. Because of that, along with his indication that a settlement could be reached, Nestlé gave serious consideration to his suggestion for a meeting of Company representatives with INFACT.

First Meeting with INFACT

Nestlé's first formal encounter with INFACT and their supporting groups such as ICCR, in October 1977, went surprisingly well. For the Company, this was also the beginning of the more intense cooperative effort between Swiss headquarters and White Plains that had been envisaged for some time. From Switzerland came Geoffrey Fookes, then assistant to the manager of the Infant and Dietetic Products Department, accompanied by Edgar Fasel, assistant for information and external relations, on what was to be only the first of several transatlantic trips. White Plains delegated its manager for community affairs and the assistant corporate secretary to a group which seemed to represent just the right mixture of expertise on the issue and managerial authority. These were corporate executives with some seniority, but not at such a high level as to inhibit discussion with the activists, who turned up with nine representatives to Nestlé's four.

This initial encounter was to a large degree given over to debate on the basic issues, with one side, then the other, mustering appropriate scientific evidence to back its answer to the familiar questions on the need for infant formula, the prevalence of breast-feeding, the incidence of malnutrition and disease among breast-fed versus bottle-fed babies, etc. When the discussion came to the matters of most immediate concern, Nestlé's marketing practices and the boycott, the Company spokesmen took the opportunity to update a rather important element in INFACT's dossier and, they hoped, to make sure that the Company would, in further public discussion, receive credit where it was due. Nestlé had, for the record, undertaken some changes in its promotional programmes since the Bern court decision, most significant among them being the phasing out of mass media infant formula advertising in key markets of the Third World.

The half-day meeting barely began to cover the ground, however. Nestlé still did not accept the principle of negotiating its marketing policy with the activists, particularly as their demands had been very loosely drawn up in terms which made them subject to wide interpretation. Nevertheless, the follow-up exchanges were for the most part encouraging. Some of the INFACT members requested additional material illustrative of Nestlé's approach to marketing and information concerning infant formula and feeding. One INFACT representative described the dialogue as positive, noting that "Nestlé is more responsive to constructive criticism than some reports had led us to believe" [3].

Both sides assumed the dialogue would continue and produce results. White Plains management, perhaps too optimistically, urged the activists to give assurance within the short space of one month that the boycott would be lifted. But any decision, INFACT answered, awaited the deliberations of the forthcoming First National Strategy Conference of INFACT scheduled for early November 1977. The group's ability to mount a national conference at this point was not an auspicious development as far as Nestlé was concerned, for it demonstrated increasing strength of the movement. Moreover, the institutionalisation of INFACT indicated that further communications would become more rigidly structured and the activists themselves more intransigent. With INFACT taking on a life of its own as an organisation whose sole interest was the campaign against Industry and more particularly the boycott of Nestlé, how could either side hope for a settlement?

Continuation of the Boycott

The decision of the INFACT conference went against Nestlé. Soliciting of support for the boycott, whose effects had not yet been felt at the level of consumer sales, would continue. The Company naturally wondered whether attempts to carry on the dialogue with the activists would serve any useful purpose, especially in the light of indications that some INFACT representatives did not intend to stay within the bounds of "constructive criticism". Shortly after the INFACT national conference, for example, three of the participants at the October meeting took part in a mock funeral service for a "victim" of infant formula in a demonstration outside Nestlé's branch office in Los Angeles.

Even without this growing acrimony, Nestlé and INFACT remained as far apart as ever in agreeing on which marketing practices were appropriate to the conditions in developing countries. Industry had already begun to adjust the finer points of promotion and marketing strategies, such as better targeting of messages to the less vulnerable consumers and more tightly controlled distribution of product samples, but INFACT was equally concerned with what it considered to be the more subtle forms of promotion. As explained by Leah Margulies, an ICCR staff member then emerging as a principal leader of the boycott campaign, restrictions on contacts between company personnel and health professionals were just as important as advertising reforms.

What INFACT meant, it seemed, was that any sort of product information, even channelled through the filter of the health professional, was to be denied to users. Equally disturbing was the implication that the professionals themselves, doctors and nurses whose job it was to advise on the most nutritionally appropriate product in individual cases when it was needed, would be denied the product information on which this decision should be based. Nestlé was convinced that such a policy would only increase the risk that the product would be misused.

Despite these discouraging developments, the Company agreed to a second meeting with INFACT, scheduled for February 1978. This time the participants more readily fell into the role of adversaries, and the discussion largely concentrated on the recent behaviour of each in the light of commitments resulting from the first encounter. INFACT found Nestlé's newly published policy statement [4] inadequate, its primary "flaw" being what Nestlé acknowledged to be simply its main feature: clarification of existing policy rather than the announcement of any radical departures. What INFACT was looking for, of course, was evidence of concessions to its specific demands. In addition, the activists claimed that Nestlé's commitment to end direct consumer advertising had not been kept. Nestlé representatives, for their part, could not conceal their annoyance at INFACT's participation in the Los Angeles demonstration. They pointed out that such public theatricals could only serve to undermine any progress that might be expected of the private discussions.

After this encounter Nestlé's relationship with INFACT was to alter profoundly, and opportunities for further dialogue would gradually disappear. One reason was that INFACT representatives committed what Nestlé considered to be a breach of good faith by releasing to other members and supporting groups detailed minutes of the meeting, unverified by Nestlé, which, in the Company's view, misrepresented the nature and tone of the discussion that had occurred. Secondly, Nestlé saw that any changes in marketing policy that might be negotiated would be expected to carry with them a confession that Industry had been wrong all along in its arguments for the need for infant formula, and in its insistence, backed by scientific opinion, that infant disease and malnutrition could be attributed principally to factors other than misuse of the product. In a personal letter to Geoffrey Fookes, who had been present at the meeting, an INFACT spokesman [5] admitted that while further studies on these basic questions of infant formula were "encouraged", the "final word" on the link between infant formula and disease and malnutrition would probably never be known. INFACT intended to continue the boycott campaign, however, employing convenient simplistic assumptions which were made to sound like the "final word".

The activists' commitment to an even more intensive campaign became more obvious as National INFACT Day was scheduled for mid-April 1978, timed to precede the annual shareholder's meetings of the US companies. Nestlé, immune to US shareholder pressure by virtue of its foreign ownership, was the target for a series of other actions designed to gain public attention. Demonstrations were held at various Nestlé facilities throughout the country and at retail outlets carrying Nestlé products. In Boston, the local INFACT chapter staged its own version of the Boston Tea Party, dumping Nestlé's brand of instant tea into the harbour.

The period of "constructive criticism" was over. INFACT saw that Nestlé did not consider its marketing policies a subject for negotiation. The Company, in turn, had become seriously disillusioned at what it saw as a breach of trust in the effort to reach a reasoned settlement of the issue. In one of its last communications to the Company, INFACT had requested the sort of data that had earlier been demanded of Bristol-Myers: expenditures on research and promotion for infant formula, salaries of employees in developing countries, sales margins and pricing policies. Although the courts had effectively supported Bristol-Myers, the decision might just as easily have gone the other way. In that particular case, those requesting the information at least had a financial interest in the company. Nestlé, however, was now facing a similar demand from adversaries who were clearly outsiders. If INFACT members could not be trusted even to keep to themselves discussions whose frankness had presumed confidentiality, what were they likely to do with proprietary data that would be most useful not to nutrition specialists, but to competitors?

Next: Political Action

As it happened, INFACT was already laying the groundwork for the next chapter in the campaign: action at the political level, with the aim of making marketing of infant formula the object of legislation and government regulations. INFACT supporters were encouraged to send letters to Senator Edward M. Kennedy, Chairman of the Senate Subcommittee on Health and Scientific Research of the Committee on Human Resources, and Senator Frank Church, Chairman of the Foreign Economic Policy Subcommittee. As influential politicians, their names meant something to the same broad public audience whose support for the Nestlé boycott INFACT was seeking. A model letter to be addressed to Senator Kennedy (which could be adapted for Senator Church) was featured in INFACT literature (see Chap. 8). Infant formula marketing had become, it appeared, a suitable subject for that peculiarly American contribution to the machinery of public policymaking, the nationally televised congressional hearing. As a reward for their efforts INFACT leaders were invited to assist Kennedy's staff in the preparations.

References

1   Ledogar RJ (1975) Hungry for profits. IDOC/North America, New York 202 pp
2   Margulies L (1977) Cracks in the bottle. New Internationalist April: 20–22
3   Sister Marilyn Uline (1977) Letter to the Nestlé company, Inc. 21 October
4   Nestlé Infant Food Policy (1978) Nestlé Products Technical Assistance Co. Ltd, Vevey 4 pp
5   Johnson D (National Chairperson INFACT) (1978) Letter to GA Fookes, Nestlé. 30 March

Chapter 6

Into the Political Arena

Maggie McComas

The news of the Senate hearing showed that the Infant Formula Action Coalition (INFACT) intended to continue its campaign along a dual track. The boycott campaign would be pursued as the means of reaching Nestlé's corporate "head". As for the US companies, the use of shareholder actions having been fairly well exhausted and only certain company practices modified as a result of this pressure, legislation or regulation that would codify the activists' demands for further change seemed the next logical step.

Business regulation whose effective implementation depends primarily upon extraterritorial application is difficult, however. The American activists had won some credibility as advocates for Third World consumers, yet it was quite another matter for US government authorities to act as global policemen for corporate activities. Even in the event that they would assume such a role, Nestlé, whose infant formula business was not connected with its US operations, would not have been affected.

Regulatory measures were not likely to be the sole outcome of the Senate hearings, in any case. The more immediate prospect was that this encounter would prove yet another attention-getting device, serving the purposes of both the activists and of publicity-minded politicians. 1978 was a congressional election year, and nationally prominent politicians with presidential aspirations were already looking ahead to 1980. Any issue of public policy on which voter opinion could be mustered could not be ignored. The infant formula controversy by now seemed to fall within that category.

Importance of Hearings

The US congressional committee hearing is a legislative tool, wielded for a variety of purposes, from investigating the behaviour of a member of Congress (or other public officials), to exploring broad policy issues that fall within such a committee's ongoing brief, to mustering expert opinion quickly for the purpose of drafting legislation. These hearings also provide politicians with the opportunity of presenting their views and influencing public opinion on a topic of their choosing, and even of arousing an apathetic constituency to take sides on an issue that might otherwise remain obscure.

The chairman of a congressional hearing has the power to organise the witnesses and thus tilt the direction of the proceedings to suit his own objectives. With Senator Kennedy in charge, the hearings on infant formula marketing were in the hands of a prominent public figure and a politician skilled in debate who could overwhelm the inexperienced, unsuspecting witness, as Nestlé was to find out. Such proceedings are conducted under varying degrees of public exposure, some closed to the public, others "open" to the extent of being televised nationwide. Regardless of the format or the motivation, the occasion is invariably one in which outside parties with a vested interest in the subject will be sure to be heard, while impartial experts who may be summoned to give their views will find it hard to refuse the invitation. In giving its assistance to Kennedy's staff during the planning of the hearings, INFACT was apparently able to exercise its influence on the calling of witnesses, its own leading supporters to be included among them. As for the companies, they waited for the call from Washington.

Preparation for Testimony

Kennedy's subcommittee staff solicited participants for the hearings, scheduled for May 1978, from what were roughly categorised as three segments of opinion concerned with the issue: the Industry, experts such as health professionals, and the activists. Nestlé, White Plains, was invited as were the US-based companies producing infant formula and marketing the product in developing countries.

It seemed to Nestlé that the hearing's organisers had missed the same point that the activists themselves had shrugged off over the past year: Nestlé was not at all involved in infant formula production or marketing in the United States. The Nestlé Company Inc., a corporate entity established in the US, was, of course, subject to state and federal laws. A congressional committee, it could be supposed, might well have the authority to summon a company representative to Washington, but to what end? In dealing directly with the activists, the US Company had for some time been relying on the expertise of managers from the infant formula business at headquarters in Switzerland. Yet it was obvious that neither these representatives of Nestlé SA (the Swiss parent Company), nor other Nestlé personnel involved in the infant formula business elsewhere in the world, could be required to submit to the subcommittee's scrutiny. These operations were unquestionably removed from US jurisdiction, and for their managers to put in an appearance might only provoke confusion on that particular point.

Yet to decline the invitation on those strictly legal grounds would only confirm the US activists' stated motivation for the boycott: the very literalness of Nestlé's being "beyond the law" and its consequent lack of response to demands for change. Management also knew that its absence from the hearings might risk misrepresenting its level of concern over the issue of infant formula marketing and the larger question of Third World nutrition being misrepresented. Finally, ignoring the proceedings would forego the opportunity to speak out in what was becoming an important public forum. If a Nestlé representative were to appear, a knowledgeable expert from Switzerland would be the logical spokesman as far as an ability to speak directly to the issue was concerned.

Choosing a Spokesman

The solution to this dilemma proved relatively simple once management had had the time to review its manpower resources. Within its midst was the ideal candidate to represent the Company and speak directly to the issue: Dr. Oswaldo Ballarin, chairman of CICOBRA, Nestlé's operations in Brazil, one of the Company's largest infant formula markets in the Third World and, in addition, the site of a pioneering dairy industry developed by Nestlé more than half a century before. The fact that Dr. Ballarin was a citizen of Brazil was not an unimportant factor in the choice. It made him an obviously more credible spokesman on the issue of Third World nutrition than any US or Swiss executive could have been. Dr. Ballarin's qualifications also went beyond his immediate business responsibilities. His interest and knowledge of nutrition outside the context of Nestlé's ongoing activities were on record, for he had participated in the 1969 and 1970 meetings of the UN's Protein Advisory Group (PAG) and had also been co-chairman of the Industry Cooperative Program (ICP), a privately financed programme within the UN's Food and Agricultural Organization (FAO), whose aims included investigation of the potential for development of low-cost weaning foods.

The ideal Company representative having been located, and his services volunteered, all that was left to do was to prepare a message appropriate for this particular forum. It would not be easy, for congressional hearings of this type do not presume a very long attention span on the part of either the politicians involved or the public viewers. As a consequence, such hearings' efficiency in generating information on a given subject is often offset by the superficiality of the discussion. In the case of the hearings on infant formula, each panelist was to be given only five minutes in which to deliver a prepared statement, with cross-examination by subcommittee members to begin at any time. To help facilitate the process, the prepared statements were to be delivered to the subcommittee 24 hours in advance. For the senators, at least, there would be no surprises.

Questionable Credentials

The case for the use of infant formula and against both the claims and actions of the activists, arguments that had been developed over years and months, would now have to be stated within the space of 5 minutes. In addition, a preliminary programme for the hearings showed that the cards were being stacked against Industry. Nestlé had expected to see the US activists clearly identified as such, yet two representatives of the Interfaith Center on Corporate Responsibility (ICCR) were to appear as members of a panel of seven now identified in rather innocuous terms as "consumer advocates and Third World health workers". The ICCR spokesmen were considerably more than "consumer advocates" in Nestlé's view, and this misrepresentation was only exacerbated by the allusion to their first-hand experience in developing countries. In fact the two had only limited knowledge of these areas, their "experience" in infant nutrition problems and infant formula marketing having come essentially from their involvement in the US campaign against Nestlé! As for the panel of experts, two of the four had adopted a clear anti-Industry stance some time ago. Dr. Jelliffe was one. The others, a World Health Organization (WHO) family health specialist and the Director Emeritus of the Pan American Health Organization, were considered impartial by Industry.

Given the uncertainty of the effects of such testimony on the subcommittee members, Industry representatives knew they could afford to do nothing less than present the strongest possible case, but in terms that the senators would find palatable. For Nestlé headquarters and White Plains, this involved reaching agreement not only on the content but also on the tone of the Company's statement. This would be the Company's first, and maybe its last chance to state its case before such an audience. While there was no strong disagreement over the basic message, the need for infant formula in developing countries (with citation of appropriate scientific support) and a brief review of Nestlé's contribution to infant health, the real problem lay in different views among members of Management as to the motivations of the US activists. These were, after all, the people who had launched a consumer boycott with potentially damaging effects. Nestlé Management was compelled to consider to what extent their presumed motivations could be used as the basis for a public counter-attack.

As Nestlé saw it, the US activists were unequivocal anti-capitalists, a point that Management both in White Plains and in Switzerland thought worth emphasising as the Company presented its case in the hearings. A general anti-Industry attitude had characterised the activists' literature and their encounters with Nestlé. These sentiments were expressed in much stronger ideological terms only a few months later when Mark Ritchie, who was to become a national INFACT coordinator, spoke on the infant formula campaign before a group of fellow activists as follows:

It's not just babies, it's not just multinational corporations, it's class conflict and class struggle . . . I think ultimately what we're trying to do is take an issue-specific focus campaign and move it in conjunction with other issue-specific campaigns into a larger, very wide, very class-conscious campaign and reassert our power in this country, our power in this world [1].

At the insistence of White Plains Management, whose reading of the political mood of the American public at large was taken at face value by headquarters Management, the "exposure" of such anti-capitalist sentiments was to figure large in the Company's statement. Nestlé may have been hoping too much, however, to expect that such evidence of political radicalism would in itself generate much sympathy for the corporate point of view. After all, headquarters Management had already had the unhappy experience, at the time of the Bern trial, of hearing a presumably impartial judge suggest musingly that causes associated with the Left were not necessarily all that bad. What had really disappointed Management, both in White Plains and in Switzerland, in their previous encounters with the US activists was something quite apart from the question of ideology. It was the evidence of bad faith in their having revealed the contents of what were supposed to be private discussions and, adding injury to this insult, misrepresenting the Company in doing so. That sort of behaviour could not really be identified with any particular ideology, but it did serve indirectly to undermine any earlier beliefs Nestlé might have held that the activists' motivations were purely altruistic.

Nevertheless, in trying to pin down the critics' motivation, Nestlé, in particular White Plains, Management, could not rid itself of the notion that the anti-Industry campaign in general, and the Nestlé boycott in particular, was only one manifestation of a broader, if more vaguely defined, programme to dismantle the very foundations of the free enterprise society. By emphasising that aspect before the subcommittee, it was thought, the Company would be assured of scoring some points. The resulting statement did indeed have considerable impact, but not the kind Nestlé intended. As soon as the words were uttered, it became apparent that the Company had committed a tactical blunder in presenting an extremely blunt, unqualified thesis before Senator Kennedy, whose position on the political spectrum was hardly a secret and whose commitment to social welfare programmes in particular was a hallmark of his political ethic.

Fateful Statement

Kennedy's opening statement had hinted that the hearing would not begin on precisely neutral ground. The question he put to the witness and the television audience was worded in a "have-you-stopped-beating-your-wife?" vein, and, as such, was to serve the activists well in their follow-up literature on the subject. The Senator asked:

Can a product which requires clean water, good sanitation, adequate family income, and a literate parent to follow printed instructions be properly and safely used in areas where water is contaminated, sewage runs in the streets, poverty is severe and illiteracy is high?[1]

Dr. Ballarin, somewhat ill-at-ease from the beginning of his testimony, speaking in a language other than his own and appearing under the glare of television lights, a setting rather different from the conclave of professionals to which he was more accustomed, had barely launched into his statement when he came to the crucial phrase that proved the undoing of Nestlé's presentation. Noting that he had been advised by White Plains of the political nature of the boycott campaign, he asserted: "A world-wide church organisation with the stated purpose of undermining the free enterprise system is in the forefront of this activity".

The response was devastating, with Senator Kennedy interrupting to confirm the credentials of the affiliates of the "church organisation" as well as those of the health workers and experts whose testimony had been heard. He went on to pour scorn on the notion that such an organisation should be involved in "some world-wide conspiracy to undermine or attack the free world's economic system". Nestlé's explanation that the claim was indeed defensible recalled a recent policy

---

[1] This question is fully discussed in Chapter 2.

document of the World Council of Churches (WCC) calling for "liberation from the present unjust international economic system" [2]. But neither that evidence nor the fact that the WCC's associate organisation, the United States-based National Council of Churches of Christ (NCC), was supporting the boycott indirectly, through ICCR, drew much sympathy. Kennedy, meanwhile, observed that the commercial boycott was a "recognised tool in a free economic, democratic system".

The subcommittee was prepared to listen to the remainder of Nestlé's testimony regarding the use of infant formula, but the damage was done. Nestlé was forced to produce yes-or-no answers to questions concerning such complex issues as safe preparation of formula and the education of illiterate populations in proper feeding methods. By contrast, the spokesmen for other companies who were to follow Nestlé's testimony were able to read through their statements almost without interruption. Once again, Nestlé had borne the brunt of the attack, but had only itself to blame for failing to obtain expert political advice on how to put over its case in such a forum.

Result of Hearings

What might have been the logical product of the Senate hearings, draft legislation on infant formula marketing, did not immediately materialise. However, just one year later the infant formula industry was to see its worst fears of unworkable marketing controls emerge in the form of a bill introduced into the US House of Representatives by Representative Ronald V. Dellums. The proposed *Infant Nutrition Act of 1979* read as though it might have been drafted by the activists, adopting as its foundation the conclusion that INFACT and its supporters had reached some time before. The bill's preliminary paragraph stated: "The Congress finds that the promotion of proprietary infant formula in developing countries has accelerated the trend away from breast-feeding toward artificial feeding, leading to increased incidence of early morbidity and mortality". The proposed legislation was built around export controls and would have:

- Established a "positive" list of developing countries permitted to receive infant formula exported by US producers
- Required all US producers to obtain a licence for sale and export to these developing countries, with authorities empowered to deny such a licence to any applicant who could not show
    "specific income groups of consumers to whom infant formula is intended to be sold or distributed"
    literacy levels of such groups
    "adequate assurance" that infant formula would be "sold or distributed only to such consumers"
    data produced through "tests or studies" to show that the sale of infant formula "will not contribute to morbidity or mortality in early infancy".

This last requirement for "data" to be submitted by a licence applicant was to include, but not be limited to, such factors as:

- Adequacy and availability of facilities for safe preparation (sterilisation and refrigeration) of infant formula
- Epidemiological studies of gastrointestinal and nutritional diseases in infancy
- Life expectancy and infant mortality rates and causes
- Cost of infant formula in relation to family income

The legislators were asking Industry to provide the kind of data over which even professionals with years of specialised experience had difficulty in interpreting, such as statistics on infant mortality and its causes. Moreover it was implied that Congress would require the potential exporter to accomplish nothing less than resolution of the issue that had now been under examination for some years: in other words to "prove" that its products did not "contribute" to infant disease and death. That the bill as law would have been applicable only to "US persons" (including corporations, which are legal "persons") was only of small comfort to Nestlé and none at all, of course, to its US competitors. The Dellums bill was eventually relegated to the legislative dustbin. Even as a footnote in the US campaign, however, it represented yet another example of support by credible public figures for the activists' cause.

As for Senator Kennedy, he subsequently recognised that US government agencies were not the proper bodies for monitoring and controlling business activities in the more remote international markets. While the US government could promulgate measures to regulate the international activities of US-based companies, the importance in these markets of firms such as Nestlé, not to mention domestic producers in developing countries such as India, was beyond its control. Attempts to police US companies' international activities only from their point of origin would be an exercise of limited value. Effective regulation of marketing practices would require control throughout the distribution chain within the developing countries, including independent agents and dealers outside the control of the manufacturers, and would require the commitment of those countries' own lawmakers and officials.

The immediate impact of the hearings was to provide INFACT with a treasure trove of quotes to fuel its campaign. Notable among these was the claim by Dr. Jelliffe, in his appearance as a member of the "expert panel", that "some 10 million cases of marasmus and diarrhoea occur annually in infants in developing countries, related *in part* to inadequate bottle-feeding" (emphasis added). Jelliffe's "guesstimate" was to be repeated by the activists, altered in a way that appeared to be insignificant, but which radically changed its meaning, to state that these 10 million cases of disease were *directly* attributable to inadequate bottle-feeding. The clear implication was that serious and widespread infant morbidity could most assuredly be avoided simply by a return to breast-feeding. The change from "in part" to "directly" is, of course, easy for the casual reader to overlook. Eventually, this was escalated into outright hyperbole by INFACT in one of its hair-raising direct mail solicitations for funds: "Ten million Third World babies are starving because of the heartless, money-hungry actions of powerful multinational corporations".

As Jelliffe's claim was repeated and exaggerated, it was forgotten that it stood in complete opposition to the view expressed by another member of the expert panel testifying before the Senate subcommittee. Dr. Abraham Horwitz, Director Emeritus of the Pan American Health Organization, had pointed out that even if governments regulate the commerce of baby foods, corporations market

and advertise their products only to those families that can afford them, and
health professionals promote breast-feeding and rational weaning practices, "the
impact on the nutritional problem in the world will be only marginal". Dr.
Horwitz's concern was precisely that which had been recognised by health
professionals and the Industry within the context of PAG several years earlier:
the urgency of assigning top priority in social and economic development plans to
improving nutrition among the population as a whole including those who live
"on the fringe of the economic process".

Although Senator Kennedy did not demonstrate a commitment to pursue
legislated controls, he dropped the hint that some sort of voluntary measures
could be adopted, with Industry participating in their formulation. Kennedy then
took up Jelliffe's suggestion that an "international infant nutrition committee" be
formed to advise the appropriate US government agency and also suggested that
the US infant formula industry serve as the "model" for appropriate marketing
practices in developing countries. Despite that continued emphasis on US
interests, Nestlé was invited to Kennedy's follow-up session, as it had been to the
Senate hearings, along with the major US infant formula producers, Ross-
Abbott, Bristol-Myers and American Home Products (Wyeth).

Follow-up Meeting

Nestlé's decision to remain involved despite its unfortunate experience in the
Senate hearings was motivated by several factors. First, the Company was faced
with the realisation that it was still a prime target of the US activists' campaign. It
had not provided the public with convincing evidence that Nestlé had the record
of a "model" company in terms of its contributions to developments in infant
nutrition. It was not well-known, for example, that Nestlé's products were among
the most advanced in terms of differentiation according to varying nutritional
requirements and even local circumstances. Some of the risk of bacteriological
contamination in tropical climates, for example, could be reduced through the
use of the acidified milks which the Company had been promoting for many
years. Nestlé had also invested in a considerable research effort to develop low-
cost weaning foods for the later months of a baby's first year, an important issue
among nutritionists but one that had taken a back seat to the controversy over the
use of formula for the younger infants.

Second, Nestlé was concerned over what was seen as its "intransigence" in
regard to marketing practices. Already the Company had undertaken certain
modifications, as it had pointed out earlier in the year to INFACT. It had,
however, received virtually no credit from the public, and certainly not from
INFACT, for having done so.

Finally, it seemed to Nestlé that the sudden shift to controls on international
marketing as developed and applied by US authorities, perhaps the inevitable
result of the activist campaign's having shifted mainly to the American arena,
ignored the realities of the markets involved. It had been fairly well-established
by this time that Nestlé was the market leader in the developing countries taken
as a whole, and Nestlé was the one firm that would not be subject to US
government regulation. Legally speaking, the Company would get off the hook,

unless the developing countries were to adopt measures themselves, following a "US model". The trouble with such a model, however, was that most of the American firms' interests in the domestic market far outweighed their business in developing countries. The prospect that these companies, through the normal lobbying activities they pursued in regard to business regulation, might have a significant influence on guidelines for marketing infant formula in developing countries did not seem to be in the Nestlé interest.

It was for all these reasons that Nestlé felt it necessary to participate in this vaguely shaped discussion of international regulation, knowing that it would require even more intense concentration on the issue by Management. Skirmishes with the more vocal critics had not abated; the boycott campaign was still in full swing. And shortly following the Senate hearings, another film documentary, made this time by the CBS network and rehashing many of the themes introduced in *Bottle Babies* managed to raise public consciousness on this issue to an even higher level.

Into the Mouths of Babes

The last thing that Nestlé wanted as the controversy moved to the political arena was a repeat of *Bottle Babies*, the provocative film account of alleged Industry abuses in which Nestlé had so heavily figured. That documentary, undertaken as a private venture during the course of the Bern trial, was transparent propaganda, very effectively alluding to Nestlé's "unethical" practices, against the visual background of Company operations and products.

When the CBS television network approached Nestlé just as the Company was preparing for the Senate subcommittee hearings in spring 1978, there seemed no reason not to comply with its request for interviews. Nestlé had only recently begun to adopt a more visible stance in the US campaign, and the chance to present its case through the CBS news feature program *Bill Moyers' Journal*, with the Dominican Republic to be presented as a case-study, seemed opportune. Interviews with an executive from the Swiss headquarters and the chairman of Nestlé's operations in Brazil were, however, abruptly cancelled immediately following the Senate hearings. Nor did the CBS production team include comment from White Plains Management, despite the fact that the documentary touched upon the US boycott campaign. An interview with the Company's managing director in the Dominican Republic was filmed, but was subsequently left unused, and comments from a member of the council of the Latin American Pediatric Association, who presented what was, in the context of the production, the "other" view, i.e. one favourable to Industry, were also deleted from the televised production. Perhaps these were coincidental victims of the editing process, but the film producers took special care to include the film sequence of Nestlé's testimony before the Senate subcommittee in which the Company, alone among the Industry firms appearing, had been submitted to harsh cross-examination.

The documentary *Into the Mouths of Babes*, presented Nestlé and other Industry companies in yet another shade of bad light by putting the label of bribery on their annual contribution, through ARAPI (Association of Representatives and Agents of the Pharmaceutical Industry), to the Dominican Medical Association. Questioned later by Senator Kennedy, Nestlé pointed out that the company was only one of 74 firms (and only a handful of those were producers of infant formula) making up ARAPI. As a member, Nestlé contributed 0.5% of the export value of its products to that country each year to the medical association. Nestlé's contribution for the last year in question (1977) came to 3383 pesos (one peso roughly equivalent to US$1) or, about $1 per doctor in the country: hardly a bribe.

The film produced a mixed response, as expressed in about 200 letters received from the viewing audience of an estimated 9 million. It was hard to know whether *Babes* actually had much effect in arousing the public at large. The National Council of Churches was interested enough to purchase the rights for subsequent distribution of the film, however, which it was to make available to other groups for a rental fee. Given the film's tone and its conclusions, that decision by NCC was perhaps more revealing of its sentiments about the infant formula issue than its subsequent face-to-face discussions with Nestlé.

ICIFI Enters the Scene

The fact that US politicians had so vigorously taken up the question of international regulation was disturbing not only to Nestlé but also to its fellow members of the International Council of Infant Food Industries (ICIFI). Industry companies, in forming the organisation just a few years previously, had recognised that a collective approach could be of considerable value in guaranteeing development of marketing practices appropriate to the local context and consistently applied by all the companies involved. ICIFI believed that a strong effort at self-regulation would avoid the need for mandatory controls, hence the development of its own code of marketing practice, and the founding members believed that the more representative the membership of ICIFI, the greater would be the validity of the code.

Yet the effort to persuade the other US companies to join had proved fruitless, their trepidation arising in part over their uncertainty about whether US antitrust law might be applied extra-territorially to what amounted to loose collaboration with competitors in international marketing activities. ICIFI nevertheless represented some 85–90% of the infant formula business in developing countries. It was here, it seemed, among this Industry group rather than among US companies with only a peripheral influence in such markets, that both the responsibility to correct marketing abuses and the right to participate in the formulation of any international controls rightly lay.

The appeal, addressed to Senator Kennedy by Ian Barter of the UK firm Cow & Gate, acting in his capacity as President of ICIFI, seemed to hit just the right note. In a concise, three-page letter, Barter quickly clarified what had been obscured throughout the Senate hearings and immediately afterwards. Resolution of the issue, he said, required the involvement of companies with headquarters in a number of countries, subject to the laws of both home-base governments and to those of the developing countries where infant formula marketing was identified as a concern. Taking the opportunity to remind the Senator that there was a precedent for international guidelines, *PAG Statement*

No. 23, Barter suggested that the discussion be adjourned to the forum where it seemed most properly to belong, an international agency such as the World Health Organization (WHO).

The proposal met with Kennedy's enthusiastic agreement and proved acceptable to the non-ICIFI American firms, polled by the Senator just before the scheduled follow-up meeting with Industry in July 1978. Removed from the eye of the television cameras, that session was considerably more relaxed than the Senate hearings had been. Discussion for the most part centred on the prospects for future collaboration with WHO. Kennedy took the initiative of contacting WHO Director-General Dr. Halfdan Mahler, asking for a commitment to a date and a provisional agenda and suggesting objectives for the meeting. These included the formulation of a "uniform code of ethics", reflecting some familiar demands of the activists; discontinuance of the use of mothercraft personnel, an end to all consumer advertising, and prohibitions on "gifts" to health professionals and organisations.

In September 1978, WHO agreed to organise an international meeting of Industry, health professionals, government officials and critics of Industry. The objectives included evaluation of the extent of alleged abuse of infant formula, determination of the appropriateness of various marketing practices, and development of programmes to promote breast-feeding. It would take a full year to lay the groundwork for this gathering, at which the seeds of an international marketing code were to be sown.

Confrontation with the National Council of Churches

In the meantime, Nestlé was to become engaged in further confrontation in the US, which had become the home front of the infant formula campaign. INFACT's boycott effort was running as strongly as ever, although the Company had not felt its impact in terms of sales volume. Having found it impossible to continue direct discussions with INFACT, ICCR and other groups supporting the boycott, Nestlé decided to try a reversal of the strategy outlined in the activists' own campaign manual. The Company would reach past the "hand" of INFACT and ICCR, approaching, rather, the activist equivalent of the corporate "head" that an INFACT spokesman had so vividly described a year before. Nestlé would go directly to the National Council of Churches (NCC), the ICCR's major sponsor.

The Company was expecting that its encounter with responsible church leaders, NCC officers, would be profoundly different from its exchanges with INFACT and ICCR, which had been hampered as much by a generation gap as by ideological differences. Nestlé executives thought that in dealing directly with NCC, they would be engaging in a dialogue with people a little more on their own wavelength, "organisation men" of a sort. The meeting, set for mid-July 1978, was of strategic importance, because NCC had not yet endorsed the boycott directly, though its indirect support, through ICCR, was quite evident. Nevertheless, Nestlé was hoping that NCC leadership would still, at this date, prove receptive to the appeal for a more constructive approach in dealing with the issue. The NCC leaders were not cordial however, nor was the encounter a meeting of like minds. The organisation's officers, as it turned out, had not recovered from the affront of Nestlé's remark before the Senate subcommittee. In the wake of that public challenge, the Company's invitation to constructive dialogue rather lacked credibility. The NCC group listened only long enough to hear the Company's review of policy changes made in recent months, including the suspension of mass media consumer advertising. But this was not considered the "significant change" that NCC thought a prerequisite for withholding its support of the boycott.

What the Company did not realise at the time, however, was that the "head", NCC, was quite prepared to act upon the advice of the "hand", INFACT and ICCR, as far as the boycott was concerned. The activists had become the church organisation's expert advisers on the issue, and their recommendations were to bear heavily upon the NCC Governing Board's final decision. This became evident only as Nestlé arrived at a late-October meeting with INFACT and NCC's then-president, Mr. William P. Thompson, Stated Clerk of the Presbyterian Church, just before the Council's annual conference. The Company had expended further effort in mustering evidence to support its basic arguments, and arrived at the meeting with two reputable outside experts, the president of the Latin American Pediatric Association and a member of the Ivory Coast's delegation to the UN. Nestlé also brought along its own filmed version of Third World infant feeding problems, recently produced in consultation with independent experts on the subject. But the Company's efforts to get the discussion back to the real issues did not succeed.

Nestlé was also promised the opportunity to meet with NCC delegates themselves only 4 days later as they convened for their annual conference. Company executives, however, found themselves yet again facing a roomful of INFACT members. Only one NCC leader was there. The sparse turnout was later attributed to the fact that the meeting simply did not capture the interest of NCC delegates, who were pressed for time between the formal sessions of the conference. "Only persons interested in the particular issue could be expected to attend . . ." NCC's President later told Nestlé. It was a curious rationalisation, given that the delegates were to express their "interest" emphatically in the boycott vote that was to follow.

Finally came Nestlé's last and, as it turned out, least productive, opportunity to reach NCC leaders, at the meeting of the Governing Board. This, too, appeared to be an INFACT-organised set piece, the meeting room plastered with activist propaganda. A comprehensive background paper that the Company had prepared and sent to the NCC secretariat a month before had not been distributed to the delegates. While speakers in favour of the boycott resolution, like Dr. Michael Latham, apparently had no time limits imposed on them, Nestlé's representative was given 3 minutes to present the Company's case, and one of the accompanying experts was not allowed to speak at all. The vote, taken immediately afterwards, was clear-cut: 280 yeas, 2 nays. The direction of the "head" was firmly set, at least for the time being.

Preparations for WHO Meeting

Following the encounter, the Company could no longer justify efforts to argue its case to its critics in the US. The meeting to be sponsored by WHO was several months off, and just as well, for Nestlé needed time to reconsider its stance. Shifting the discussion back once again to an international forum might not result in a quick resolution of the controversy, but it would surely help to focus attention once again on the real issues and, at the same time, put Industry back on an equal footing. After its unhappy experience in the US Nestlé looked forward to the opportunity of receiving a fair hearing and equal time.

References

1   Ritchie M (1978) Remarks. In: Symposium The human costs of corporate power. Aug 16–17. Clergy and Laity Concerned (CALC), New York 6 pp
2   World Council of Churches (1977) Programme unit on justice and service. Report of the Geneva consultation on a proposed action/reflection programme on transnational corporations, 13–18 June. WCC, Geneva 14 pp

Chapter 7

Developing International Recommendations: The WHO Code

Maggie McComas

The October 1979 conference on infant feeding, sponsored jointly by the World Health Organization (WHO) and UNICEF, which specialises in aid programmes directed to children among the world's needy populations, brought together several different points of view. The most apparent was the desire of Industry, as expressed in particular by Nestlé and other companies belonging to the International Council of Infant Food Industries (ICIFI), to shift the discussion on infant formula marketing back to the sphere of relevant government authorities, health professionals and Industry experts, where, it was believed, the responsibility for resolution of the problem actually lay.

WHO Programme

Having been formally requested by Senator Edward Kennedy to assume responsibility for any further development of international marketing regulations, WHO was stimulated to act on an issue that fitted neatly with its permanent programme of activities, which included promoting the health of mothers and children, combatting malnutrition, tackling the problem of safe water supplies and training health personnel. The questions raised by the marketing of infant formula seemed related to those objectives. Yet WHO staff soon found themselves wrestling with the distinction between health and nutrition goals whose achievement could be aided by more "appropriate" marketing practices, and those objectives more properly categorised as a precondition to the correct use of infant formula. Whose responsibility was the provision of safe water supplies, for example, if not that of governments?

WHO's growing interest in the relationship of infant formula to the larger issue of nutrition in developing countries had run in parallel with the development of the public controversy throughout the 1970s. The 1974 World Health Assembly, for example, the annual meeting of WHO member-state delegations, mainly representatives from national health ministries, had approved a resolution noting the general decline in breast-feeding and asking member countries to "review sales promotion activities on baby foods and to introduce appropriate remedial measures, including advertisement codes and legislation where necessary" [1]. That initiative immediately followed the article in the *New Internationalist* and War on Want's publication of *The Baby Killer*. Then in 1978, just about the time Industry was stating its case before Senator Kennedy's Senate subcommittee in the US, the World Health Assembly passed a similar resolution issuing an even stronger call for the promotion of breast-feeding and for the regulation of "inappropriate sales promotion of infant foods that can be used to replace milk" [2].

Resolutions may amount to no more than the word implies: intentions, presumably good ones. In the context of international bodies, such communiqués, couched in appropriately diplomatic language, allow the members to show political accord and to state their collective commitment to a certain principle, not necessarily imposing on them formal obligations to take action. After WHO decided to act on Kennedy's request later in 1978 the Organization was to become committed to more than mere resolutions.

Politics of Policy-Making

Industry, and Nestlé in particular, was hoping that WHO's assumption of the responsibility for guiding the debate on infant formula marketing would have the effect of removing the strong political flavour the issue had by then acquired. Moving the debate to this international forum did not fully depoliticise the issue even though WHO is recognised as one of the more professional and least political of the UN bodies. Since its objectives are tied essentially to scientific matters, a high degree of professionalism, along with neutrality, usually prevails in the projects carried out by the secretariat's staff, who cooperate with health professionals of the member states. Yet WHO administrators themselves are careful to point out that WHO is technically the collective body of member states, and in any such body, representing in this case more than 150 countries from East and West, industrialised and developing states alike, it is difficult for national representatives always to act like professional civil servants in a truly neutral fashion.

The other influence upon a delegation's objectivity in approaching any health issue on its own merits is the more subtle internal clash of interests. Political realities at home may decide how, or even whether, commitments made in an international forum such as WHO are translated into action. This problem is particularly acute in the case of developing countries, whose limited resources must be carefully allocated in an effort to meet several objectives that are collectively defined as the "national interest". Hard-pressed to build a stronger position in international trade, for example, such a country may give priority to the production of exportable cash crops over the development of food crops destined for local consumers. Similarly, the kind of social legislation that provides time off for working mothers may not be compatible with the level of productivity that such countries require in order to be competitive in international markets and which makes them attractive as sites for productive investment. No country in this position would like to be characterised as putting economic goals before the objectives of better health for its people. Nevertheless, improved health and reduced infant mortality are almost invariably a by-product of upgraded collective economic well-being. In practice, health ministers of such countries, once they have unpacked their bags after the annual World Health Assembly, have to compete with other public officials for limited financial and physical resources as they seek to make good their commitment to develop a better trained, more extensive public health network, improve water supplies, and promote breast-feeding. They do not always win.

Planning the Meeting

As the preparations for the meeting of "interested parties" were being made, ICIFI suggested to the WHO secretariat that two major objectives guide the discussion: first, determination of the actual need for infant formula and, second, taking that need into account, the delineation of appropriate promotion practices. Nestlé had some ideas of its own on how the conference should be organised. These, too, were communicated to Kennedy's aides to be forwarded to WHO [3]. The Company suggested discussion of factors which, in addition to promotion, had been recognised as having an influence on infant feeding practices: maternal nutrition, maternity legislation and provision of breast-feeding facilities at the work site. Most of these were put on the agenda without further discussion, for they largely reflected WHO's own thinking on the subject.

As the meeting date, 9–12 October 1979, approached, it became increasingly evident that the proceedings would be rather different from what Nestlé and other companies had envisaged. They had seen it as an opportunity for an exchange of views among a small group of acknowledged experts from government, academia and Industry (Nestlé understood about 30 participants). But when the day came, over 150 people were to appear, among them the more vocal critics of Industry, including representatives of the Infant Formula Action Coalition (INFACT), War on Want and even the Arbeitsgruppe Dritte Welt (ADW).

At the same time, increasing polarisation in the health profession resulted in pressure upon WHO to assure a "balance" of opinion among the experts. This was perhaps inevitable, despite the desire of most professionals, who were not involved with activist groups, to avoid the confrontational mode that had come to characterise the relationship between Industry and the activists. With the exceptions mentioned above, such experts had been careful to avoid aligning themselves overtly with one side or another, but the inclination of both Industry and the activists to cite the findings of experts whose views were favourable to a particular argument meant that health professionals almost unavoidably, even though mistakenly, became identified as either for or against Industry.

Industry's hopes for the conference were further deflated when it was learned that only one working document, to be prepared by WHO/UNICEF, was to be circulated as the basis for discussion. This document laid out essentially the same conclusions as the critics had employed in their campaign over recent years. It noted, for example, that "widespread use" of breast milk substitutes (including infant formula) had had an "adverse effect" on breast-feeding practices, and proceeded to outline a programme of reform for Industry marketing [4]. Corporate executives were angered to see WHO endorsing the activists' claims, and found the background paper additionally disappointing because of its cursory review of "current knowledge" in infant feeding practices. Here, even professionals who had maintained a careful distance from the conflict between Industry and activists felt compelled to comment on the turn this supposed effort to bring the discussion to a neutral plane had taken. *The Lancet*, for example, stated in an editorial: "The WHO/UNICEF document takes a stance which seems too authoritarian and restrictive to set the meeting off on the right note. It implies that the difficulties of all families in all Third World countries are so similar that they are amenable to common solutions. And it is already under criticism for its lack of reference to data sources" [5].

Taking exception to a great many points in the document, as well as its general tone, ICIFI prepared a point-by-point critique to guide its participant companies in the discussion. Other firms outside the ICIFI group did the same. ICIFI also prepared its own background paper presenting the Industry case and drawing attention to important reference sources quite clearly belonging to the body of "current knowledge" on infant feeding, but which Industry felt had been glossed over by WHO/UNICEF [6].

Arriving on the scene in Geneva, the activists, too, sought to present their particular views, but using methods bordering on the most blatant sort of political lobbying. The day before the meeting was due to begin, INFACT and its allies announced plans to hold a "Bottle Baby" seminar for participants, indicating that WHO and UNICEF officials would deliver presentations. The World Council of Churches (WCC), whose interest in the controversy dated back to the Bern libel suit, offered its nearby headquarters as a meeting place. Industry was relieved to be assured directly by the WHO secretariat that INFACT had misrepresented the situation and that its officials had no intention of participating in such an event, but this brief flurry added to the tenseness of the atmosphere. The seminar turned out to be as virulently anti-Industry as any INFACT had held previously, which did not augur well for any possible reconciliation.

Working Groups

Since the meeting was organised into five working groups, it looked as though the issue of marketing practices would at last be placed in the proper context of the larger question of Third World infant nutrition. Sessions were devoted to the other four topics: encouragement of breast-feeding; promotion of appropriate weaning practices; information, education, communications and training; and health and social status of women. These topics certainly deserved the attention of participants who were experts in those areas. But the fifth working group, on "appropriate marketing and distribution of breast milk substitutes", was understandably the justification for the presence of most Industry representatives at the conference, and it also became the equivalent of the "centre court" for the meeting as a whole as far as press coverage was concerned.

This fifth working group therefore attracted not only Industry representatives, but also health professionals and a full complement of activists: ICCR, INFACT, War on Want and ADW. The presence of these critics inevitably cast the session into a confrontational mode. Nestlé representatives, for example, found themselves face to face with the US boycott leaders, whose good faith in pursuing a constructive dialogue they had ample reason to doubt.

The other obstacle to progress during this working group's four-day session was the fact that Industry and the critics were still not speaking the same language, even at this late date in the controversy. The two sides were still deadlocked, for example, over the question of promotional (sales-related) advertising as opposed to educational and informational advertising and communication. In the critics' view this distinction was a red herring. They believed that any communication dealing with infant formula or breast milk substitutes, even in a generic sense, inherently discouraged breast-feeding. This line of argument seemed to Industry to be illogical, as both sides had agreed on the need to curb product-misuse arising out of ignorance. Because Industry maintained that such information was essential to the proper preparation and safe consumption of its products and because the possibilities for company representatives to communicate personally with mothers were being further limited, the distinction between promotional and informational advertising and communication was crucial to development of a responsible marketing practices code.

Although an uneasy truce was reached within the working group as some loose definitions on the different types of advertising and promotion were discussed, renewed conflict on these and other aspects of marketing practices threatened to disrupt the final plenary session and undo the work of the previous days' discussions. However, WHO met the hopes of ICIFI and Nestlé by providing a "strong and rigidly impartial chairman" to steer the tense debate through its course. This task fell to Dr. Fred Sai, a Ghanaian whose credentials as a World Hunger Program health professional struck exactly the right note of credibility. Anyone lacking direct experience with the problems of nutrition in developing countries or whose sympathies were the least bit one-sided would have been immediately suspect. Even more important than the fact of such neutrality, perhaps, was the personal diplomatic skill needed to keep the remaining discussion on a narrow track. Dr. Sai's blend of good humour with reasoned consideration of the various arguments presented was just what the meeting needed to prevent the final hours from breaking up in disorder.

Consensus on Marketing

Bringing to a close four days of intense debate, participants in the October 1979 Meeting on Infant and Young Child Feeding sponsored by WHO/UNICEF agreed to a "consensus" on each of the five areas of concern discussed. On the controversial subject of infant formula marketing, these conclusions were to serve as a foundation for the development of a formal international code. The key points of the consensus were as follows:

– Governments have a duty to ensure the supply and availability of adequate infant food products to those who need them, in ways that will not discourage breast-feeding

– There should be no sales promotion, including promotional advertising to the public, of products used as breast milk substitutes or supplements, or of feeding bottles. (This includes the use of mass media and other forms of advertising directly to the mother or general public, designed to increase sales of breast milk substitutes, to the detriment of breast-feeding)
– A government mechanism must be established to ensure that through continuous screening and monitoring, information and publicity relative to maternal, infant and young child feeding are correct and appropriate and that undesirable and inappropriate messages and publicity are eliminated
– Promotion to health personnel should be restricted to factual and ethical information
– Promotional distribution of samples of breast milk substitutes through health service channels should not be allowed
– Artificial feeding should not be openly demonstrated in health facilities
– No personnel paid by companies producing or selling breast milk substitutes should be allowed to work in the health care system
– Infant formula and weaning foods should be governed by strict legal standards and labelled to indicate proper and safe home preparation. Governments should adopt the recommended international standards developed by the Codex Alimentarius Committee
– There should be an international code of marketing of infant formula and other products used as breast milk substitutes, supported by both exporting and importing countries. WHO/UNICEF were requested to organise the process, with the involvement of all concerned parties
– Monitoring of marketing practices, usually under government auspices, was recommended
– There should be no marketing or availability of infant formula or weaning foods in a country unless marketing practices were in accord with the national code or legislation if these exist, or, in their absence, with the spirit of the meeting and the recommendations contained in the report or with any agreed international code

Nestlé's Response

Labelling the meeting's conclusions a "consensus" was a misnomer of sorts. The activists had sought an even more restrictive approach not only to the marketing of infant formula but to the justification for its use. Nestlé's reaction was mixed. Some of the principles outlined in the consensus had already been adopted as Company practice. Nestlé brands conformed to international product standards, for example. And the Company had some time ago, albeit reluctantly, eliminated instructions for their use in the feeding of infants from the labels of its sweetened condensed milk products.

Other parts of the consensus were less to Industry's liking and thus met resistance as they were later translated into provisions of a formal international marketing code. Nestlé was convinced, for example, that the ban on "open" demonstrations of correct artificial feeding methods, together with the prohibition on the participation of Company personnel in such public health activities, would lead only to increased product-misuse and its attendant hazards for the consumer. Conducting such demonstrations in private, that is, on a one-to-one basis involving a single mother and health worker, was a luxury that few health services could afford, and seemed clearly impracticable.

Despite a few misgivings on the part of Industry and other participants over certain aspects of the consensus, the one point on which all could agree was the commitment to develop a more clearly defined international code of marketing of infant formula and other breast milk substitutes. On the basis of these informally stated principles, Industry looked forward to the prospect of playing a positive role in the discussions that were envisaged.

It would be a refreshing change from fending off direct attacks by the activists, as had been the pattern of the past few months. On the whole, Nestlé was satisfied with the outcome of the meeting. Dr. Arthur Fürer, the Managing Director of Nestlé, expressed this view shortly afterwards. "We do not feel at all limited in our entrepreneurial freedom by these recommendations. On the contrary, the changes Nestlé have gradually introduced over the last five years correspond to these recommendations", he said in an interview given to a Swiss newspaper [7]. Unfortunately, the critics were later to use Dr. Fürer's remarks to underscore the Company's commitment to "entrepreneurial freedom". Translated into the critics' own terms of thinking, this was construed to mean that Nestlé put profits above all else. What they conveniently continued to ignore was the little-publicised modification of Nestlé's marketing practices since the Company had undertaken a full scale review of its policies following publication of *The Baby Killer*.

Nestlé's Checklist for Marketing Practices

Over the years, Nestlé had periodically modified its marketing practices to take into account the changing needs and welfare of its consumers, determined by the Company's own resources or upon recommendation of responsible, knowledge-able third parties (usually, the medical profession).

In the case of infant formula, however, the Company's most ardent critics, in particular those leading the US boycott campaign, refused to give Nestlé credit for the way in which its marketing policies evolved. By mid-1979, at the height of the boycott campaign, for example, Nestlé had eliminated most consumer sales promotion. In addition, new restrictions had been imposed on marketing personnel providing assistance to health professionals and mothers, in order to ensure that these activities, aimed at encouraging better feeding practices, were not construed as "promotional" in nature.

Extracts from Nestlé's internal guidelines dated June 1979 show to what extent actual corporate policy in the developing countries complied with the critics' demands.

Advertising
– No mass media product advertising

Sales Promotions

– No coupons, raffles or discount price offers
– No baby accessory give-aways carrying product brand names
– No in-store demonstrations
– No participation or sponsorship of baby shows, even at the invitation of health authorities

Product Samples and Free Supplies

– No direct distribution to mothers
– Samples given to physicians are not to exceed quantities actually needed
– Free supplies to health institutions are not to exceed their actual needs, as stated in writing
– Charity and welfare requests are to be considered only on the basis of written requests

Information and Educational Materials

To the medical profession:

– Materials concerning branded products are to be clearly indicated as intended for distribution to the medical profession only
– Educational materials such as charts and posters on infant feeding are not to mention brand names, but may mention the Company name

To mothers:

– Product information leaflets indicating brand names to be distributed only through the medical profession
– Educational materials such as booklets on infant feeding, and weight/height charts may bear only the Company name and must be distributed only through the medical profession
– Books for mothers may include only generic information on infant formula
– Health education activities such as films or demonstrations are to be conducted only by Company personnel who are professionally qualified (nurses, nutritionists) and only upon the request of health authorities
– Such personnel may not wear uniforms that can be confused with those of public health personnel

Remuneration

– Bonuses or incentive payments based on sales of infant formula are not to be paid to staff engaged in medical-related activities or health education

Activists Resurgent

The October 1979 meeting signalled a new chapter in the controversy for both Industry and its critics, but there were no moves towards conciliation. No sooner had the participants left the conference room than representatives from various activist groups jointly announced the formation of IBFAN (International Baby Foods Action Network). The inclusion of INFACT and ICCR, the groups that had organised the US boycott of Nestlé products and its organisational links with the IOCU (International Organization of Consumer Unions), seemed particularly ominous. With the activists now dedicating themselves to making the general campaign against Industry more international in scope, it was not difficult to imagine that the boycott, too, could be stretched beyond the borders of the US and that Nestlé would again become an even larger symbolic target for all the Industry.

Those fears were not groundless. An International Nestlé Boycott Committee (INBC) was soon founded, its membership including some familiar faces from INFACT, along with representatives of the European and Asian activist groups now joining their American counterparts under the IBFAN label. Despite a brief flurry of globe-trotting following the meeting, however, public support for the boycott in other countries failed to gain momentum. The International Nestlé Boycott Committee at that time seemed to be more symbolic than real. For Nestlé it was the same actors parading under yet another banner. It justified its existence, however, by taking up where INFACT had left off in calling upon Nestlé to negotiate terms for an end to the boycott. Nestlé for its part was not prepared to negotiate its marketing policies with what it saw as a self-appointed group lacking any kind of authority for determining how the WHO/UNICEF consensus should be put into practice. Even when Nestlé agreed to recognise this bureaucratised sort of advocacy several years later, it refused to regard the dialogue which ensued as negotiations.

Development of ICIFI Model Code

Anticipating that the development of the WHO code and its subsequent implementation would be a long-drawn-out process, ICIFI companies decided that an Industry initiative in self regulation could have some value in showing just what sorts of controls on marketing and promotion were actually workable. So ICIFI, working from the October 1979 consensus, developed a model code to serve both as the basis for discussion with governments in the formulation of national codes, and to be followed voluntarily by ICIFI member companies where government action was not forthcoming [8]. However, this ICIFI code differed in one important way from the international guidelines that were to be developed under the auspices of WHO. The Industry Council's rules were devised to guide marketing practices specifically in developing countries where the risk of serious nutrition problems and formula misuse was greatest. It would have been redundant, even inappropriate, ICIFI believed, to apply these same standards to industrialised countries, where the need for such controls had simply not been demonstrated.

In working out this Industry code in late 1979, ICIFI hoped for the support of the governments of many developing countries. The Council had already collaborated with some of them, such as those of Malaysia and Singapore, that had been pioneers in the development of national codes. In these cases, government authorities assumed the task of monitoring compliance, and ICIFI claimed that the experience in both countries had shown that voluntary regulation could indeed prove effective in preventing abusive marketing practices.

Meanwhile, the task of drafting the official International Code was formally entrusted to the Director General of WHO at the May 1980 World Health Assembly [9]. Endorsement of the project came in a formal resolution that received almost unanimous approval, the only dissension coming in the form of eleventh-hour objections from the US delegation. At issue, it seemed, was the Code formulation process rather than the principle of the Code itself. Only at the last minute had the US policymakers realised that a precedent of sorts would be set in turning the development of such guidelines over to the administrators of an international organisation. It seemed that the Americans had expected that WHO member-state representatives would be full participants in the code-drafting process, and the fact that extensive consultations were to follow did not mitigate the US delegation's reservations, which foreshadowed the Reagan administration's objections to the final draft of the Code a year later.

Industry "Violations"

The 1980 Assembly gave a foretaste of the activists' use of the meeting as a public platform from which to denounce alleged Industry malpractices, in this case, violations of a code that had yet to be developed. In their IBFAN incarnation, the critics held a press conference at which they cited a long list, containing some 200 incidents of alleged abusive marketing practices [10]. This performance caught Industry quite unawares and drew the media focus away from the deliberations of the Assembly proper. The accused companies had no opportunity to deliver even a preliminary rebuttal and were not even sure where to begin to do so, given the confusion over interpretation of the October 1979 recommendations. Nevertheless, once the Assembly was over, ICIFI began the painstaking task of investigating each charge. This involved tracking the alleged violations to their sources in quite a number of developing countries around the world. The process was to take several weeks, and the eventual announcement of ICIFI's findings [11], three months later, well after the World Health Assembly was no longer a news event, generated far less attention than had the original charges.

Many of IBFAN's citations proved to be without substance or quite incapable of being verified. Details on places and names were obscured from many of the citations of "violations". In a few cases the activists were actually right. There *was* some breach of stated Industry policy. Typically this involved the failure to remove outdated educational or promotional material. An independent retailer, for example, may have been reluctant to give up these "decorations". In still other instances the reported violations resulted from an interpretation of the 1979 consensus and differed markedly from Industry's understanding of the guidelines. Thus many more of the alleged abuses were discounted. In the final analysis, ICIFI's verdict was that only 15 of the 202 citations could be reasonably substantiated and attributed to its member companies.

The activists' evaluation of Industry's conduct according to their own interpretation of generally agreed standards was not surprising to ICIFI. For years now the critics had been sitting in judgement on Industry practices. What irritated ICIFI was the indication that the activists seemed to be less concerned about enforcing ethical marketing practices than assuring their own place in the media spotlight. Had the alleged abuses been reported first to ICIFI or to the companies implicated, they could have been investigated more quickly. This successful activist tactic was to be repeated on subsequent occasions. An IBFAN publication distributed to delegates at the 34th World Health Assembly in May 1981, at which the WHO Code was adopted, claimed to have documented over 1000 violations of the WHO/UNICEF October 1979 recommendations [12]. By January 1983, IBFAN regaled members of the WHO Executive Board and the press with a "year end compilation of violations" of the WHO Code [13]. No less than 14 985 160 violations had been recorded in 50 countries and involving 83 companies. One method used for arriving at this figure was to calculate the circulation of a newspaper or magazine in which an offending advertisement had appeared and to count each published copy as a separate violation.

Difficult Drafting Job

The WHO/UNICEF drafting group, made up of staff from the organizations' secretariats and outside consultants, was in the unenviable position of developing a major policy document in matters on which it had little expertise. These were experts in nutrition, not in product-marketing. It was not surprising, therefore, that the first drafts did not eliminate the earlier confusion over the role of sales personnel as opposed to company medical representatives, and over the now-familiar issue of "informational advertising" versus "sales promotion". The process of consultation, which the drafting group followed by meeting with Industry representatives, health professionals and the critics, was meant to clarify the ambiguities and eliminate confusion. But the consultations did not eliminate conflict. The code-making process, rather than rising above the controversy, seemed to become more deeply enmeshed as one stage followed another.

From early 1980 until May 1981, the code went through four drafts, each reviewed by the "interested parties". The proposals were to go through considerable modification over this period, yet the resulting set of guidelines was less than satisfactory, leaving many questions of interpretation and of practicability of implementation and enforcement.

In January 1981, the fourth and final draft was approved by the WHO Executive Board which, in turn, was to present the document to the 1981 World Health Assembly for consideration by the WHO member states. Despite the painstaking consultations that had taken place and the number of modifications that the draft had undergone, this final version still left a lot to be desired not only in the view of Industry, but also in that of health experts as well as, for different reasons, the critics. Nestlé was encouraged, however, by the final version's inclusion of a provision stating the code's aim. This showed that WHO/UNICEF officials appreciated the larger issue of nutrition and health that lay behind pressure for the code. The code's aim, as stated in Article I, was "to contribute to the provision of safe and adequate nutrition for infants" not only through the "protection and promotion of breast-feeding", but also by recognising the role of breast milk substitutes, "when these are necessary", whose "proper use" was to be assured through "adequate information" and "appropriate marketing and distribution". Both in the preamble to the code and in its aim, the legitimacy of the market for infant formula was formally recognised.

Regulation or Recommendation?

Having made considerable efforts to produce a workable draft, WHO secretariat officials turned to the political issue of how the draft could best be steered through the Assembly. Should the measure be introduced in the form of a Regulation, a measure directly binding on member states (except where a government notifies WHO of its intention to reject it in part or as a whole)? Or, would the code succeed better as a Recommendation that would give member states considerable flexibility in translating the principles into practice by choosing a form of implementation and enforcement appropriate to local conditions? The activists were hoping to see a binding Regulation, despite their claim that the code as drafted was not strong enough. Industry meanwhile, continued to take issue with some points of the code which seemed to be far too restrictive as well as expressing grave doubts about its form of implementation.

The WHO secretariat quietly considered what it knew to be political realities. Endorsement of the code as a general principle, as in the case of the previous year's resolution, would be easy enough for most countries. Expression of good intentions does not cost much. When it came to a binding Regulation, however, ideological qualms and political conflicts were more likely to surface, possibly leading to hard lobbying to forge alliances for a vote. In still other instances, some member states might be compelled to withhold their approval on purely technical grounds, such as conflicts with existing business regulation, in particular antitrust laws. Even a few dissenting votes would seriously detract from the effectiveness of a Regulation meant to be truly international in scope. This was a risk that WHO and the drafting group, in particular, were reluctant to take.

The Executive Board thus endorsed the code and forwarded it to the World Health Assembly in the form of a Recommendation. This approach would allow those countries who fully approved of the draft to translate it directly into national regulation, while those with legal or administrative conflicts could either formally implement only certain parts of the measure or simply suggest that the guidelines as a whole serve as a voluntary standard for Industry.

Approval was overwhelming: 118 votes for the Code, with 3 abstentions. The sole negative vote was cast by the US delegation, which refused an opportunity to appear diplomatically in tune with its fellow WHO member states and then later, once back home, slipped out through the back door of implementation by citing the conflict with the US constitution. Its vote was a blunt "no". A US State Department spokesman declared later: "It is true that the Code was only a Recommendation to member governments and could have been rejected or ignored. But the US administration considered it hypocritical to vote in favour of a Code we could not implement ourselves. And under the circumstances, we did not believe it proper to recommend the Code to others" [14].

References

1 World Health Assembly Resolution 27.43 (1974)
2 World Health Assembly Resolution 31.47 (1978)
3 Nestlé Letter (1978) To Mr. David Winston (Minority Counsel, Subcommittee on Health and Scientific Research) 29 December
4 WHO/UNICEF (1979) Meeting on infant and young child feeding, background paper. October 1979
5 Leading Article (1979) Uneasy prelude to meeting on infant feeding. Lancet ii:680–681
6 WHO/UNICEF (1979) Meeting on infant and young child feeding ICIFI supplementary background paper. October 1979
7 Tagesanzeiger (Zürich) (1979) 19 October
8 International Council of Infant Food Industries (ICIFI) (1980) A prototype national code of marketing in developing countries, for infant formula and other products intended for use as breast milk substitutes. July ICIFI, Zürich
9 World Health Assembly Resolution 33.32 (1980)
10 IBFAN (1980) Infant formula promotion
11 ICIFI (1980) The WHO/UNICEF meeting on infant and young child feeding, October 1979; Is the industry observing the recommendations? August ICIFI, Zürich
12 IBFAN (1981) Infant formula promotion. A report by the international baby food action network which exposes the aggressive promotion of powdered milk products for babies, May 1981
13 IBFAN (1983) Breaking the rules – 1982. January 1983
14 Abrams E (Assistant Secretary of State, US) (1981) The US position on infant feeding. Nutrition Today July/August

Chapter 8

Escalation of the Campaign and Nestlé's Response

G. Veraldi

Escalation: Further Observations on the Controversy from Industry's Standpoint

The events described in the preceding chapters took place before I began my own study of the controversy which, up to then, I had followed only in the press. In the seven years which had passed since the affair first caught the attention of the public, every conceivable aspect of the problem of infant feeding in the Third World had been exhaustively debated. Medical, scientific, socio-cultural, economic, ethical, legislative, administrative and political issues had been raised, with profound differences of opinion emerging on practically every point.

When, finally, the World Health Assembly adopted an unprecedented International Code in May 1981, it was understandable that some observers considered the matter closed. After all, the Code had been approved by most of the WHO member states, and it was now up to the health authorities in each country to take appropriate action in line with its principles and aim. In fact, the matter was far from closed. On the contrary, before the ink on the Code was dry, the activists were busy trying to extend their boycott action, up to that point confined to Anglo-Saxon and Nordic countries, to continental Europe and elsewhere. How can we explain this paradox?

No doubt the very suggestion that the escalation of the controversy following adoption of the WHO Code was a paradox, will expose me to accusations of naivety, for the activists considered the Code, not as an end in itself, but as a new beginning. By adopting the Code the WHO member states had legitimised the activist campaigns which preceded it, and since there was little prospect of effective implementation without continued pressure, the activists were prepared to fight on for years to come. Moreover, by riding on the back of this movement, the highly diverse components of the activist network could advance their own causes in their other fields of interest.

It is easy to see, therefore, that the extension of the controversy which we are about to examine was a world-wide phenomenon with profound implications for the relationship between industry and society, a subject I had been studying for nearly twenty-five years. Would the companies concerned know how to face such a challenge on unfamiliar issues in which they lacked professional expertise? As far as Nestlé was concerned, the boycott could not be described as an economic threat. Insult, rather than injury, might be the best characterisation. Yet it was a fundamental challenge to the social role of industry. Would companies be overtaken by events? Would they put up an inept defence? Or would they develop creative approaches to resolve these issues? Whatever the answers, it was clear that we would be witnessing some hotly disputed developments from which many interesting lessons would be learned, as we shall see.

The Power of a Simple Message

Any communicator who wishes his message to penetrate and be retained by a wide audience knows the importance of simple, memorable slogans. However inexperienced activist leaders may have been in matters of Third World nutrition, they were accomplished professionals in the art of promoting simple messages.

It would be difficult to conceive of more evocative and attention-grabbing headlines than *The Baby Killer*, *Death in the Bottle*, *Milk and Murder*, *Breast against Bottle*, *Profit at any Cost*, and, above all, *Nestlé Kills Babies*.

Each slogan was supported by copious statistics, anecdotes and facts, either lifted directly from the writings of one of the activists' scientific resource people, or creatively modified to retain the flavour (and authority) of the original statement, while playing more directly on the reader's sense of outrage. In this way Dr. Jelliffe's bland, "we have calculated that if breast feeding could be re-instituted . . . some 10 million babies would be saved from diarrhoea and marasmus each year," was adapted by Douglas Johnson, writing on behalf of INFACT under the heading, "The Nestlé Boycott", to read: "Ten million Third World babies are starving because of the heartless, money-hungry actions of powerful multinational corporations. Only you can stop the scandal!" [1].

In a similar vein, the pronouncement by UNICEF's Executive Director James Grant, to the effect that one million infant lives a year could be saved "if all of us in the international community who are working to promote and protect the practice of breast-feeding are successful in our efforts" [2], was turned by the activists into: "One million babies will die this year from infant formula abuse" [3]. These messages were backed by graphic illustrations of the suffering alleged to be caused by Nestlé's "heartless, money-hungry actions".

Playing on the Emotions

Following the launch of the Nestlé boycott, the organisers persuaded Americans in their thousands to send postcards to Nestlé Management, bearing the illustration of a pitifully under-nourished (marasmic) baby. The caption on some cards read:

When I see an emaciated, dehydrated, seriously ill baby . . . when I find that the mother was persuaded to bottle-feed[1] rather than breast-feed because of the immoral promotion of infant

---

[1] See discussion of terminology pp. 10–11.

formula[1] then I do become angry. (The statement on the postcard was signed: Dr. Michael Latham, Program on International Nutrition, Cornell University, Nov. 1978.)

Another caption read:

West Indian baby, bottle-fed[1] from early weeks of life with dilute, contaminated bottle feeds[1] resulting in marasmus, diarrhoea and death. (The source was quoted as Dr. Derrick Jelliffe MD, Professor of Pediatrics and Head of the Division of Population Family and International Health, School of Public Health, UCLA.)

However, direct mail promotion on these lines paled in comparison with the emotional appeal achieved through the medium of film. *Bottle Babies* was produced in 1975 by a German filmmaker, Wilhelm Gladitz. It was given its world première during the 5th Assembly of the World Council of Churches held in Nairobi in November 1975 and subsequently was distributed throughout the United States. It became, for the activists, one of their most powerful tools in drawing public support. The film was an effective propaganda piece that reached more people, and stated the critics' side of the case in more emotional terms than was possible through the medium of print. In the words of a guide distributed to groups showing the film, *Bottle Babies* was "not just a documentary". The film was, rather, meant to be a "subjective, emotional, unequivocal – and quite devastating – polemic against the manufacturers of infant formula and the harm the indiscriminate marketing of the product is doing" [4]. It certainly was that.

The visual medium, especially for those not yet accustomed to the scenes from famine-stricken areas which are now on all our television screens, was much more provocative than either *The Baby Killer* or *Nestlé tötet Babys*, and the film footage was even more dramatic than the still photographs that had accompanied the published accounts. For many of the viewers, it was time to leave the room when the film came to the sequence in which a needle was inserted through the scalp into the head of a malnourished infant, as preparation for a rehydration treatment. This routine manoeuvre, like many ordinary hospital procedures, is upsetting for those not familiar with it. Corporate practices were linked to what appeared to be torture rather than ordinary medical procedure. Also, in the context of *Bottle Babies*, infant formula and corporate practices were made synonymous with Nestlé.

The filmmaker, working under the name of Peter Krieg, explained that the focus on Nestlé came about primarily because of its position as infant formula market leader in the Third World. He noted that Nestlé's actual policies and practices were "no worse than other corporations in this respect", but the film portrayed lengthy images of Nestlé, including a review of earlier published charges, the Bern libel suit, an array of Nestlé food products and even a new wing of the Company's headquarters building. These suggested that the new wing was "built from the profits of sales in Third World markets", and left the unmistakable impression that Nestlé, among all the companies in the Industry, was an offender of the first order.

That portrait of Nestlé was far from satisfactory to some of the outside experts who had assisted in the project and who found that their trust in its purported objectives had been violated. At the University of Nairobi, for example, where much of the footage had been shot, one of the medical professors, Professor Nimrod Bwibo, who had reviewed the film's original script and was interviewed

---

[1] See discussion of terminology pp. 10–11.

on camera, protested that his comments had been deleted and that the finished film misrepresented health professionals' attitudes on infant feeding. He also refuted directly the film's claim that milk companies used high-pressure sales techniques in their battle for market share. He pointed out in a letter that among the companies, Nestlé had for some time been collaborating with local health professionals, and that he was happy with the way the Company had followed his advice [5].

Alarmed at the prospect of their major promotional vehicle being discredited, the activists claimed that Nestlé had put pressure on Professor Bwibo. It was their word against Nestlé's, and the implicit insult to the integrity and intelligence of the Professor was ignored. In any case the question became academic since the major US television network, CBS, shot a similar documentary in the Dominican Republic to coincide with the Kennedy Hearings (see p. 75). It was a faithful replica down to the last emotional climax: the needle inserted through the baby's scalp. Showing these two films around the country (well over 300 copies were in circulation) certainly did more than any other single action to recruit supporters to INFACT's cause and finance their on-going campaigns.

Professional Endorsement

However simple the message and emotional the appeal, it is hardly likely that the campaign against the infant formula manufacturers could have had such an impact without some direct medical support and encouragement. The names of two British-born experts, Dr. Derrick Jelliffe and Dr. Michael Latham, were indissolubly linked with the campaign from its very early days, and while their critics would not question their sincerity, there are, as we have seen in Chapter 2, legitimate scientific grounds for challenging many of the allegations and assumptions they make, which formed the basis for the case against Industry.

Most scientists are professionally reluctant to express themselves in stark unqualified black-and-white terms on matters as complex and controversial as infant feeding and malnutrition in the Third World. They usually confine their exchanges to the columns of scientific journals and the podia of medical congresses. Dr. Jelliffe made it clear in his court testimony in Bern [6] that he felt the time had come to move the debate out of these refined circles and into the public arena. Others followed him, their contributions to the debate being characterised by the activists as those of "leading medical experts", "world authorities", etc.

But if the reader could think of one man more than any other, to whom mothers have turned for advice and comfort over the past few decades, there is little doubt whose name would spring to mind. And if that trusted adviser said that Nestlé was "actively encouraging mothers in the developing countries in Africa, Asia and South America to give up breast-feeding and turn to powdered milk formula instead", and went on to describe the tragic results, it is hardly surprising that thousands of sincerely-concerned American parents would heed his call. Dr. Benjamin Spock said: "boycott *all* Nestlé products, and send a generous contribution to help us spread the word" [7]. Few stopped to question Dr. Spock's credentials as an authority on the problems of Third World infant nutrition.

Church, Politics and Press

Added to all this was the moral endorsement of the activist case by the churches, the sympathy of prominent politicians like Senator Edward Kennedy, and wide coverage of the issue (often in simplistic and sensationalised terms) by the national and local media. It can now readily be appreciated that the dimensions of the problem faced by Nestlé management were substantial.

Mention has already been made of the formal endorsement by the National Council of Churches of the Nestlé boycott (p. 77). This action was followed (and in some cases preceded) by resolutions from many of the principal Christian denominations and religious orders in support of the boycott. Not only did church endorsement add to the credibility of the boycott movement, but it provided both organisational support through the staff of important church agencies, and more important still, gave a platform, or perhaps more accurately, a pulpit, from which to spread the word to the grass roots.

With this background in mind, the outrage of decent American citizens genuinely concerned about hunger in the Third World can be readily appreciated; and although postcards and form letters accounted for the bulk of the protest mail received by the Company in Switzerland and in White Plains, many correspondents expressed their own individual sentiments in unequivocal terms:

I think what your company is doing to promote the use of its formulas for babies in the undeveloped countries is shameful, inhuman and immoral. I don't know how anyone with a conscience can be a party to such practices (signed SM 13.3.79).

What I don't understand is how supposedly intelligent people can take advantage of the poor and uninformed and still sleep at night (signed GJA 11.2.79).

[. . . Will not purchase Nestlé products again] until you have ceased your exploitations and made amends to the families of babies you have *murdered* and *maimed* with your powdered milk (signed EMKF 15.3.79).

And from a pastor:

I hesitate to use even a salutation to begin this note, since I don't think those who contribute to mass suffering and murder should be even politely recognized. You are a money-hungry pig . . . I have joined their boycott and intend to fight you on the local level in *any* way possible. This means . . . don't personally come to Lincoln if you value your life. (signed Rev. P.P. 22.2.79).

Similar incitement at the grass roots had already led to the congressional hearings referred to earlier. The text of the model letter reproduced below was included in INFACT publications early in 1978.

MODEL LETTER

Senator Edward Kennedy
U.S. Senate Office Building
Washington, D.C. 20510

Dear Senator Kennedy,
    At least thirteen major companies produce infant milks and promote them in developing countries. In recent months, I have become more and more conscious of the injustices done by corporations involved with the manufacture and sale of infant formula in these areas.
    The hard-sell promotion tactics associate infant formulas with modernity and higher status, imply that breast-feeding is a thing of the past and suggest the possible inadequacy of the mother's milk. Studies from Third World countries confirm that bottle-feeding has resulted in greater infant disease, malnutrition and mortality. The use of infant formula requires sanitary water, bottles and nipples. Lacking these conditions, the formula can become a deadly transmitter of severe bacterial infections

leading to diarrhea, dehydration and death. Moreover, infant formula is very expensive, so poor mothers dilute it to make it last longer. This causes malnutrition.

These injustices lead me to support the Nestlé boycott. I encourage your support of this boycott and further request that you support investigation into, and government control of corporate sales practices in the infant formula market.

I urge you to be responsible for promoting the requested investigation within the Senate Antitrust and Monopoly Sub-committee.

Sincerely,

INFACT introduced this text by telling their supporters that in order to ensure that congressional hearings would be held, citizens should demonstrate their support for them through letters to the two senators most likely to hold them: Senator Edward Kennedy and Senator Frank Church. In addition, INFACT pointed out that it was vital to provide "all senators and representatives with the same information so that they also will know about the issue and support appropriate hearings". Finally, supporters were exhorted to express personal criticism in letters to congresspersons by changing the model letter to make the message "an individual one" [8].

Encouraged by local INFACT workers, the media took up the story throughout the United States and Canada. Nor was it only the local media. In the first half of 1981 the *Washington Post* ran more than 80 articles related to the Nestlé boycott and the impending discussions at the 1981 World Health Assembly on the WHO Code. The primary cause of the *Post*'s interest, however, was the controversial nomination of Mr. Ernest Lefever to the post of Assistant Secretary of State for Human Rights and Humanitarian Affairs in the new Reagan administration. The nomination issue was linked to the fact that Nestlé had donated funds to the Ethics and Public Policy Center (EPPC) in Washington DC, directed by Lefever, in order to finance a mass mailing in the US of reprints of a June 1980 *Fortune Magazine* story entitled, *The Corporation Haters*. This article focussed on the activities of the organisations behind the infant formula campaign, and had also been given wide distribution by the US infant formula manufacturers.

Interest in the links between Nestlé and Lefever was sparked off by an internal memo written to the Nestlé Chief Executive Officer by the head of Nestlé's Infant and Dietetic Products Department, which fell into the hands of INFACT. The memo was dated after the *Fortune Magazine* article attacking the boycott movement was published. It discussed, among other things, how the article could be used to maximum advantage to inform public opinion about the nature of the boycott movement. The memo stated: "The interest of the Ethics and Public Policy Center is the best opportunity we have had yet *to put the record straight* . . ." [9] (emphasis added).

Mention was made of the need to rebut "the unfounded attacks on Nestlé", and of the determination of the activists to "use the IBFAN international network to promote anti-Industry propaganda to influence government delegates to WHO consultations and medical opinion in Third World countries".

The mailing of the *Corporation Haters* article to opinion leaders throughout the United States could hardly be expected to enhance the credibility of the boycott campaign. Accordingly the INFACT response was coordinated and orchestrated with great care. It is not known precisely when or how the memo was leaked to INFACT although mention had already been made of it in a Canadian INFACT newsletter dated September 1980. However plans were being made for a "major story" to break in January 1981, in time to influence members of the WHO executive board which would then be meeting in Geneva to consider action on the WHO Code.

Even the internal Nestlé memo might not have provided the spark for the flurry of unfavourable press reports without the subsequent revelation that the *Fortune* article's author, Herman Nickel, later to be US ambassador to South Africa, had been engaged by Lefever to conduct a study on infant formula. It took the activists no time at all to invent a conspiracy linking Nestlé, the journalist, and Lefever. In fact Nestlé, whose US management had been interviewed briefly for the article, had nothing to do with Nickel's engagement by Lefever.

The story broke in the *Washington Post* on 4 January 1981, under the title *Infant Formula Maker Battles Boycotters by Painting them Red*. This referred to a subtitle in the *Fortune* article *Marxists Marching under the Banner of Christ* which was contributed by a *Fortune* editor and approved by the managing editor himself. It insinuated that Nestlé had inspired the article. This was untrue. In fact the article was uncomplimentary to Nestlé and relied for much of its background on information supplied by a US formula manufacturer. Of course Nestlé purchased large quantities of reprints from EPPC because the Company considered that it gave an accurate picture of the motives and methods of the boycott organisers and of some of their supporters.

The *Washington Post*, however, made it sound as if the whole episode was a carefully planned "campaign" financed by Nestlé. The article was followed by world-wide press coverage. The *Toronto Star*, 12 January 1981, referred to the leaked Nestlé memo, already available to INFACT in September as: *The lid is blown off Nestlé-gate*, and reported that "Secret Nestlé documents tell a story of corporate deviousness" and that the Company "has surreptitiously financed anti-boycott propaganda".

If the wide dissemination of third-party views which support one side in a controversy can be described as "corporate deviousness", then Nestlé was undoubtedly guilty, but certainly less so than the activists who relied on such tactics for virtually their entire propaganda effort. The *Washington Post* and *Toronto Star* reporters appeared to overlook the conviction in the memo that Nestlé considered its cause to be well-founded.

In retrospect, it is doubtful whether the *Fortune* article could have won the support of people who already had a pro-activist bias, for it was hardly a model of objectivity. However, it is understandable enough that it appealed to Nestlé, particularly to those individuals in Management whose encounters with the activists had left them convinced that organisations such as the ICCR and INFACT were more committed to attacking Industry than to promoting the resolution of infant nutrition problems.

The lesson was learned the hard way: endorsement of a company's stance in an issue such as this by traditionally pro-business publications or organisations can at best have a minimal positive effect on the public at large. At worst, they can undo any credibility that the company may have established. This was certainly the case as far as Nestlé's relations with church organisations was concerned. Several such organisations were deeply offended by the role they perceived the Company as having played in the *Corporation Haters* affair, and as a result became active supporters of the boycott movement.

Such was the situation facing Nestlé in mid-1981 as the WHO Code was being adopted in Geneva. It is worth examining at this point how Nestlé and a broad cross-section of the infant formula industry (represented by the International Council of Infant Food Industries) had attempted to respond to the boycott campaign and to the broader international efforts aimed at "de-marketing" infant formula.

Nestlé's Response

Nestlé strategy in dealing with the infant formula controversy had to take two distinct, but obviously inter-related, issues into account. One was the actual infant formula marketing policies practised by the Company in the Third World, the charges against which were outlined in Chapter 1; the other was the whole complex problem of convincing a large and sceptical audience that these policies were appropriate and beneficial. It had become evident that what the Company *said* to its critics was just as important a factor in resolving the controversy as what it actually *did* in the field.

A source of major difficulty was the fact that in the early 1970s , when the campaign against Nestlé began, there were no internationally accepted standards against which to measure marketing policies. The United Nations Protein Advisory Group (PAG) had indeed criticised certain activities, but its recommendations to governments, the health professions and Industry clearly recognised an important role for Industry, and even actively encouraged certain practices which were in direct contradiction to the demands to be made later by boycott leaders. For example, governments were invited to initiate specific legislative actions to reduce direct and indirect fiscal burdens on processed infant formulae and weaning foods. They were also urged to stimulate the use of mass media channels for both "educational and ethical product promotion communication". Indeed "promotion" was recognised as an "essential component of any marketing program to establish widespread consumer use of nutritious foods for children". Cooperation between the infant food industry and paediatricians was actively encouraged, and although Industry was exhorted "to avoid sales and promotional methods that could discourage appropriate breast-feeding in any way", equal emphasis was given to the need for development of improved product instructions.

In Nestlé's eyes, what amounted to United Nations endorsement for its own ideas on appropriate marketing shaped the Company response to the marketing issues in the early stages of the controversy. Moreover, the PAG recommendations were the basis on which ICIFI defined its voluntary code and its programmes. Unfortunately, the Industry critics were dismissive of the PAG recommendations. Mike Muller, author of the *Baby Killer* report [10], referred to them as, "vague and timid".

With the demise of the PAG in 1977, the credibility of its recommendations as a basis for action was seriously compromised. In their place, and backed by the horrifying picture of destruction caused by Industry which was painted by the activists and their supporters, the INFACT demands became the standard against which Nestlé marketing activities were "judged". These demands were based on the concept of "de-marketing" promoted by a Boston City University professor, James Post, together with Edward Baer, the co-director of ICCR's infant formula program [11]. This concept may well have influenced the tone of successive drafts of the WHO code. The crux of "de-marketing", as described by Post and Baer, was "the recognition by management of the need to target sales at a level appreciably lower than that otherwise possible in the absence of knowledge about the adverse public effects". They went on to say that senior management "must recognize that no public purpose is served by the commercial marketing of these products in the LDC's".[1]

With such a philosophy being preached by the activist leadership through its growing network of supporters, now extending well beyond North America, it became an uphill task to defend Industry marketing practices. Even when practices which Nestlé itself acknowledged as inappropriate were eliminated, the reforms were perceived as a sign of weakness and greeted with stepped-up demands.

Development of Product and Marketing Policy

Emphasis on Breast-Feeding

Industry's responsibility to ensure that its products are correctly used, and only by those who really need them, can be fulfilled in part by emphasising the benefits of breast-feeding. This notion existed long before the arrival of the critics who emerged in the 1970s. Such messages have been an integral part of Nestlé's marketing policy for infant foods from the Company's earliest days of operation. A guide to infant feeding, prepared for new mothers by the Company's founder in the nineteenth century, put it this way: "During the first months, the mother's milk will always be the most natural nutriment, and every mother able to do so, should herself suckle her children" [12]. Such a message was even more relevant in 1869 than 1981, as modification of the then-available breast milk substitutes involved quite painstaking efforts in what, even in West European or American kitchens, were fairly primitive conditions by today's standards.

This theme continued to be an important element of Nestlé's educational material throughout the early part of the twentieth century. A 1932 version of the international Nestlé's mothers' guide said "Breast milk is nature's gift to baby and every mother should endeavour to give this ideal food to her infant. Every drop is precious and whatever is available should be given." That message reflected what Company specialists already knew about infant feeding patterns: that the bottle was frequently used as a complement to, rather than a total replacement for, the breast.

The increased use of commercial breast milk substitutes during the post World War II period, first in industrialised countries and then in the Third World, was at first accepted as an inevitable development by health professionals. By the end of the 1960s Jelliffe and others were pointing to an abrupt decline in breast-feeding in poor communities and claiming that mothers were being encouraged to use substitutes unnecessarily. This shortcoming on the part of the profession in developing countries was recognised by the PAG in 1969: "A major responsibility

---

[1]"LDC's", meaning "Less Developed Countries" is terminology commonly used by the United Nations.

for the apathetic or misguided attitude to the current dangerous decline in breast-feeding rests with the health services, particularly pediatricians and obstetricians, nurses and midwives" [13].

If the medical profession had become remiss in its obligation to encourage breast-feeding, it was not surprising that the superiority of breast-feeding was sometimes omitted from Nestlé infant formula advertising and medical literature in some countries, and the superiority of breast-feeding was not mentioned on labels. In retrospect this neglect was illogical since the importance of breast-feeding was stressed in employee-training and in educational materials aimed at mothers.

Nevertheless, as the result of Management's policy review following the Bern libel case, Nestlé began to modify its promotional and educational materials to place greater emphasis on breast-feeding. Because this required adjustments in a wide variety of communications directed both at consumers and professionals, disseminated through various media, including product labels and educational materials distributed by doctors, in numerous markets, the implementation process begun in 1976 was gradual. In taking this initiative, Nestlé was running a step ahead of the move towards international policy formulation. By the time the question of Industry's role in emphasising breast-feeding was raised at the WHO-sponsored meeting in 1979, Nestlé's new policy was in effect.

When the critics first spoke out on the subject of infant formula marketing in the early 1970s, their views on advertising controls were fairly narrowly focussed. The *New Internationalist* article of 1973 went only so far as to condemn the use of inappropriate messages rather than product advertising *per se*. At that time Nestlé was already making substantial modifications to the content of its advertising for developing country markets. The Company had realised, for example, that radio messages featuring catchy jingles, a style common to a wide variety of consumer goods, were really not appropriate for infant formula promotion. This type of commercial was eliminated in the mid-1970s as the Company adopted a more educational approach that emphasised the importance of breast-milk and included reminders about correct formula preparation and feeding.

By 1978, mass media advertising had merged even further into the background of Nestlé's marketing strategy for infant formula and was being phased out altogether in the English-speaking countries in Africa and the Caribbean. In the few remaining Third World countries where Nestlé continued to use mass media, it did so only if the following conditions were fulfilled [14]:

- The general economic, cultural and intellectual level of mothers in the audience addressed by the specific media is such that they are in a position to take a responsible decision in consultation with a doctor, nurse or health worker as to the form of infant feeding to be adopted
- The message is predominantly educational, with clear emphasis on the importance of breast feeding as the preferred method of feeding during the first months of life
- Use of the media concerned is approved by the local health authorities

Even this considerably more stringent approach did not go far enough for the critics, who attempted to discredit the notion that audiences exposed to vehicles of mass media could be as carefully circumscribed as Nestlé contended. The burden of proof lay with Nestlé to show that its advertising did not reach the eyes and ears of consumers who could neither afford to purchase the product in sufficient quantities nor ensure that it would be prepared under safe and hygienic conditions.

Pressure from the critics continued to mount, particularly in the United States, where the call for elimination of all mass media product-advertising headed the list of demands made by the boycott leaders. So, in 1978, Nestlé decided to withdraw all mass media advertising for infant formula, even that which was primarily educational in nature, from Third World markets. This decision gave rise not to plaudits, but simply to more frustration. It did not seem to affect the stance of the activists, who virtually ignored Nestlé's initiative, leaving their demands unchanged.

Equally troubling to Management was the inconsistency in corporate policy that this decision implied: the Company had just recently enlisted the cooperation of authorities in screening advertisements for those markets where such promotion was allowed. Some national codes, such as that for Singapore, also recognised that media advertising could play a positive role:

The development of media communication has an important educational role in instructing the correct and safe use of infant formula products. Such communications should be approved by the Vetting Committee, appointed by the Ministry of Health [15].

Now, practically overnight, Nestlé was having to withdraw all mass media advertising, including information messages that such authorities had considered a positive contribution to their own efforts to educate consumers in infant nutrition and feeding.

Mothercraft Activities

Probably the single most damaging accusation levelled at Nestlé in the course of the campaign was the charge that the company employed "sales girls dressed as nurses". That accusation arose in part from a misinterpretation of what was the Company's candid description of various Industry marketing practices in the course of the interviews with the author of War on Want's *The Baby Killer* report. Nestlé itself had not disguised sales personnel in nurses' uniforms, but once *The Baby Killer* was published, its name was irretrievably linked to this particularly damaging charge.

The fact was that, even before World War II, the Company had employed qualified nurses and midwives to assist the medical profession in instructing mothers how to prepare and administer milk products correctly for infant feeding. These "Nestlé nurses" were not involved in direct sales, nor was their reward linked directly to product sales. The more delicate point of debate, however, was the extent to which mothercraft activities could be considered promotional in nature.

As part of their duties, Company nurses called on homes where mothers were encountering specific feeding problems which had been attributed to the use of a Nestlé product. Professionals that they were, these nurses did not take lightly what they saw as a general responsibility to assist mothers and babies in any aspect of feeding or infant care, including counselling on breast-feeding. In some countries, where the health services were strained to provide the most basic of services, these Company employees came to be regarded as an Industry-subsidised godsend. As such, they frequently spent days and nights on calls helping mothers to cope with colicky babies whose problems often had no connection with the use of a Nestlé product. Those efforts had the result in some markets of making the Nestlé nurses a feature of daily life where infants were concerned. It was this high visibility which subsequently made the Nestlé nurses vulnerable to charges of aggressive product promotion.

It is paradoxical to note that a report submitted as evidence by ADW to the court in Bern (see Chap. 4) confirmed that Nestlé nurses were fully qualified and were actively encouraging breast-feeding. The same report, from CFNI, the Caribbean Food and Nutrition Institute in Jamaica, also confirmed that Nestlé nurses only addressed mothers with the permission of public health staff, and that they were not paid sales-related commissions [16].

Although, on balance, the CFNI report felt that the potential conflicts of interest outweighed the advantages of company-employed nurses, it was by no means categorical. A government-employed clinic nurse, a public health nurse and a midwife who were interviewed, all felt that the commercial nurse had a place, but only "if and when there is no alternative to bottle-feeding". The report concluded: "If the nurses are to continue in an educational role they must *not* be sales agents, and they need re-education concerning nutrition in the weaning period".

In the context of Dr. Jelliffe's condemnation of company-employed nurses it is particularly ironical that the Caribbean Food and Nutrition Institute had participated in training programmes for Nestlé nurses, even when Jelliffe himself was Director of the Institute. However, as a result of the report's findings and Nestlé's own analysis of the situation, policy was defined as follows in February 1978:

. . . appropriately qualified personnel (e.g. nurses, dieticians, health educators) may assist in nutrition and health education work if requested to do so by the appropriate health authorities. In order to avoid any possible confusion with public health service personnel, Nestlé personnel will not wear official uniforms even when their qualifications entitle them to do so.

In order to underline their educational function in accordance with the philosophy outlined earlier, the salary paid to Nestlé representatives is not related to sales and they are not permitted to sell our products to mothers [14].

It was fully recognised that instruction on infant feeding was primarily a public health matter and hence the responsibility of the health authorities. On the other hand, in countries where the value of such advisory services to mothers was recognised by national codes and where the conditions under which these services were rendered were clearly defined by the health authorities and under their supervision, as was the case for example in Singapore, Nestlé felt that it had a responsibility to continue this service. However, these clarifications of policy and the restriction of mothercraft activities to a handful of countries where this service was approved by the authorities did nothing to deflect criticism.

The activities of Company-employed nurses continued to be characterised by the activists in the following terms:

Dear Friend,

Please imagine you are a young woman in a poor village in Africa, or Asia or South America, with a newborn son. By God's mercy, you are healthy enough to breast-feed him.

But a woman in white, the company "milk nurse" who comes to your village, tells you there's a *better* way than giving your breasts to your baby . . . that "old-fashioned" mother's milk may be inadequate and inconvenient.

She says the *modern* way is to give your child infant formula, a powdered milk preparation. "Your baby will grow fair and strong on it!".

The "milk nurse" gives you a free sample of the formula. She mixes it . . . so easy . . . just add water . . . look how the child drinks . . . such a beautiful child, and how he'll grow!

You want your baby to be healthy, so you vow to spend what little money there is in the house for a can of formula.

After the milk nurse has left, you discover that you don't know exactly how much powder to add to the water. You find it difficult to understand the instructions on the label (which may not even be in your language, if you can read at all).

You've never even heard of sterilizing, and you couldn't afford the necessary fuel anyway. You want to make the expensive formula last as long as possible, so each time you mix it you add a little more water.

After a few weeks your son develops a high fever, and becomes dehydrated from severe diarrhea. Each day his cries become fainter, his eyes seem to stare more blankly.

Finally, he dies.

You bury him, sadly. On the tiny grave you place a loving tribute – the empty bottle you used for his formula. You still believe that his formula was his most valuable possession . . . you don't for a moment suspect that *it actually caused his death!*

Let's go back to that woman in uniform. The "milk nurse", as she's known throughout the Third World, may or may not be a real nurse. She is one of hundreds of women employed by several big multinational corporations to promote infant formula products.

Make no mistake. She wasn't hired to work as a nurse, she was hired to *look* like a nurse and to push baby formula – to exploit every mother's desire to do what's best for her baby – regardless of what the cost in babies' lives may be.

The cost in babies' lives is staggering.

Dr. Derrick Jelliffe of the UCLA School of Public Health reports that 'as many as *ten million* cases of malnutrition a year can be traced to bottle feeding.' (Not all artificially fed babies die, of course. For many, malnutrition leads to permanent brain damage.) [17]

Faced with this kind of misguided, emotive, but effective propaganda, it finally became a political impossibility for Nestlé to maintain its mothercraft activities and the service was completely withdrawn in 1981.

Phasing out mothercraft activities had the effect of placing the entire burden of instruction in infant feeding back to where the critics said it belonged: the medical profession and public health services. It is to be hoped that the latter will be able to find the resources, both in time and personnel, to fill this gap in providing mothers with direct personal assistance.

Medical Representatives

Meanwhile, Nestlé continued to employ medical representatives. These Company personnel are men and women with specific training in health and nutrition, but whose contacts in the market are generally confined to health professionals. Their function is closely akin to that of the pharmaceutical companies' "detail men", whose job it is to inform doctors about prescription drugs.

Nestlé's medical representatives provide physicians and health workers with information on different types of infant formula and other infant foods. This sort of communication is a two-way street, for the medical representative seeks constant feedback from health professionals. This is an important element in product development and the improvement of labelling and feeding instructions. It is through this relationship with the health professions at all levels that Industry can attempt to ensure that infant formula is used safely and when necessary.

As the development of the international marketing Code progressed, it became evident that the critics' suggestions for a "hands-off" policy in regard to the

and outside consultants, an ICIFI working group developed prototype standard preparation procedures and ethnically neutral symbols for teaching these procedures, together with simplified graphic presentation of feeding instructions. It also attempted to develop an improved, easy-to-clean feeding bottle. By the late 1970s these innovations had undergone field testing which revealed the need for further improvement.

It was just about that time that the activist campaign began to pick up, and Industry's resources had to be diverted to answering its critics, while the cooperative effort with international organisations halted as polarisation on the issue of infant formula marketing set in. By mid-1978 it became apparent to Nestlé Management that Nestlé's low-key approach to handling public criticism was ineffective. The Company's entry into the public arena had only added fuel to the fire, and the boycott movement was gaining strength daily, as organisation after organisation pledged its support for INFACT.

In spite of the valiant efforts of the volunteer speaker panels composed of Company employees sent out by Nestlé White Plains to confront the activists, it was felt necessary to hire public relations expertise in an effort to communicate Nestlé's case more effectively. However, this approach also failed. The problem of gaining credibility at the grassroots and taking the initiative from the boycott movement could not be resolved by conventional communications techniques. What was needed was a comprehensive strategy to respond, not so much to the activists' demands, but to the perceived concerns of opinion leaders, those who came to be described as "critics of conscience".

Responsibility for planning and implementing this comprehensive strategy was given to a new corporate affairs group established in January 1981, called the Nestlé Coordination Center for Nutrition Inc. (NCCN), located in Washington DC, and headed by Mr. Rafael Pagan, a veteran public affairs professional with long experience in both industry and the government sector. Creation of the Center was a departure from Nestlé's traditional policy of letting its actions speak for themselves.

In addition to professionals in public affairs, the Center staff included two highly qualified scientists and a health worker, each with several years of Third World experience behind them. If a former director of nursing, whose experience included "front line" work in Vietnam, Nicaragua and Bangladesh, could not convince audiences that the activist's characterisations of Third World problems were off-base, then nobody could!

NCCN jumped in at the deep end, just as the "Nestlé-gate" controversy was breaking. In spite of the distractions of these "brush fires" they began a programme of contact with the main supporters of the boycott movement: church groups, women's organisations, unions, public health organisations, academics and, not least, the media. However, the most significant responsibility of NCCN, in those early days of its existence, was to pursue the dialogue which had begun between the United Methodist Church and the Company, a few months earlier.

United Methodist Task Force

At this point it is necessary to go back to the creation of the United Methodist Task Force, as this event was a crucial turning point in the history of the Nestlé boycott.

Up to April 1980, many mainline US church demoninations and their agencies had followed the lead of the National Council of Churches in giving support to the boycott. Although Nestlé representatives would be allowed the opportunity to state their case at the general assemblies of their organisations, the activist groups, aided by supporters on the church staffs, overwhelmed the meetings. They mounted exhibitions, graphically portraying Nestlé "crimes", showed films, and personally lobbied key representatives. The result, when the boycott issue came up for voting, was virtually a foregone conclusion. So there was a sense of *déjà vu* when Nestlé was invited to present its case at the general conference of the United Methodist Church, one of the biggest Protestant denominations in the United States, with some 10 million members.

However there was a difference at this meeting. In addition to a majority report which would have committed the Church to boycott Nestlé, a minority report had been submitted. This report pointed to the "considerable scientific, economic, psychological and political complexity" of the issues, and called on the General Conference to authorise the General Council on Ministries to establish "a representative task force of persons from the Council and the Church at large". This task force would review the debate, establish "constructive dialogue" with Nestlé and with its American competitors seeking modifications of advertising promotion and distribution methods which may contribute to nutritional harm to infants. The task force would be charged with recommending to the General Council on Ministries (GCOM), no later than July 1982, appropriate action by the GCOM and other United Methodist agencies. Such action might include a continuation of dialogue – if considered fruitful and effective in producing constructive change, or, alternatively, formal participation in a boycott "of the company or companies involved" [20].

The promoter of this minority report, Dr. Paul Minus, had already pointed to weakness in the critics' campaign. Although critical of the way Nestlé "clumsily questioned the motivations and intelligence of its critics", he wrote that the critics "often appear to have ignored that stream of Christian tradition warning against the theological and ethical blunder of seeing only virtue in one's own position and only vice in the adversary's". Minus went on to say "proper regard for the present state of knowledge would not have allowed INFACT, in its recent mass appeal for funds, for example, to claim simplistically that Third World mothers are shifting from breast-feeding to bottle-feeding because of the crass marketing practices of profit-hungry companies like Nestlé!" According to Minus, a substantial body of anthropological study indicated that this shift was due to a variety of factors [21].

In spite of determined efforts by INFACT and its supporters, the minority report calling for the creation of the Task Force was adopted by a vote of 510 to 398. Some credit for this must go to the team from Nestlé White Plains. Their's was a difficult and thankless task. Twenty-three annual conferences and two of the general boards of the United Methodist Church had already voted to participate in the boycott by the time the 1980 general conference convened. The Nestlé team demonstrated on this occasion that, when the odds were not entirely stacked against them, they could get results.

The first decision by the Task Force was to commission Dr. Minus to write a comprehensive background paper on the controversy. The 114 page report [22] was completed in September 1980, and Nestlé was invited to comment. Those responsible for monitoring boycott developments in Switzerland viewed the Task Force with a certain amount of scepticism. At least one influential member had written a highly critical report of an earlier visit to Nestlé Management in Switzerland, and Dr. Minus' report certainly did not give Nestlé a clean bill of health.

Nevertheless, the Company decided to cooperate with the United Methodist Task Force (UMTF). They had, after all, chosen the path of dialogue rather than confrontation and Nestlé could hardly afford to reject an outstretched hand at this point. Detailed comments on his report were therefore sent to Dr. Minus, and when Nestlé was invited shortly afterwards to send representatives to meet members of the Task Force a small delegation including Geoffrey Fookes from Corporate headquarters in Vevey, and Dr. Thad Jackson (an immunologist with several years' field experience in Bangladesh who had recently joined Nestlé staff in Switzerland and was later to join NCCN) made the trip to the Wesleyan Seminary in Washington, whose Dean, Dr. Philip Wogaman, had been appointed chairman of the UMTF.

The meeting was cordial, if a little tense at times as both sides sought to put aside suspicion of each other's motives. Agreement was reached to continue the dialogue, and when NCCN opened for business in January 1981, the Task Force was invited to use NCCN as its point of contact with the Company.

The part played by the on-going dialogue between NCCN and the United Methodist in resolving the conflict will be described in the next chapter, as we examine Nestlé policy towards the *WHO International Code of Marketing of Breast Milk Substitutes*.

References

1 INFACT (1979) Fundraising letter: The Nestlé boycott. The Newman Center, Infant Formula Action coalition (INFACT), 1701 University Avenue SE, Minneapolis, Minnesota 55414, February 1979
2 Grant J (Executive Director, UNICEF) (1981) Speech at *NGO* Forum, United Nations, New York City, 12 January 1981
3 Baby Milk Action Coalition (BMAC) (1983) BMAC petition, reported in International Baby Food Action Network (IBFAN) News, April 1983
4 Leader's Guide for using *Bottle Babies* (1977) Interfaith Center on Corporate Responsibility (ICCR), 475 Riverside Drive, New York, NY 10027, June 1977
5 Nimrod O Bwibo (Professor and Chairman Department of Paediatrics, University of Nairobi) (1978) Letter to Miss June Noronah, 14 April 1978. In: Marketing and promotion of infant formula in the developing nations, 1978. Hearing before the subcommittee on health and scientific research of the committee on human resources. US Government Printing Office, Washington DC (United States Senate 23 May 1978) pp 621–622
6 Audienz des Gerichtspräsidenten VIII von Bern (1976) Fortsetzung des Hauptverhandlung wegen Ehrverletsung (Hearing in Bern libel suit, 1974–76, 26 February 1976, witness Prof. Derrick B Jelliffe)
7 Spock B (1979) Letter which accompanied INFACT Fundraising letter (reference 1 above)
8 Catholic Church Investments for Corporate Social Responsibility V (1978) Special Issue, Justice & Peace Center, 3900 N. Third Street, Milwaukee, Wisconsin 53212
9 Internal Nestlé memo (1980) Addressed to Mr. A Furer (Managing Director), US Boycott. Conclusions based on US visit (2/4 August 1980), 13 August 1980. (Reproduced by INFACT under the title: Nestlégate secret memo reveals corporate cover-up, 1980)
10 Miller M (1974) The baby killer. War on Want, London
11 Post JE, Baer E (1979) Demarketing infant formula: consumer products in the developing world. Contemp Business 7: No. 4

12 Nestlé H (1869) Memorial on the nutrition of infants. Loertscher & Son, Vevey (Switzerland)
13 WHO (1969) Report on the meeting of the protein advisory group's *ad hoc* working group on feeding the pre-school child. Geneva, WHO, December 1969
14 Nestlé Infant Food Policy (1978) Issued by the infant and dietetic products department, Nestlé Products Technical Assistance Co. Ltd, Switzerland, February 1978
15 Ministry of Health, Singapore (1982) The code of ethics on the sale of infant formula products in Singapore
16 Caribbean Food and Nutrition Institute (1974) A report on some aspects of the sales promotion of proprietary brands of milk for feeding infants. Caribbean Food and Nutrition Institute, Kingston, Jamaica
17 INFACT (1978) Fund-raising letter; The Nestlé Boycott. Infant Formula Action Coalition (INFACT), San Francisco 1978
18 May CD (1981) The "infant formula controversy": a notorious threat to reason in matters of health. Pediatrics 68: 428–430
19 Leah Margulies (Program Director Interfaith Center on Corporate Responsibility (ICCR)) (1979) Interview in International Herald Tribune, 13 October 1979
20 Committee on Church and Society (1980) Report No. 71 (Minority). Subject: Infant Formula, 20 April 1980. In: Daily Christian Advocate, 24 April 1980
21 Minus Paul M (1979) The infant formula issue: other perspectives. The Christian Century 96: 662, 663
22 Minus Paul M (1980) A background paper on the infant formula controversy, prepared for the United Methodist task-force on infant formula, 17 September 1980

Chapter 9

Implementing the WHO Code

G. Veraldi

On 21 May 1981, the day that the WHO Code was adopted by the 34th World Health Assembly, Nestlé issued a statement supporting its principles and aim, which pointed out that no single measure could hope to solve the problems caused by widespread poverty, lack of food, contaminated water, poor sanitation and frequently insufficient coverage by public health services. It went on to stress the need for improved maternal nutrition, adequate maternity leave, better education and other measures, with infant formula continuing to fill a vital need when mothers were unable to breast-feed, or when breast milk had to be supplemented during the first months of life. The statement ended:

Nestlé is totally committed to achieving the aims of the Code, and will consult with the government in each individual country in which it operates, on the specific measures to be introduced. Nestlé will abide by any such measures and will work with the medical profession and health authorities in their implementation.

This expression of support was given little coverage, and was greeted with scepticism by the critics. After all, Nestlé and its partners in the International Council of Infant Food Industries (ICIFI) had strenuously opposed the idea of an inflexible international regulation, and had campaigned to the last minute for changes in certain ambiguous passages in the Code text. Moreover, a statement issued by ICIFI, adopted by an uneasy consensus of a bare quorum of members, placed emphasis on the fact that the Code had been adopted as a voluntary measure rather than accepting its principles and aim [1].

ICIFI Disbanded

In the following months, disagreements over policy led to serious divisions within ICIFI and the resignation of several member companies. These internal dissensions, aggravated by ICIFI's failure to obtain the status of non-governmental organisation in official relations with WHO, led to the disbandment of the Council in 1983. Although new, and more broadly-based international representation of the Industry has since been established[1], it was largely left to the initiatives of individual companies to determine how the WHO Code should be implemented in terms of their policies.

As far as Nestlé was concerned, with its adoption by an overwhelming majority, the Code had become a political reality and would shape all future debate on the marketing of breast milk substitutes. For all its faults, its aim clearly recognised that the infant formula industry has a legitimate role which corresponded closely with long-standing Nestlé philosophy. There was, therefore, nothing very extraordinary in the Nestlé commitment to support the Code. What *was* different, however, was the fact that within a month of its adoption, Nestlé was testifying in front of subcommittees of the US House of Representatives, alongside its US competitors and critics, and this time attracted no negative comment. The testimony before a joint subcommittee hearing of the House Foreign Affairs committees which was then reviewing United States policies towards the WHO Code, marked a kind of public debut for the Nestlé Coordination Center for Nutrition (NCCN, see p. 110). It had been carefully planned in close consultation with Management in Switzerland, and emphasised Nestlé's willingness to work with individual countries in the development of codes based on the WHO recommendations, as well as reiterating Nestlé's full support for the aim of the WHO Code [2].

Dialogue with the United Methodists

NCCN also quickly took up the dialogue with the United Methodist Task Force, whose chairman, Dr. Philip Wogaman, had attended the sessions of the World Health Assembly and had discussed Industry policies with ICIFI and with Nestlé representatives while he was in Geneva. In September 1981, NCCN submitted an *aide mémoire* to the Task Force outlining the Company's policy and activities in relation to the WHO Code [3]. The paper pointed out that the Company was in the process of consulting with governments to clarify specific provisions of the WHO Code which were "open to different interpretations", and listed the countries where the Company had offered cooperation or where dialogue was already in progress. Of particular importance was the proposal that, as an interim measure pending implementation of the Code by governments, a "hot-line" be established between the Task Force and Nestlé, in order to examine complaints about Company marketing activities.

It should be mentioned that although the governing body of the United Methodist Church had opted for an investigation rather than endorsing the boycott, over 30 annual conferences (out of 75) and 2 national agencies of the Church had already lent their support to the boycott and continued to do so. The Task Force activities therefore came under intense scrutiny and criticism both from those within the Church who had opposed its establishment, and from the

---

[1] International Society of Dietetic Industries (ISDI) which includes in its membership the International Association of Infant Food Manufacturers (IFM). In January 1987 ISDI was admitted into official relations with WHO as a non-governmental organisation.

boycott leaders, who identified it as a threat to their leadership and ability to dictate the terms on which the boycott could be lifted. This was indeed true for, as pointed out in a press report, the United Methodist membership (9.6 million) was larger than the combined membership of the six US "boycotting" denominations which had only 8 million members between them [9]. It was therefore no surprise that the Task Force meeting in open session on 25 September 1981 was "bombarded by conflicting arguments" [4].

The Infant Formula Action Coalition (INFACT) chairman, Douglas Johnson, warned the Task Force "against accepting Nestlé officials' claims 'at face value' " [4] and "bescecched it to stop diluting the efforts of most other large mainline (church) denominations", which were already boycotting Nestlé [5]. Lest it be thought, in the light of subsequent events, that the Task Force adopted a "soft line" towards Nestlé, it should be mentioned that, in addition to these external pressures, several of its members were rather sceptical at that time about the outcome of the dialogue with the Company. Just one year later, its chairman was quoted as saying that when he first got involved with the task force, he thought that they would very soon be going back to the Church and asking for a boycott [6].

In reply to the Company's "hot-line" proposal for the examination of complaints, the Task Force said, in essence, that before the idea could be considered, the changes Nestlé said it had made, and was making, to comply with the Code would need to be documented [7]. Task Force members regarded the Company's willingness to produce internal memos, letters and other documents "as a crucial test of Nestlé's sincerity" [8].

Nevertheless the Nestlé presentation was welcomed, and even if the "hot-line" proposal was not accepted, it was described as "suggestive of hopeful lines of further development" [7].

In spite of continuing opposition pressure, including charges that it had been "hood-winked" by Nestlé [9], the Task Force continued its work. In a letter dated 9 October 1981, the Company was requested to supply:

– Documents to substantiate assurances that Nestlé had made important voluntary changes in marketing even before the adoption of the WHO Code

– Similar documents relating to voluntary adjustments being made in response to the adoption of the WHO Code

– Country-by-country analysis of Nestlé policy towards the Code

All this information was to be made available by early December 1981. What in fact the Task Force was requesting, was disclosure of private corporate policy communications. Although the preliminary contacts had been constructive, it would be going too far to suggest that mutual trust and confidence had been fully established. Perhaps the "Nestlé-gate" affair had made Nestlé over-sensitive, but the thought of confidential Company memos falling into the hands of the boycott leadership, to be misrepresented and quoted out of context, was hardly appealing. Yet the dialogue with the Task Force represented the most promising avenue for re-establishing Company credibility. Failure to cooperate would inevitably lead to full and determined endorsement of the boycott by the entire United Methodist Church. Moreover, the Company was confident that the record of its efforts to implement its publicly stated commitments could be convincing to any observer of good faith. The Task Force letter accepted assurances that the

Company regarded the WHO Code as "the normative frame of reference". Internal memoranda to Nestlé managers confirmed that substantive changes in marketing practices had been imposed well before the adoption of the WHO Code. Documentary evidence could also be provided to demonstrate affirmative action in support of the Code in the weeks following the May World Health Assembly: Nestlé managers had been instructed to consult with government health authorities, leading paediatricians and nutritionists to offer cooperation in the development of national codes based on the WHO recommendations. Label texts, educational materials and medical documentation were all being modified to reflect the Code's requirements. Intensive study of alternative label designs in line with the Code's ban on the use of baby illustrations was in progress.

Management therefore took the decision to accede to the Task Force request. Over the next few months over 300 private corporate documents were shown, in confidence, to Task Force members. Never was there the slightest reason to believe that confidentiality was betrayed, and there is little doubt that the trust established in this way played a very significant part in moving the infant formula debate into a more constructive phase.

In the meantime the boycott leadership had not abandoned its efforts to torpedo the Task Force approach. A letter sent by INFACT to delegates attending the United Methodist General Council on Ministries (GCOM) meeting at the end of October 1981 asked whether the Task Force was the servant of Nestlé or of the one million children "who unnecessarily die each year". It contrasted the actions of other churches who had endorsed the boycott with those of the United Methodist Church which "refuses to see the weight of evidence as necessitating a boycott of Nestlé". These criticisms were countered by other voices. An editorial in the *United Methodist Reporter* said that instead of "catching heat" the General Council of Ministries (GCOM) "should be receiving commendation for the even-handed mediating role its leaders are seeking to play". Although the decisions of other churches and of institutions within the United Methodist Church were "understandable, to be respected as well-intentioned, and consistent with the usual style of many religious groups in recent years", it was also possible, according to the editorial, "that the controversy could have been resolved sooner if Nestlé's critics had been less confrontational in orientation" [10]. This editorialising did not deter the boycott lobby, ten of whom were passing out literature in support of the boycott as GCOM members entered the plenary session. Their efforts were to no avail: the GCOM endorsed the Task Force approach and postponed any decision on the boycott [11] until their report had been submitted, no later than July 1982.

Code Implementation at the National Level

Meanwhile, efforts continued to encourage government action to implement the international code, which WHO member states themselves had adopted the previous May. According to a review carried out by Nestlé late in 1981, Codes had been published, or were about to be published, in 21 countries. "Active consultation" was said to be taking place in a further 38 countries. Even assuming that these consultations would come to fruition, the results of the review meant that little or no action was being taken in about 100 member states. At the same time, Nestlé's efforts to encourage Code development at the national level were being characterised by the International Baby Food Action Network (IBFAN), as "anti-WHO Code lobbying" in 36 countries [12]. This was a reference to the *Aide Mémoire* to the United Methodist Task Force [3] in which Nestlé had detailed the countries where cooperation had been offered, or where code discussions were known to be already in progress. This accusation of IBFAN highlighted basic differences in philosophy with regard to the Code.

As pointed out earlier, the Code was adopted as a *recommendation*, and like any other WHO recommendation was addressed to member states. Article 11.1 of the Code states the following:

Governments should take action to give effect to the principles and aim of this Code, as appropriate to their social and legislative framework, including the adoption of national legislation, regulations or other suitable measures.

Nestlé and other manufacturers regarded this as meaning that the operative clauses of the Code could be adapted by governments according to their local requirements, provided that the measures actually taken were in line both with the principles stated in the Preamble to the Code and with the aim of the Code, as stated in Article 1. This point of view has since been confirmed by a number of governments. For example, a statement at the 36th World Health Assembly made it clear that Brazil had voted in favour of the Code on the understanding that member states would be free to adjust the recommendations to local conditions and specific needs [13]. The same point was made by the Malaysian Minister of Health when he launched his country's revised national code in April 1983. He stated that the WHO Code was only a guideline for member countries; it did not imply that it had to be followed in all respects [14].

This was not the opinion expressed by the boycott leaders and other Industry critics. They pointed to the Resolution adopting the WHO Code [15], which stressed that "adoption of and adherence to the International Code . . . is a minimum requirement". It went on to urge all member states:

to give full and unanimous support to the implementation of the recommendations made by the joint WHO/UNICEF Meeting on Infant and Young Child Feeding (October 1979) and of the provisions of the International Code *in its entirety* as an expression of the collective will of the Membership of the World Health Organization. (Emphasis added.)

According to the critics' reasoning, member states did indeed have the flexibility to modify the Code, but only in the sense of making it more restrictive. In other words, the Code "in its entirety" is "a minimum requirement", they claimed. They went on to argue that Article 11.3 gave Industry a moral obligation to implement the Code, whether or not the authorities had decided on action:

Independently of any other measures taken for implementation of this Code, manufacturers and distributors of products within the Scope of this Code should regard themselves as responsible for monitoring their marketing practices according to the principles and aim of this Code, and for taking steps to ensure that their conduct at every level conforms to them.

The key question was whether practices in accordance with the "principles and aim" could be taken to mean the practical application of each and every detailed provision of the Code, including those which engaged the responsibility of the Health Care System. According to the boycott leadership, that was exactly what it meant.

By the end of 1981 it had become clear that it was unrealistic to expect widespread promulgation of national codes based on the WHO model. The Nestlé policy of "encouraging national measures" while expressing "support" for the aim and principles of the WHO Code was rapidly losing credibility. Members of the United Methodist Task Force were beginning to question the policy and to ask for evidence of substantive application by the Company of the Code's detailed provisions.

The Nestlé Instructions

A clear policy statement was necessary to remove confusion over Nestlé's commitment to the WHO Code, and to maintain the momentum created by the dialogue with the United Methodists. Early in 1982, a first draft of such a policy was circulated at headquarters in Switzerland. It took the form of detailed Code implementation instructions addressed to all companies of the Nestlé group, as well as to agents and distributors marketing infant formula under trade marks owned by the Nestlé group. Each and every article of the WHO Code was printed alongside a corresponding instruction, which translated the necessarily generalised recommendations into specific and practical examples of "do's and don'ts". Although much of the document simply confirmed policy already in force, it also contained new voluntary commitments to apply specific Code recommendations. These included the removal of baby illustrations from labels of Nestlé infant formula, and specific instructions on the provision of samples to health workers and donations to hospitals and other institutions. A model *Investigation Form* was attached, specifying the information required to investigate complaints on any Nestlé activity claimed to be incompatible with the principles and aim of the WHO Code.

The Nestlé Instructions, as they came to be known, were intended for application in countries "where no specific measures have been, or are being taken" to give effect to the WHO Code.

In order to ensure conformity with national needs, Nestlé managers were instructed to draw the policy document to the attention of the appropriate authorities.

After going through internal revision and refinement, the United Methodist Task Force was given advance information about the Nestlé Instructions at a meeting in Dayton, Ohio, on 13 February 1982. This meeting marked another positive stage in the relationship between the Company and the Task Force in that the two top Company executives, Mr. Helmut Maucher, President, and Dr. Carl Angst, Executive Vice President, went to Dayton to meet Task Force members. In doing so they underlined the importance attached by the Company to the ongoing dialogue, and were able to demonstrate that the initiatives being taken by Nestlé had the full backing and commitment of Nestlé corporate management.

Although the official communiqués covering the meeting were perhaps a little low key, appearing to place more emphasis on a Task Force request to remove some of the proprietary information from the "confidential list", and on the continued postponement of the Nestlé "hot-line" proposals, there can be no doubting the political significance of the event. The head of the new Nestlé office in Washington (NCCN), Mr. Rafael Pagan, who was also present at the meeting, described it later as "the Dayton Entente", and this aptly expressed the "chemistry" of the meeting. The Task Force appear to have been impressed by the open and frank attitude of the new Nestlé Management, and the Nestlé managers were reassured by the sincerity and objective approach of the Task Force.

Audit Committee

Meanwhile another important initiative was being considered. NCCN had pointed out, quite correctly, that the credibility of the new Nestlé policy would depend largely on the extent to which it was perceived as being strictly applied in practice. Over the past three years Nestlé had allowed its critics to take the initiative in monitoring its practices. The INFACT and IBFAN reports of Code violations, using their own criteria for interpreting the Code, had been widely publicised and had seriously affected Nestlé's efforts to convince groups supporting the boycott of its sincerity. There was little doubt that with the publication of the new policy, the boycott organisers would redouble their "monitoring" efforts. In order to forestall this strategy, NCCN proposed an imaginative solution, which also conformed with the WHO Code recommendation (Art. 11.3), that the Company establish its own monitoring system. The key point of the NCCN proposal however, was that Company monitoring measures should be highly visible and should include the creation of an international committee composed of prominent and respected clergy, scientists and lawyers, as well as a senior Nestlé executive. An international figure, with high credibility among the groups supporting the boycott, would be needed to chair the committee. NCCN proposed the name of former Senator and US Secretary of State, Edmund S. Muskie.

The mandate of this "Infant formula marketing ethics audit committee" (as it was then called), would be to:

– Monitor Nestlé compliance with the Code and report to the Nestlé Executive Committee with recommendations
– Investigate allegations of violations of the Code when they were reported by church leaders, public interest groups or local authorities
– Work in conjunction with WHO and UNICEF in dealing with Code issues

This proposal, which was a more elaborate version of the original "hot-line" idea discussed with the United Methodists, was well received by Management. It was suggested, however, that for logistical reasons it would be preferable for the committee to consist only of Americans, and that in order to underline its complete independence there should be no Nestlé representative in the committee itself, but that a liaison person be nominated to ensure good communications. Third-party complaints, received by the Audit Commission, could be evaluated to ensure that sufficient detail had been supplied to allow proper investigations, and then channelled to the Company. Nestlé could forward its report on the investigations to the committee together with details of remedial action taken, if needed. The committee would then decide whether the complaint was justified, and whether Nestlé's actions were in conformity with its commitments to the WHO Code. Its findings would be made public.

With this green light, NCCN went about the task of approaching potential candidates for the committee, including leaders of churches which were boycotting Nestlé, and above all, Senator Muskie himself.

Nestlé Announces its New Policy

Towards the end of February 1982, the Nestlé Instructions were sent out to Nestlé operating companies. Copies were then addressed to the World Health Organization and to UNICEF, as well as the United Methodist Task Force. In his covering letter to WHO and UNICEF, dated 12 March, Dr. C. L. Angst stated that the policy was a logical sequence to the unqualified support given to the Principles and Aim of the WHO Code when it was adopted in May the previous year.

The way was now clear to announce the Nestlé Instructions to a wider public. This was done by means of press releases issued simultaneously in Washington and Switzerland on 16 March 1982. Under the title "Nestlé completes WHO Code Implementation Process", the announcement described the Nestlé Instructions as "comprehensive policy guidelines to be applied in countries that have not yet taken measures to implement the World Health Organization's International Code". In addition to highlighting specific policy changes, the announcement went on to point out that the Instructions confirmed earlier Nestlé infant formula policy directives in developing countries, which prohibit mass media advertising, direct sampling to mothers and participation in trade or consumer promotions of any kind. Finally, Nestlé announced that it was forming an audit committee in the United States, composed of "prominent clergyman, medical scientists and chaired by an individual of high international repute".

Media reaction to the announcement was more extensive and more favourable than might have been expected. This could be explained by the fact that it was the first time Nestlé had been perceived as abandoning its low profile and defensive posture and taking its own positive initiative. Of greater significance to Nestlé, however, was the reaction of the boycott leadership. Immediately after the announcement, the International Nestlé Boycott Committee (INBC) addressed a telex to Nestlé Management in Switzerland, welcoming the initiative taken by the Company and suggesting a meeting aimed at identifying "any differences that may remain between us". A press release issued by the Infant Formula Action Coalition (INFACT) welcomed the Nestlé initiative "with cautious optimism". [16] It went on to say that the instructions suggested a new Company policy on compliance with the WHO Code.

In view of this positive, if guarded, reaction, Management agreed to delegate Geoffrey Fookes from the Vevey staff (who was in Washington to help with press enquiries) and Dr. Thad Jackson of NCCN, to meet INBC representatives. Their brief was simply to respond to queries about the Instructions, and not to enter into negotiations of any kind. The Company also requested the chairman of the United Methodist Task Force to attend the meeting as a neutral observer. The meeting developed into a veritable cross-examination of the Nestlé representatives, both on the Nestlé Instructions and on the audit committee proposal. INBC wanted to know in particular how Nestlé would ensure the "acceptability" of the committee members to the critics. It was made clear that advice would be sought from different sources, including the United Methodist Church. Not surprisingly, in view of their criticism of the Task Force, INBC were unhappy at the presence of its chairman at the meeting, and even suggested that as the United Methodists were not "part of the boycott" they should have nothing to do with "negotiations" leading to the lifting of the boycott. To this, Dr. Wogaman retorted that the primary interest shared by all concerned was the health and welfare of infants, and not the future of the boycott. Afterwards INBC addressed a letter to Nestlé describing the discussion as "informative and helpful", and proposing a follow-up meeting.

Meanwhile, an informal reaction from WHO had described the action taken by Nestlé as a positive and welcome step. UNICEF, which perhaps had been more critical and outspoken than WHO in its public statements about the infant food industry during the Code development, gave the Nestlé policy an even warmer reception. The UNICEF Executive Director, Mr. James Grant, stated: "Our preliminary in-house reaction to your new policies is most positive, although we have noted some specific areas we wish to study further, for possible clarification by you". These areas would be studied further by UNICEF and would be communicated in further detail once the analysis had been completed [17].

As for the United Methodists, their Task Force met on 2 and 3 April 1982 and commended Nestlé's action, which expressed clearly "The Company's respect for the WHO Code". They went on to express the hope that Nestlé would be open to suggestions for improvement and to this end looked on the announcement of an independent audit commission as "an especially welcome development" [18]. The Task Force had nevertheless received a statement from boycott leaders expressing reservations about the guidelines. Its chairman, Dr. Wogaman, reporting on the recent contacts with INBC, said that the latter apparently did not see the Task Force playing a mediating role on the boycott issue.

Events were now moving fast. By early April, Senator Muskie had agreed in principle to chair the audit committee. The United Methodist Task Force approved the participation of Dr. Philip Wogaman provided that it would be truly independent, and that its findings could be reported publicly. Within a few weeks, the Committee's members had been appointed and its Charter (see Appendix 1) and Statutes finalised.

It had by now become quite clear that the boycott leaders were doing everything possible to discredit the audit committee concept. They could see that it would threaten their status as arbiters of acceptable marketing practice. A Chicago INFACT Newsletter published on 31 March claimed that Nestlé had refused to meet with INBC to discuss their new position (this was not true) and went on:

We will not be fooled by Public Relations Statements. It is the Nestlé boycott that compelled Nestlé to make the changes they have already made. We demand that Nestlé meet with the boycott organizers. The Nestlé boycott will continue to grow until Nestlé proves its sincerity.

As a result of pressure brought to bear by the boycott movement, two prominent church leaders refused invitations to serve on the audit committee. Nevertheless when the Nestlé Infant Formula Audit Commission (NIFAC), as it was finally called, was launched at a press conference in Washington on 3 May

1982 it *did* include the General Secretary of the American Baptist Churches of the USA, Dr. Robert Campbell, and Dr. Henry Andersen, a prominent pastor of the Presbyterian Church. Both their denominations had endorsed the boycott.[1]

The announcement of the Commission was given wide, and favourable press coverage, but just three days later INFACT hit back with its own press conference. Under the title *Nestlé fraud denounced worldwide*, the INFACT press release reported 226 Code violations by the Nestlé Company. It went on to announce the publication of a document analysing the Nestlé Instructions under the title *Nestlé Distorts Code*, and claimed that the new policy was simply a rehash of the guidelines sent to Nestlé marketing personnel in July 1979. The INFACT press release described the "attempt to reissue them now as the Code", as "an act of extreme bad faith", and congratulated the two senior church leaders who had declined to serve on the Nestlé Infant Formula Audit Commission. INFACT's May 1982 *Update* described the commission as "seriously flawed" and "unacceptable at this time", which was hardly complimentary to Senator Muskie and the distinguished members of his Commission. INFACT's chairman, Douglas Johnson, added that there seemed little reason to report violations to the commission since it was "chartered only to investigate violations of Nestlé's weak marketing instructions". Johnson was careful, however, to leave the way open for future accommodation with the commission, by expressing the hope "that a man with Senator Muskie's prestige" would prevail upon Nestlé to "*adopt* the WHO/UNICEF Code, not *adapt* it".

Just one week after the public announcement of the Muskie Commission, Nestlé received a disquieting letter from the Executive Director of UNICEF, stating that his staff had now completed a careful examination of the Nestlé Instructions and had conveyed to him "their serious misgivings on Nestlé's interpretation of significant aspects of the Code and on the possible harmful effect of its instructions in the implementation of the true spirit and intent of the Code". Unfortunately for the Company the letter was leaked to the boycott movement and to the press, which responded with such headlines as: "UNICEF hits Nestlé on Infant Formula" [19].

The controversy was far from over, but it is doubtful whether more than a handful of people understood what the remaining argument was really about.

Interpreting the WHO Code

The fact that there should have been such wide differences of opinion on the interpretation of the WHO Code ought not to have surprised anyone. International recommendations are usually the result of compromise in order to achieve consensus, and this one was no exception. Certain provisions in the Code were phrased in such a way as to make it almost inevitable that both Industry and its critics could agree on the text, yet totally disagree on its meaning in practice. A few examples will help to illustrate the difficulties:

---

[1] For a more complete description of the Muskie Commission, as it came to be known, see Chap. 10.

Code Scope (Article 2)

The WHO text reads as follows:

The Code applies to the marketing, and practices related thereto, of the following products: breast milk substitutes, including infant formula; other milk products, foods and beverages, including bottle-fed complementary foods, when marketed or otherwise represented to be suitable, with or without modification, for use as a partial or total replacement of breast milk; feeding bottles and teats.

This presents no difficulty as far as infant formula is concerned, since it is a category of product officially defined by the Codex Alimentarius [20]. There could be no argument, either, about "feeding bottles and teats". But "other milk products, foods and beverages" used as a "partial or total replacement of breast milk" seemed to open the scope of the Code well beyond "breast milk substitutes". After all, the whole weaning process can be defined as leading to the "total replacement of breast milk"; hence any part of the weaning diet would fall within the scope of the Code. Certainly this was (and remains) the interpretation of the International Baby Food Action Network (IBFAN) [21].

So much confusion was generated by the wording of the Scope that a statement explaining its meaning had to be made by a member of the WHO Executive Board when presenting the Code for the approval of the 34th World Health Assembly [22]. This statement made it clear that "breast milk may be replaced (substituted for)" during the first four to six months of life, by "*bona fide* breast milk substitutes, including infant formula". It went on to say that "any other food, such as cow's milk, fruit juices, cereals, vegetables, or any other fluid, solid or semi-solid food intended for infants and given after this initial period, can no longer be considered as a replacement for breast milk (or as its *bona fide* substitute)". These foods *complement* breast milk, and may be referred to as complementary foods, weaning foods or breast milk supplements.

These remarks seemed to confirm, once and for all, that weaning foods, promoted for use after the age of 4–6 months, were not included in the scope of the Code. However, since this explanation is contained only in the annex and not in the body of the Code, the fundamental issue as to which products are really covered by the Code still remains a point of controversy even today. The Nestlé Instructions nevertheless attempted to eliminate any such confusion:

These instructions apply to the marketing of infant formula covered by Codex. Other Nestlé products which may be inappropriately used as breast milk substitutes but which Nestlé does not market, or otherwise represent as suitable, for feeding babies before the age of 4 months, are not included.

This was presented by IBFAN as improperly narrowing the scope to infant formula alone for babies under 4 months old [23].

Advertising (Article 5.1)

According to the Code "There should be no advertising or other form of promotion to the general public of products within the scope of this Code".

The problem with this provision is that the words "advertising" and "promotion" are not defined. Although this may seen unimportant, in fact practically the whole debate on appropriate marketing at the WHO/UNICEF Meeting on Infant and Young Child Feeding in October 1979 had centred on the differentiation between advertising and *bona fide* educational activities, designed, in the words of the Code's Aim, to ensure "the proper use of breast milk substitutes, when these are necessary, on the basis of adequate information . . .".

Nestlé attempted to resolve this issue by prohibiting the communication directly to mothers of "information relating to specific brands of infant formula" whether through public media, or by personal contact, between Company representatives and the public. This could leave the door open for generic educational activities, including, if appropriate, illustrated instructions for the safe preparation of breast milk substitutes (a poster doing just this was at that very time being used by UNICEF in some West African countries).

Ironically, criticism of this and other Nestlé interpretations of the Code led WHO and UNICEF staff to issue their own internal (and unofficial) notes on what the Code really meant [24]. In the case of Article 5.1, the WHO/UNICEF notes read "Such advertising and promotion include *brand* and *non-brand*, *direct and indirect*, advertising and promotion".

Although they went on to point out that "informational and educational materials" were covered by Article 4, the lack of any definition of "advertising" and the all-embracing terms, "brand and non-brand, direct and indirect", meant that IBFAN was soon reporting perfectly bona fide educational materials, such as the posters being used by UNICEF, as Code violations.

Consumer Contacts (Article 5.5)

This article states that "Marketing personnel in their business capacity, should not seek direct or indirect contact of any kind with pregnant women or with mothers of infants and young children".

Quite apart from the absurd interpretations that can be given to this provision if one happened to be interviewing female candidates for staff vacancies, Nestlé, rather logically, formulated its policy on the basis of the word "seek". The Instruction to Nestlé personnel on this article of the Code therefore read:

In accordance with current instructions, Company personnel may not solicit direct contact with mothers either individually or in groups.

This does *not* prevent appropriately qualified personnel from responding to complaints or unsolicited requests for information.

This was described by INFACT/IBFAN as "leaving the door open . . . to contact between 'qualified' personnel and mothers" [23]. The WHO/UNICEF notes [24] were categoric: "This provision prohibits any contact between marketing personnel, acting in their business capacity, and mothers and pregnant women, whether such contact be direct or indirect".

Taking this interpretation literally, it would mean that the Company could neither allow its employees, nor even delegate a third party, to answer any simple consumer query. Nor, according to the unofficial WHO/UNICEF notes, could Nestlé respond to complaints.

Since Nestlé received over 100 questions and criticisms on its instructions from the boycott leaders, it is clear that a longer book than this could be filled with detailed discussions of this nature. These would probably be of interest only to the serious student of the Code; nevertheless one more example relating to the question of samples is necessary because of its implications for the relationship between the Company and the health professions.

Samples (Articles 5.2 and 7.4)

Article 5.2 states that "Manufacturers and distributors should not provide, directly or indirectly, to pregnant women, mothers or members of their families, samples of products within the scope of this Code".

This had long been Nestlé policy and therefore the Instructions made it clear that samples could only be given to health workers and not to mothers. However, Article 7.4 (part of the section dealing with Health Workers) is worded as follows:

Samples . . . should not be provided to health workers except when necessary for the purpose of professional evaluation or research at the institutional level. Health workers should not give samples of infant formula to pregnant women, mothers of infants and young children, or members of their families.

This provision raises a number of issues. First of all, "samples" are defined in Article 3 as "Single or small quantities of a product provided without cost". It is difficult to see, therefore, how meaningful "research at the institutional level" could be conducted with "samples" (a clinical trial to evaluate growth and development of infants when fed on a specific product would require substantial quantities of infant formula). Furthermore, if doctors were not able to give a sample tin to a mother, what sort of "professional evaluation" did the Code have in mind? Nestlé decided to leave it to the individual health worker's discretion how this should be interpreted:

Samples may be provided *upon written request only* to individual health workers for the purposes of professional evaluation. Recipients must be reminded of WHO Recommendations related to samples (the relevant articles were to be printed on the reverse side of Request Forms).

The Instructions went on:

Recognizing that there is a legitimate interest on the part of doctors to familiarize themselves with the characteristics of a specific infant formula, samples of infant formula to be used for feeding a doctor's own baby may be given.

. . . .

Samples supplied for the purpose of clinical research are permitted subject to the conclusion of a research protocol.

The Nestlé interpretation of the provisions dealing with sampling was probably attacked more strongly than almost any other. It was an extremely complicated and sensitive issue.

Any company marketing health-related products depends to a greater or lesser extent on the goodwill of the health professions. Although Nestlé was committed to efforts aimed at preventing samples from being distributed in such a way as to discourage breast-feeding, no company is in a position to *dictate* to health workers how they should use samples. Nestlé felt strongly that sampling had a legitimate role to play, consistent with the aim of the Code. A health worker could use a sample to instruct a mother on correct preparation technique, or monitor the progress of a baby after a few days on the product. Not least, the sample could be of real service to a mother if shops were closed.

However badly formulated the Code's provisions on sampling were, Nestlé believed that its policy respected the spirit. This view was not shared by the critics. In point of fact it was *they* who were re-writing the Code to match their own interpretation, as can be seen from this INFACT/IBFAN version: "Samples are for evaluation or research only at the institutional level" [25].

The WHO/UNICEF notes, for their part, stated that "this prohibition of the

giving of samples also applies to the *health worker's own family*" [24]. Incidentally, neither the boycott leaders nor the UN officials involved have ever
explained exactly what sort of "professional evaluation" *is* intended by the Code,
using "single or small quantities of product".

Revising the Nestlé Instructions

As has been pointed out earlier, the Code is addressed to governments, and it is
up to governments (the member states of WHO) to interpret and implement
WHO recommendations as most appropriate to their local situation. For this
reason, if no other, the WHO Code was broadly drawn in order to allow for
flexibility in application. In the absence of government action, however, how was
a company to go about interpreting the Code without incurring the wrath of its
critics? The obvious answer, surely, would be to consult WHO, but it is not quite
so simple as that. The World Health Organization is an inter-governmental
agency, and does not have the authority to interpret the Code (the notes referred
to above were unofficial and for "internal" use). Only the member states acting
individually or collectively as the World Health Assembly can give an official
interpretation. According to Article 11.1 of the WHO Code, WHO, UNICEF
and other UN agencies, can lend their cooperation to member states in measures
aimed at giving effect to the principles and aim of the Code, but they have no
official mandate to advise private industry.

Nestlé did indeed receive an informal reaction from individual WHO officials
with reference to its own "interpretation" of the Code before its policy was made
public. But even where the reactions were supportive, WHO could not be quoted
as endorsing any particular company policy.

Moreover, there could be quite wide differences of opinion between different
officials at WHO and between WHO staff and UNICEF staff on the practical
interpretation to give to various provisions. In many cases the unofficial WHO/
UNICEF notes confused the issue even further. It was therefore an easy matter
for the boycott leaders to dissect the Nestlé policy document, and claim by the use
of their own interpretation that Nestlé was distorting the Code. Yet even had
Nestlé found it appropriate to negotiate its policies directly with INBC, the final
result would have carried no greater weight with governments, or even other
consumer movements, far from the boycott battle-front.

What was needed was an authoritative, independent, body to advise Nestlé on
its Code implementation measures, and this was precisely the role filled by the
Muskie Commission.

Having been thoroughly briefed in Switzerland on the Nestlé policy in May
1982, and having heard Nestlé's reaction to the line-by-line criticisms, Senator
Muskie and members of his Commission met with top WHO and UNICEF
officials, leaders of the boycott movement, and church leaders, in an attempt to
take into account reasonable criticism, and recommend appropriate modifications to the Nestlé policy.

As can be imagined, Nestlé Management was less than enthusiastic at the
prospect of revising a policy which had been sent out only a few months earlier,

which had been drawn to the attention of the health authorities everywhere, and which had necessitated detailed information and training sessions at all levels in all the operating companies. On the other hand, Nestlé could hardly afford to be dogmatic about its interpretation, as it was the first to admit, indeed to claim, that other interpretations were possible. Therefore, after what could be described in diplomatic terms as "frank discussions" with Senator Muskie, the Company agreed to modify a number of points in the Instructions. Most of these modifications were by way of clarification, such as the revised scope, which made it clear that infant formula products are covered by the Instructions, "regardless of the age of the babies by whom they are consumed". Others were substantive; for example, it was no longer permitted to provide formula free of charge for use by doctors' own families. It was also agreed to urge the retail trade not to promote infant formula at the point of sale (another very delicate area).

Nestlé also made a major concession with respect to one of the main reproaches levelled at its original Instructions, namely that they did not apply to countries where a national code was in place, or was under consideration. According to the critics this caveat eliminated virtually all countries where Nestlé operated and allowed the Company to give precedence to codes which were less restrictive than the WHO recommendations or its own Instructions. It was therefore made clear that the Revised Instructions applied to all countries outside Europe, whether or not a national code was in force. The only case in which they would not be followed would be if the national code or legislation specifically precluded practices permitted by the Instructions. As far as Europe was concerned, the Company announced its intention to comply with the codes then being developed in consultation with the Industry by the European Community and individual nations.

The Revised Instructions were announced at a joint press conference in Washington held on 14 October 1982. The two principal speakers were Senator Muskie on behalf of the Nestlé Infant Formula Audit Commission, and Dr. Carl Angst on behalf of the Company.

Senator Muskie presented the Commission's first quarterly report [26] pointing out that in the absence of complaints submitted by the boycott movement, which in effect had decided to boycott the Commission too, the Commission had decided to address itself to the central issue of the "repeated challenge to the credibility of Nestlé's commitment to the WHO Code" [27]. The Senator went on to say that Nestlé had "responded promptly and forthrightly" to the Commission's recommendations and "essentially adopted all of them". WHO and UNICEF, as well as other groups, had been consulted as to the acceptability of the Instructions and as to any remaining problems. On the basis of this review, the Commission had decided to accept the Revised Nestlé Instructions. The revisions were then described in detail.

Senator Muskie stated that, in the experience of the Commission, Nestlé had "demonstrated a willingness to respond positively to the imperative of change in its marketing policies", and that in doing so the Company had "responded positively to the public interest, as stated in the WHO Code". He ended by exhorting "members of the public and interested groups" (a thinly-veiled reference to the boycott movement) "to contact the Commission if they have questions about Nestlé's compliance with its commitments". In his statement, Dr. Angst re-iterated the Company's commitment to the Code and confirmed its full support for the Commission. He pointed out that Management in Switzerland had absolved Company executives of responsibility for loss of sales resulting from strict observance of the WHO Code.

Support for the Boycott Wanes

Media reaction to the press conference and the announcement of the Revised Nestlé Instructions was generally positive, in spite of continued criticism from the Infant Formula Action Coalition (INFACT). INFACT held its own press conference in Washington on the same day. The press release carried the headline: "Nestlé Violates Marketing Code, Boycott Leaders demand real changes". However, no doubt recognising that efforts to discredit the Muskie Commission had rebounded on them, the boycott leaders now announced that they would submit more than 30 (alleged) Nestlé violations of the Code to the Commission.

The Commission thus entered into the second phase of its activity, and the one for which it was originally established, investigating Nestlé compliance with its commitments towards the WHO Code. Although the Commission's investigation procedures led to a number of other policy clarifications during the course of 1983, the October 1982 Revised Instructions remain the basis of Nestlé policy for marketing infant formula today and thereby the Company's implementation of the WHO Code.

Whatever the boycott leadership may have thought and said about the Nestlé initiatives, one important body of opinion was now convinced of the Company's sincerity. On 28 October 1982, the United Methodist General Council on Ministries voted by a two-to-one majority to accept its Task Force's recommendations that the United Methodist Church should not boycott Nestlé, and that general agencies and annual conferences of the Church which were participating in the boycott "re-examine their position and consider concluding their participation in the boycott" [28].

In its report [29] the Task Force justified its recommendations by referring to the positive results of the dialogue with the Company, leading to "substantial changes in policy and practice". The fact that the Company had established the audit commission "with sufficient resources for this group" to do its work "with no strings attached", was particularly emphasised. In other terms, the report went on, "the company has put a group of independent people in a position to 'blow the whistle' with maximum public effect if any of them feel the need to do so". By so doing, the Company had "made itself vulnerable to a degree perhaps unprecedented in corporate circles".

The Task Force report did not imply that the Company's revised policy instructions were perfect, but it did pose the question to those engaged in the boycott as to whether their action should continue until "every conceivable objection to Nestlé policy has been answered or dealt with in a satisfactory way". Remaining problems were described as "relatively trivial", reflecting "points of honest disagreement about interpretation", and "not weighty enough to warrant boycott action". Furthermore, and this was music to Nestlé's corporate ears, the Task Force pointed out that if the most negative interpretations were to be placed upon all Company policy instructions, "we cannot conceive of any statement of company policy that could not be questioned – and answers to questions will only lead to further questions". Since it was in the Company's interest to "keep faith with its new commitments", was there really a justification for the boycott leaders to insist on a formal negotiating process to end the boycott, the Task Force asked. Such an inflexible attitude could have the effect "of *diminishing* public respect for the corporate responsibility movement".

The boycott leadership was unimpressed by these arguments, and in January 1983 IBFAN published their new report announcing 14 985 160 Industry violations of the WHO Code, including well over 4 million Nestlé violations [30]. In March 1983, INFACT launched a "new citizens' initiative" aimed at Tasters' Choice, one of the Company's instant coffee products with the expressed hope of bringing Nestlé "to its moral senses" [31]. The press release quoted a telegram from the then President of the International Organization of Consumers Unions (IOCU), Mr. Anwar Fazal, stating that in Malaysia:

. . . our babies continue to sicken and die because their mothers are lured into abandoning breast feeding by Nestlé's promotion . . . The new Nestlé guidelines might make it appear in the US as though the company has changed its policies. But in fact that is wrong.

However, the tide was already on the turn. In January 1983, for the first time, the boycott movement lost a major supporter, the powerful American Federation of Teachers. Other organisations were following suit in a slow but steady trickle.

The United Methodist Task Force, for its part, was continuing to follow the controversy, and three of its members had conducted their own spot-checks of Company marketing practices in several Third World countries. Through the participation of its Chairman, it was cooperating extensively with the Muskie Commission. It was therefore in a good position to comment on the continued activities of the boycott movement. But for the first time, in its April 1983 report [32], the Task Force did not mince its words. While expressing appreciation for the role of the boycott movement in calling "an important problem to the world's attention", the report went on to state that the Task Force experience with the movement had revealed "serious flaws in it".

Concluding this lengthy chapter, an extensive quotation from the Task Force report will help to explain the accelerating loss of support which the boycott movement suffered during 1983, and which led to the resolution of the conflict described in the next chapter. The report stated:

Those who are inclined to follow the leadership of this movement uncritically should be aware of such facts as these:
a) Boycott leaders sought strenuously to prevent the formation of the Nestlé Infant Formula Audit Commission, subjecting it to public ridicule and seeking to prevent religious and medical leaders of independent mind from serving on this monitoring body. The effectiveness of NIFAC is in spite of the boycott leadership, not because of it.
b) Nestlé policies and actions have been subjected to substantial and sometimes gross misrepresentation. For example, during the summer and fall of 1981, Nestlé was flatly accused of being unwilling to commit itself to the provisions of the WHO/UNICEF Code – while the reality was that it accepted some key provisions and was in the process of working the others through. For example, when Nestlé issued its public commitment to the WHO/UNICEF Code in March, 1982, INFACT issued a press release saying that "INFACT Welcomes Nestlé Initiative with Cautious Optimism;" but then, after the boycott movement decided to deepen the polarization, another press release proclaimed "Nestlé Fraud Denounced Worldwide".

Actual interpretations of the Nestlé Code Instructions frequently placed the most negative possible construction upon the new policies. Nestlé had clearly excluded payment of bonuses to infant formula marketing personnel, but the Company was accused of disregarding the WHO/ UNICEF Code at that point. The boycott movement criticised the Company for applying the Code only in those countries not having national laws (which might be weaker than the Code), although the Company made it clear that it would observe the WHO/UNICEF Code except in those countries where some provision or other might be *against* the local law. The Company was accused of substituting its own Code for the WHO/UNICEF Code, when it was clear that Nestlé had developed its Instructions to guide its marketing personnel in observing the WHO/UNICEF Code. NIFAC was alleged to have been set up to police only the Company's "code" and not to hold Nestlé accountable to the WHO/UNICEF Code, while the Company's mandate to NIFAC called upon it to assess Nestlé's guidelines and practices in the light of the WHO/UNICEF Code itself. Some of these distortions and others published by the boycott movement were understandable – sometimes Nestlé was responsible for difficulties in communication. But it is noteworthy that the boycott movement has always seized upon the most damaging possible interpretation of Company policy or practice, has publicized it widely, and has rarely corrected its mistaken judgements.

c) INFACT and other boycotting organizations have recently intensified their campaign with inflammatory rhetoric. An INFACT ad refers to "crimes committed against mothers and infants by Nestlé". Graphics show a stirring spoon with a skull on its handle dipped in a jar of (Nestlé) Taster's Choice coffee or depict the Company as a snake encircling a baby. An INFACT fund-raising letter refers to "Nestlé's deadly infant formula marketing", and demonstration placards, pictured approvingly in boycott newsletters, carry slogans proclaiming that "Nestlé Kills Babies". Claims are frequently advanced that more than a million babies die each year as a result of formula marketing. Such rhetoric neither accurately states facts nor promotes the climate necessary for successful negotiation to end the boycott.

d) In its reporting of incidents of violation of the WHO/UNICEF Code, IBFAN reports from several hundred thousand to more than two million reported violations for each month in 1982 by Nestlé and the other formula companies. Most casual readers are led to suppose that this means that many separate, documented instances where the companies violated the Code. In fact, such wildly exaggerated figures are arrived at by multiplying particular offensive periodical advertisements or leaflets by the total readership (thus, one offending ad in the *New York Times* might constitute a million separate violations!).

Such facts make us regret that some United Methodists supporting the boycott have apparently acquiesced in tactics of villification without publicly holding critics of Nestlé to standards of fairness and truthfulness. At the very least, these tactics should make United Methodists and others be very cautious about taking the boycott leadership simply at face value.

References

1   International Council of Infant Food Industries (ICIFI) (1981) Industry comments on WHO marketing code. Press release 21 May 1981. ICIFI, Geneva, 2 pp

2   Jackson TM (1981) Prepared statement. In: Implementation of the World Health Organization (WHO) code on infant formula marketing practices. Hearings before the subcommittee on international economic policy and trade-and the subcommittee on human rights and international organizations. US Government Printing Office, Washington DC, pp 58–60 (US House of Representatives 16–17 June 1981)

3   Nestlé Coordination Center for Nutrition (NCCN) (1981) Aide-mémoire to the United Methodist task force on infant formula, from the Nestlé coordination center for nutrition, Inc. 25 Sep 1981. NCCN, Washington DC, 2 pp

4   Allbaugh D (1981) Hazard to infants claimed. Church group hears formula arguments. Dayton Daily News, 26 Sep

5   Beck RH (1981) Nestlé asked for proof of change. United Methodist Reporter, 2 Oct

6   Beck RH (1982) UM task force OK's Nestlé plan, rejects boycott. United Methodist Reporter, 17 Sep

7   Perryman LM (1981) United Methodist Communications News, 28 Sep: 1–4

8   Beck RH (1981) Nestlé asked for proof of change. United Methodist Reporter, 2 Oct: 2

9   Beck RH (1981) Friends stoke boycott fire. UMC "hoodwinked" by Nestlé, say numerous critics. United Methodist Reporter, 9 Oct

10 Editorial (1981) Nestlé boycott, mediation efforts and Christian ethical teaching. United Methodist Reporter, 30 Oct: 2

11 Anonymous (1981) GCOM supports infant formula code, takes no action on boycott. United Methodist NEWSCOPE, 6 Nov: 2
12 Anonymous (1981) United States – Nestlé reveals government lobbying targets. IBFAN News, 3 Dec
13 Chaves R (1983) Statement. In: World Health Organization. Infant and young children nutrition, including nutritional value and safety of products specifically intended for infant and young child feeding and the status of compliance with and implementation of the international code of marketing of breast-milk substitutes. 36th World Health Assembly: verbatim records; Document WHA 36/1983/REC/3. WHO, Geneva, pp 302–312 (Committee B, 6th meeting)
14 Tan Sri Chong Hon Nyan YB (1983) Speech at the launching of the revised code of ethics for infant formula products in Malaysia 7 April 1983. Ministry of Health, Kuala Lumpur, 4 pp
15 World Health Assembly Resolution 34.22 (1981) International code of Marketing of breast milk substitutes 21 May 1981. WHO, Geneva, 2 pp
16 Infant Formula Action Coalition (INFACT) (1982) INFACT welcomes Nestlé initiative with cautious optimism. Press release 17 Mar 1982: 1–2
17 Grant JP (Executive Director, UNICEF) (1982) Letter to Pagan RD, President NCCN, 31 March
18 Perryman LM (1982) United Methodist Communications News, 5 April: 1–4
19 Hilts PJ (1982) UNICEF hits Nestlé on infant formula. Washington Post, 10 June: 29
20 Codex Alimentarius Commission. Codex standards for foods for special dietary uses including foods for infants and children and related code of hygiene practice. Rome: FAO, Secretariat of the joint FAO/WHO Food standards programme, 1982. 89 pp
21 Allain A (1984) Not just formula. Health Now (3)
22 Mork T (1981) Statement. In: World Health Organization. International code of marketing of breastmilk substitutes. 34th World Health Assembly: verbatim records; Document WHA/34/1981/REC/3. WHO, Geneva (Committee A, 13th meeting) Excerpts of Dr Mork's statement are reproduced in Annex 3 of the International Code of Marketing of Breast Milk Substitutes, WHO
23 INFACT/IBFAN (1982) Preliminary analysis: Nestlé's WHO code interpretation. INFACT Update, April
24 World Health Organization/UNICEF (1982) Infant and young child feeding. Notes on the international code of marketing of breast milk substitutes. Document WHO/UNICEF/IC/July 1982 WHO, Geneva 13 pp
25 INFACT/IBFAN (1982) Preliminary analysis: Nestlé's WHO code interpretation. INFACT Update, April, p 2
26 Muskie ES (ed) (1982) Nestlé infant formula audit commission (NIFAC). First Quarterly Report, 30 Sep: 1–4
27 Nestlé Coordination Center for Nutrition Inc./Nestlé Infant Formula Audit Commission. Transcript of proceedings. Press Conference with Hon. Edmund S. Muskie, Chairman, Nestlé Infant Formula Audit Commission and Dr. Carl Angst, General Manager Nestlé SA, Switzerland. 14 Oct 1982. Washington DC: ACE-Federal Reporters. 53 pp
28 Lovelace JN (1982) UMC "as a denomination" won't join Nestlé boycott. United Methodist Reporter, 5 Nov
29 Wogaman JP (ed) (1982) Recommendations of the United Methodist Infant Formula Task Force to the General Council on Ministries and the Church. October 1982: 1–13
30 International Baby Food Action Network (IBFAN) (1983) Breaking the Rules – 1982. A year end compilation of violations of the International code of marketing of breast-milk substitutes. IBFAN, Minneapolis 10 pp
31 Johnson DA (1983) Statement to the press. INFACT Press Release, 1 March, 14 pp
32 Wogaman JP (ed) (1983) Fourth Report of the Infant Formula Task Force to the United Methodist General Council on Ministries. 28 April: 1–11. (GCOM Plenary document 5. April 1983)

Chapter 10

Resolution of the Conflict

G. Veraldi

Throughout 1983, attempts by the Infant Formula Action Coalition (INFACT) to revitalise the boycott against Nestlé failed. A much publicised international petition drive aimed at collecting one million signatures for delivery at the Nestlé Annual General Assembly "to demonstrate international concern over this issue" and symbolise the one million babies estimated to die each year "from infant formula abuse" [1], succeeded in achieving only 10% of its aim.

The Muskie Commission continued its work, publishing comprehensive reports every 3 months. These included reports of field trips made by individual members of the Commission, and the Commission's determinations on the result of investigations into complaints of Code violations alleged to have been committed by Nestlé operating companies. As a result of the investigation procedure, further refinements and clarification of Nestlé policies were announced. These included the question of donations of infant formula to hospitals, health hazard warnings on labels and revision of education materials more in line with Code requirements, improvement of scientific information for health professionals, and the difficult area of what does or does not constitute a "financial or material inducement" for health workers.

Discussion of controversial scientific issues was not neglected either. In June 1983, the Commission sponsored a two-day conference on breast-feeding and infant nutrition at the University of California, Berkeley. Its aim was to bring together experts of various backgrounds to discuss the merits of the inter-related and multidisciplinary issues involved in breast-feeding and infant nutrition. In sponsoring this conference the Commission demonstrated its awareness of the importance for its work of a better understanding of the fundamental scientific issues.

The meticulous and objective approach adopted by the Commission was not lost on the leadership of church groups, professional associations, unions, and others whose support had been vital for the boycott movement. The Commission's quarterly reports were mailed to all interested parties, and resulted in a more general understanding of the complexities of the controversy and of the efforts made by Nestlé to respond positively to the concerns expressed by its critics.

By June 1983, more than half of the United Methodist regional conferences which had originally endorsed the boycott had rescinded that support. The support of other religious denominations and Catholic religious orders was waning. In October, a highly significant breakthrough occurred: the Church of the Brethren, a relatively small, but influential Protestant denomination, rescinded their February 1979 endorsement of the boycott. A letter enclosing the resolution pointed out that there had been some hesitation to act separately from other boycotting organisations, but the primary point was that the Company was now in compliance with the original objectives stated by the General Board of the Church, and "it would be wrong, to fail to recognize that improvement in the Company's conduct" [2].

Meanwhile, Nestlé contacts with the International Nestlé Boycott Committee (INBC) had continued intermittently. Attempts were made to find a peace-making process which would reflect creditably on both sides in the dispute. These attempts fell through because the Company had accused certain members of the boycott leadership of bad faith and refused to carry on a dialogue at senior management level with them. By the end of the year this objection had been partially resolved by the departure of two particularly hard-line leaders from the activist ranks. The stage was thus set for the end-play.

The "Four Points"

There is enough circumstantial evidence available to suggest that by December 1983 the boycott leadership was facing the prospect of massive defections from the movement, and thereby the potential loss of any credit for its undoubted achievements.

After all, it is unlikely that an International Code of Marketing would have existed without the efforts of these critics, and there were plenty of people who approved sufficiently of the end result to ignore the means by which it was achieved.

Whatever the motives, it was INBC who tendered the olive branch, in a letter dated 14 December 1983, addressed to Nestlé SA's Executive Vice President, Dr. Carl L. Angst. The letter passed no judgement on the reasons for the breakdown of earlier discussions and revealed instead that "an extensive review of Nestlé's policies" had just been completed. The result was a clearer idea of the "issues (which) have been dealt with satisfactorily" and those which "remain of concern". Over two dozen areas of discrepancy with the WHO/UNICEF Code (sic) had been identified, INBC went on, but progress had also been noted in many areas of concern. In particular, INBC claimed to have undertaken an evaluation of those areas "significant enough to warrant our continued recommendation of the International Nestlé Boycott". These had been narrowed down to just "four significant areas of concern":

1. Free supplies to hospitals should be limited to mothers with a real need, based on medical criteria
2. All personal gifts to health professionals, regardless of the economic value, should be halted

3. Information to mothers and health professionals must provide objective and balanced information regarding use and misuse, the benefits and hazards of the product

4. Strong warnings of hazards should be provided on labels

The INBC letter went on to announce a "strategic conference" to be co-hosted in Mexico City on 2–5 February 1984 by INBC and the International Baby Food Action Network (IBFAN). The conference would bring together "the activist base" of the "10 boycotting countries" under the theme "International Baby Milk Campaign: Strategies for Action".

If Nestlé could demonstrate "adequate progress" in the four areas outlined above, the INBC would be "prepared to recommend to the entire conference that the Nestlé boycott be suspended, worldwide". Conciliatory as it was, the letter ended on a somewhat threatening note: "It is in the best interests of the company to seek additional avenues to communicate its intentions regarding these four critical avenues".

This letter was received with mixed feelings. There was little doubt in the minds of Nestlé Management that INBC were looking for a face-saving device in order to end the boycott on an up-beat note. The question was whether or not the Company should afford INBC this satisfaction. Support for the boycott was waning fast, and the four areas highlighted by INBC had all been dealt with in the refinements of policy worked out as a result of the Muskie Commission's Code interpretations. Above all, Nestlé had no intention of changing its policy in refusing to negotiate marketing policy, including label texts, with what it continued to regard as a self-appointed group of advocates.

On the other hand, failure to seek a resolution of differences with the boycott movement would inevitably entail a long, drawn-out, and probably bitter, conclusion with the ever-present risk of the campaign flaring up at any time.

Within a week of receiving the INBC letter, therefore, a reply was sent stating that the Company had been encouraged by the letter, and recognising that the "four points" were difficult to interpret clearly and that this might be the cause of misunderstanding. It was therefore agreed that "discreet discussion at various levels on these points" might be useful.

In view of the fact that the Company could not agree to settle Code interpretations through bi-lateral discussions with INBC, Management proposed that a procedure be developed which would lead to understanding with WHO, UNICEF, the Muskie Commission and INBC.

Such a procedure may sound an obvious enough solution, but it must be remembered that it is the member states of WHO and not the Director General or Secretariat of that Organization who can provide official interpretations of the Code (see Chap. 9). Hence the procedure worked out for settling the differences between Nestlé and INBC would not have an official nature and even the interpretations hammered out after such consultation could be rejected or ignored by individual governments.

January 1984 Discussions

The key to reaching an understanding with INBC was the willingness of WHO and UNICEF to cooperate in the procedure. Private and off-the-record talks were held with WHO staff on 2 January in which the Company's policies on the INBC four points were discussed. The willingness of WHO staff to meet on a public holiday gives some measure of the desire to replace confrontation and controversy by cooperation.

It is fitting at this point to pay tribute to the help and encouragement given by the WHO staff members most closely involved with the issues. They had had to tread a very narrow line to maintain strict impartiality, while at the same time attempting to give genuinely useful advice. In view of the more public, but no less vital, part played by UNICEF, the role of WHO in the events of January 1984 tends to be overlooked.

It will be recalled that during 1983, as a result of the Muskie Commission's investigation of complaints, agreement had been reached to modify "hazard warnings" on label texts, as well as define policy more clearly with respect to the donation of infant formula to hospitals (p. 135). As both of these issues had been the subject of detailed discussion with WHO staff, there was some bewilderment as to what more could be done to satisfy INBC concerns. Code requirements on educational materials and labelling included giving information on the "health hazards of unnecessary or improper use of infant formula" [3], as well as stating the "social and financial implications" of infant formula use [4].

On the question of health hazards, Nestlé had resisted including explicit warnings which might alarm a mother unnecessarily and even provoke incorrect use. For example, if a mother was told that over-dilution of formula could lead to undernutrition, she might well over-concentrate the feed in an attempt to provide "extra security" and this too is known to have undesirable consequences for the baby's health. Then there was of course the question of which health hazards should be mentioned. It is not difficult to come up with a list of potential hazards, which might vary considerably according to environment, and it would be quite impossible to include them all on the limited space available on a label. The Company had therefore given a warning in very general terms. "When using an infant formula, it is important for your baby's health that you follow the instructions carefully".

Following consultations with the Muskie Commission, WHO, and others, the statement was modified as follows:

Follow the instructions very carefully. Using unboiled water or unclean feeding utensils can make your baby ill. The amount of powder per feed indicated in the instructions should never be increased or reduced except on medical advice.

This new label statement was announced in October 1983 [5], yet INBC maintained that the warning statements used by some of Nestlé's competitors came closer to meeting Code requirements. This, of course, was a matter of opinion and hardly a serious reason for maintaining the campaign against Nestlé. Nevertheless, the Company was ready to admit that there was little evidence to confirm the effectiveness of different messages intended to convey the warnings recommended by the Code.

The suggestion now made by WHO staff was that Nestlé should enlist the help of an agency specialised in the development and testing of health messages to illiterate and semi-literate audiences. This agency, Program for Appropriate Technology in Health (PATH), and its sister agency, Program for the Introduction and Adaptation of Contraceptive Technology (PIACT), had worked with WHO and UNICEF in developing educational materials for the use of oral rehydration solutions and family planning devices. Their experience was clearly relevant to the problem of developing appropriate and understandable instructions for infant feeding. Moreover, an agreement to develop warning statements following field research by PATH could hardly be rejected by INBC.

The same considerations applied to the question of the "social and financial implications" of infant formula use. Such implications could obviously vary from case to case. Nestlé policy had therefore been to confine its observance of this Code requirement to reminding the health professions of the need to keep social and financial implications in mind when advising mothers on the use of breast milk substitutes. This was regarded by INBC as a dereliction of responsibility and hence, implicit in their "four points", was the requirement to tackle the question of the "social and financial implications" explicitly in Nestlé educational materials.

It does not take a great deal of imagination to understand that such implications include the *advantage* for some mothers to give up breast-feeding in order to pursue their careers. However justified from a socio-cultural point of view, a statement to this effect would hardly have been likely to satisfy the INBC demands. Past experience did not augur well for consensus on this point, therefore the use of field-tested research techniques aimed at determining what messages would be meaningful to mothers seemed a much more sensible approach.

As for the question of "financial or material inducements", it should be noted that the Code does not prohibit the presentation of "personal gifts", which in many countries are part of cultural tradition. What it does prohibit is "inducements to promote products". Nestlé did not consider that the presentation of a box of its own chocolates at Christmas, as a sign of appreciation for the working relationship with an individual health worker, could be interpreted as "an inducement". INBC's opinion differed. On the advice of WHO, Nestlé was prepared to make further concessions by restricting "personal gifts" to inexpensive technical service items, such as measuring and weighing devices, growth charts and similar diagnostic materials, rather than boxes of chocolates.

Finally, and by far the most difficult area, came the question of infant formula donations to institutions. Nestlé policy, based on Articles 6.6 and 6.7 of the Code, permitted such donations, but had been refined (and announced to health authorities and hospital administrations throughout the world) as follows:

1. Free or reduced cost supplies of infant formula provided by Nestlé are intended for use in hospitals and clinics only for infants who have to be fed on breast milk substitutes, in accordance with Article 6.6 of the WHO Code

2. In line with the spirit and letter of the Code, discharge tins of infant formula should not be given to breast-feeding mothers. Free or reduced cost supplies provided by Nestlé are not for this purpose

3. Mothers who are unable to breast-feed, and who cannot afford infant formula, require special attention. Nestlé will continue to consider written requests for the donation of infant formula to feed individual needy infants on a case-by-case basis in consultation with the hospital in accordance with Articles 3 and 6.7 of the WHO Code.

On the basis of its discussions with WHO, Nestlé did not feel that this policy required any further modification, since in the final analysis, responsibility for implementing those Code recommendations addressed to health care systems lay with the health authorities in each country rather than with Industry. The Company therefore felt that agreement might be possible on the basis of a joint statement by INBC and Nestlé calling for government action to define policy, which would apply both to the health services and to all infant formula suppliers.

The next step for Nestlé was to discuss its response to the INBC "four points" with UNICEF, and to devise a procedure for reaching consensus on an acceptable way in which to meet INBC concerns. This task fell to the Nestlé Coordination Center for Nutrition (NCCN) in Washington. Following intensive discussions a process was finally agreed. UNICEF would host meetings at which the Nestlé response, based on WHO advice, would be presented to INBC. The latter would be able to pose questions and present objections, and UNICEF staff would moderate and give their opinion as to how the positions adopted corresponded to the Code requirements. WHO staff in Geneva would be consulted throughout and representatives of the Muskie Commission would be present as observers at all times. In parallel with these "technical" discussions, bilateral meetings would take place between Nestlé and INBC representatives to reach agreement on procedures for terminating the boycott.

Some of the boycott leaders were unhappy with this procedure. They were insisting on direct Nestlé/INBC negotiations. By bringing UNICEF and other parties into the picture, the perception of a clear-cut "victory" over Nestlé by the boycott movement might be lost. Finally, it appeared that the personal gratification sought by these hard-liners gave way to the more pragmatic view that successful resolution of the differences between Nestlé and INBC was the real aim. UNICEF agreed to the role proposed by Nestlé, and so began an intensive two-week round of meetings, aimed at seeking a common understanding on how only four points of the Code should be interpreted and implemented.

Nestlé Statement of Understanding

On the basis of its informal discussions, first with WHO and later with UNICEF staff, Nestlé summarised its position with regard to the INBC "four points" in a draft paper entitled *Statement of Understanding*. This paper was given to INBC on 12 January 1984, and formed the basis for the first "plenary" discussions held at UNICEF headquarters in New York on Saturday 14 January.

Agreement on Nestlé policy for dealing with "hazard warnings" on labels and improvement of educational materials, using the PATH agency recommended by WHO, was reached without much difficulty.

The Nestlé representatives estimated that field research, discussion of the findings, with all concerned parties (WHO, UNICEF, NIFAC and INBC), re-design of labels, and phasing in of the new labels around the world, would take approximately 18 months.

The similar procedure envisaged for dealing with educational materials was also agreed, but a sticking point arose over Nestlé insistence on including the product brand and an illustration of the product (known as a "pack shot") on preparation leaflets. The Nestlé Instructions issued in February 1982 had already made it clear that pack shots could not be included in publications of a general nature intended for mothers, such as baby-care books, growth charts and similar materials. What was at issue now was the inclusion of product identification on instruction leaflets distributed through the health services. These are intended to complement the instructions given on labels, particularly for use by minority language groups and semi-literate or illiterate mothers.

There was little doubt that inclusion of pack shots, even on instruction leaflets, was not in conformity with Article 4.3 of the Code, which states that educational materials should not refer to a proprietary product. However, Nestlé felt that in drafting the Code, the practical implications of this particular restriction had been overlooked. The Nestlé representatives pointed out not only that different infant formula manufacturers used different methods of reconstitution, but also that with the elimination of baby pictures from labels, infant formula could not be distinguished easily by less literate mothers from other types of powdered milk (sold in similar-shaped tins). These included skimmed milk products, which are totally unsuitable for use by young infants, and full-cream powdered milks which need to be specially modified before being given to babies. The product identification on the infant feeding instruction leaflet was, therefore, one way of ensuring that the mother bought the product to which the instructions applied.

Although some of the UNICEF staff appeared to sympathise with this position, there was concern that endorsement of such an exception to observance of the Code "in its entirety" might open a flood-gate of exceptions. The matter was resolved finally by describing it as an area of "honest disagreement". Nestlé agreed to take note of UNICEF and INBC concern that the inclusion of a pack shot should not be exploited for promotional purposes. An undertaking was given that instruction leaflets should only be given to mothers by health professionals *after* a decision to bottle-feed had been taken.

The question of financial or material inducements also proved relatively easy to resolve. INBC characterisation of the Code requirement as a ban on "personal gifts" was in itself an interpretation, since neither the Code, nor the WHO/UNICEF explanatory notes on the Code [6] refer to "gifts". UNICEF accepted the position that the Code text was ambiguous and suggested that a "rule of reason" be applied, using the criteria of the value of the item and whether it was of a professional or personal nature. On this basis, Nestlé's proposal to allow Company personnel to distribute inexpensive technical service items under the terms of Article 7.3, rather than personal gifts, was considered to be in conformity with the spirit of the Code.

Predictably, it was the question of supplies of free or low-price infant formula to hospitals which presented the greatest difficulty. It involved many difficult issues. Not least among these was the generally acknowledged fact that if a mother decided, for whatever reason, that her baby would be bottle-fed, then there was a high probability that she would continue to use the brand of infant formula given in the hospital when she returned home. Thus it is of obvious commercial importance to the infant formula manufacturer that his brands be used by the hospital in preference to a competitor's. Equally important is the fact, mentioned earlier, that this section of the Code (Article 6) is addressed specifically to "Health Care Systems". Neither Nestlé nor its competitors could impose WHO policy on hospitals or other health care system facilities.

Last, but not least, the Code lacks clarity on this point. This should not be a matter of surprise, since it was always intended that the Code be flexible enough to take account of widely different situations in different WHO member states. For example, the word "supplies" in Article 3 is defined as "quantities of a product provided for use over an extended period, free or at a low price, for social purposes, including those provided to families in need". Use of the word "including" seemed to make it clear that there were other "social purposes" in mind than just economic need. Also the limitation of use in Article 6.6 to "infants who have to be fed on breast milk substitutes", begged the question as to *which* infants this referred to.The widest interpretation could be "any infant not being exclusively breast-fed", while the narrowest might be, "any infant whose mother was unable to breast-feed". The latter definition would eliminate any possibility of choice by the mother.

On top of all these considerations, there was an interrelation between the "supplies" problem and "sampling", which is dealt with in Articles 5 and 7 of the Code. Article 5.2 seeks to prevent manufacturers from providing samples of infant formula to mothers either "directly or indirectly", while Article 7.4 states that health workers should not give samples to mothers. In fact it was a common practice for hospital staff to provide mothers with a free tin of the infant formula on which their babies had been fed when the mother and baby returned home. Such a practice had been endorsed by at least one government, the United Kingdom, in a circular addressed to health workers [7]:

The practice of handing out samples of infant formula to mothers who are leaving hospital with the intention of continuing to breast-feed is to be deprecated. On the other hand, where a mother is already using artificial feeds it is reasonable to ensure that she leaves hospital with an adequate supply for her immediate needs.

This was precisely the policy announced by Nestlé (see p. 135). On the other hand, INBC, supported by the UNICEF staff, argued that if hospital personnel provided "discharge tins" of Nestlé infant formula to mothers, regardless of how their babies had been fed in the hospital, the Company was in effect making an indirect distribution of samples, in violation of Article 5.2. As for which babies had to be fed on breast milk substitutes, the WHO/UNICEF notes [6] stated that supplies of infant formula (i.e. donation or low-price sales) "should only be used when necessary, for example on medical, economic or social grounds". According to Nestlé this "definition" succeeded only in clouding the issue further.

Nestlé/INBC Agreement

Discussions aimed at narrowing the differences on the above issues continued on the next day, Sunday 15 January, and throughout the following week. As agreements were reached, Nestlé amended its draft *Statement of Understanding* accordingly, and the text was reviewed by the other participants to ensure that it reflected the consensus.

On the complex "supplies" issue, Nestlé accepted that the aim of the WHO Code provision was to discourage bottle-feeding as a routine procedure in maternity wards and agreed to make its policy more explicit with this aim in mind. In order to provide the basis for the re-formulation of Nestlé policy, UNICEF agreed to study clearer definition of the expression "infants who have to be fed on breast milk substitutes" with WHO. Once this definition was available, Nestlé would support it, and fill requests for supplies only for uses intended by the Code. However, both on the question of infant formula use within the hospital and that of the hospital practice of providing "discharge tins" to mothers, Nestlé insisted on a multilateral approach to the problem. This approach recognised the fact that respect for the Code provisions on supplies and samples was the direct responsibility of the health services. The very notion, implicit in the INBC demand, that a company could question the decisions of medical personnel and, moreover, demonstrate its disapproval for such decisions by withholding services, is quite unrealistic.

For example, in order to implement a commitment to ban discharge tins, the Company would be obliged to carry out routine checks on mothers leaving maternity wards, in order to establish whether the mother had actually received a tin of infant formula free of charge or at a reduced price. It would then be necessary to threaten to withhold further infant formula donations if the hospital persisted in the practice. The result of such action on the Company's relations with the hospital concerned needs no explanation. Moreover, unless the policy were enforced by the health authorities and applied to all infant formula suppliers, hospitals would simply switch to suppliers who were not under pressure to apply the Code. The basic problem would remain unsolved.

Throughout the discussions, however, UNICEF had made it clear that their interpretation of the Code would not allow supplies to be used for distribution as discharge tins except as provided for in Article 6.7 (this deals with charity requests where the free supply is maintained for as long as the infant needs it). Since Nestlé had already stated its agreement to support whatever definition was produced by WHO and UNICEF on the supply question, a form of wording was agreed and incorporated into the final *Statement of Understanding* (Appendix 2). Attachment 2 of this statement makes it clear that Nestlé was now prepared to work for the elimination of "discharge tins":

As company policy, Nestlé's goal is to have free or low-cost formula supplied to hospitals used only for infants who "have to be fed" on breast milk substitutes within the health facility, except as provided for in Article 6.7 of the Code. This goal must apply to the entire industry.

On the basis of this understanding and the agreements reached on the other points raised by INBC, no further obstacles lay in the way of lifting the boycott. This however posed some delicate problems for INBC. Nestlé's chief executive, Mr. Helmut Maucher, had given the responsibility for bringing the controversy to an honourable conclusion to Dr. Carl Angst; the latter, however, was available only on 25 January 1984 to sign an agreement with a high-ranking church leader representing INBC. No other opportunity would be available, due to demands on his time, for several weeks. Neither side wished to lose the momentum or see the terms of the agreement leaked.

On the other hand, INBC represented an international constituency and had planned to reach a decision on the future of the boycott at its conference in Mexico, scheduled for early February (see p. 137). The INBC representatives at the meetings hosted by UNICEF were all American, with the exception of a Canadian who had attended in the later stages, and it was therefore necessary for INBC to consult overseas supporters.

Boycott Suspension

Agreement to suspend the boycott for a period of six months was obtained following an international telephone conference call on 24 January 1984. Next, agreement had to be reached between Nestlé and INBC on a joint declaration, on the form of the signing ceremony and on the announcements to be made to the press.

After many hours of discussion, the following joint statement of INBC and Nestlé was finalised:

The International Nestlé Boycott Committee has decided to suspend its international boycott of Nestlé Company products.

Over the last decade a controversy has grown over the proper role of infant formula in the Third World, ways of marketing the products there, and the health hazards for infants resulting from improper use.

Much of this controversy has been directed at infant formula manufacturers, and in 1977 INFACT, supported by other organizations, initiated a boycott of the products of Nestlé, the world's largest manufacturer of infant formula.

Out of concern for the health of infants, the World Health Assembly in May 1981 adopted the International Code of Marketing of Breast Milk Substitutes (WHO/UNICEF Code) which provides guidelines to industry, governments, health authorities and non-governmental organizations. Nestlé made a firm commitment to implement that code. Since that time there has been considerable pressure on all infant formula companies to fully comply with the Code, and much progress has been made.

INBC continued to express concern about differences it had with Nestlé's interpretation of some provisions of the Code. In December 1983, INBC announced four areas of concern: educational materials, hazard warnings on labels, gifts to health professionals and free supplies to hospitals. Both Nestlé and INBC sought further explanation and guidance from WHO and UNICEF on these areas of the Code.

As a result of intensive discussions involving UNICEF, Nestlé further clarified its policies in these four areas of concern and INBC has recommended a suspension of the boycott.

Both parties praise UNICEF's assistance in clarifying provisions of the Code.

INBC commends Nestlé for taking the leadership role in Industry's compliance with the International Code.

Nestlé recognizes and supports the commitment of INBC and its members to safeguard the children of the Third World from hazards related to the inappropriate marketing of infant formula.

On Wednesday 25 January 1984, the joint statement was signed in a ceremony at a New York hotel, by Dr. Carl L. Angst and Mr. William P. Thompson, Co-stated Clerk of the Presbyterian Church, representing the International Nestlé Boycott Committee. The latter, incidentally, had been President of the National Council of Churches of Christ when it officially endorsed the Nestlé Boycott (see pp. 77–78).

Even up to the very last minute, the agreement could have fallen through. In his opening statement, Mr. Thompson pointed out that INBC did not accept two elements of Nestlé policy. First, INBC maintained that Nestlé should apply the Code in Europe in the same way as it does in the developing countries, and secondly, INBC continued to disagree with the inclusion of pack shots on instruction leaflets. However, these areas of disagreement would not impede the decision to suspend the boycott. At the same time, however, INBC still had lingering doubts about Nestlé commitment with regard to the supplies question and wanted further clarification.

It was as if the endless debates of the preceding two weeks were about to be re-opened. Nevertheless, Dr. Angst launched into an explanation of the Company policy. He stated his regret that discharge tins should be eliminated since he believed they provide a genuine service to mothers. However, Nestlé accepted UNICEF views on the matter, and would cooperate in efforts to prevent their distribution. On the other hand, Nestlé could not be expected to eliminate them single-handed, unless the object was for the Company to go out of business. He hoped that the wording in the Nestlé *Statement of Understanding* was acceptable. Mr. Thompson then asked whether the Company's commitment to implement the steps outlined in Attachment 2 of the *Statement* depended on action being taken simultaneously by competitors. On being told that moving ahead with the procedure depended only on the clarification to be provided by WHO and UNICEF, Mr. Thompson stated his satisfaction with this response and the INBC/Nestlé joint declaration was duly signed.

Company executives and INBC supporters, who had been bitter adversaries for years, suddenly found themselves sitting together at a lunch hosted by Nestlé. Even more extraordinary was the scene the following day, when Nestlé and INBC representatives faced the media at a joint press conference held in Washington. There was Douglas Johnson, chairman of INFACT and author of the infamous Nestlé Boycott fund-raising letters (see p. 96), making the following statement:

Nestlé has moved forward to become a model for the whole industry, a model which creates a new standard of corporate behaviour. This will protect the health and lives of infants around the world from the abuses of marketing at any cost. In this commitment our interests, and Nestlé's have become parallel. [8]

He went on to announce that INFACT was suspending all boycott-related activity against the Nestlé Company, and would urge "colleague activist organizations" building the Nestlé boycott in nine other countries to support the INBC recommendations.

Termination of the Nestlé Boycott

In spite of some grumbling at the INBC–IBFAN Conference in Mexico about lack of consultation by the INBC leadership with INBC supporters in reaching the agreement with Nestlé, the decision to suspend the boycott was confirmed.

In the following months many of the organisations which were still officially boycotting Nestlé decided to withdraw their support without waiting for the "official" termination.

Nestlé immediately went to work to implement the agreements. PATH (Program for Appropriate Technology in Health) was commissioned to begin field-work on appropriate hazard warnings and other messages required by the Code, WHO, UNICEF and INBC being consulted at each stage in the process. The results of the research have now been incorporated into new labels and educational materials throughout the world, and the development process has been described in a detailed paper as an example of cooperation between multinational corporations and private voluntary organisations [9].

A list of inexpensive materials of professional utility that could be given to individual health workers was drawn up, and instructions given to Nestlé operating companies to eliminate all gifts of a personal nature to health workers.

Once again, however, the major difficulty proved to be in implementing the agreement on donations of infant formula: the "supplies" question. It will be recalled that the Nestlé commitment concerned support for a definition to be provided by WHO and UNICEF. However, in the heat of the moment it appears that in making the commitment to provide a definition the UNICEF staff had omitted to consult with their WHO colleagues. No sooner was the ink dry on the Nestlé/INBC agreemeent than WHO officials were informing all concerned that neither WHO nor UNICEF was in a position to interpret the Code, and that the responsibility for defining "infants who need to be fed on breast milk substitutes" lay with the competent health authorities on the basis of the health and economic circumstances in each case.

Efforts were then made to work out a process by which a number of countries would request WHO assistance in developing guidelines which could then be circulated to all member states as a model for action. Nestlé and INBC agreed to participate in the development process. This plan had made little progress by September 1984 and what had been the key concession made by Nestlé in the January 1984 agreement looked increasingly hollow.[1] The question was, how would this problem, which was beyond the control of either Nestlé or INBC, affect the decision with regard to the termination of the boycott? A meeting of INBC had been scheduled for late September to consider this question.

Nestlé policy with regard to "supplies" and, more specifically, "discharge tins", continued to be the main focus of attention. These concerns were expressed in person to Dr. Carl Angst during a visit to Nestlé headquarters in Switzerland, by Mr. William Thompson, on 25 September. As a result of the discussions between the two, Dr. Angst sent the following telex to INBC leadership in New York:

I agree that, in order to remove even the slightest risk of discouraging breast-feeding and to prevent any possibility of even unwillingly promoting routinisation of bottle-feeding, discharge packs should be stopped. While this has been our stated objective ever since our New York meeting of January 1984, I also had to make it clear at the same time that a single member of industry cannot bring about this change in isolation and that therefore a cooperative effort is required. I also stated in January in New York – and I repeat it – that Nestlé would welcome and even initiate such an effort. It must be recognised that it would be an empty gesture for Nestlé to apply such a policy unilaterally since other manufacturers would simply fill the gap and the objective of encouraging mothers to breast-feed would not be achieved. Therefore, if a meeting could be convened between WHO, UNICEF, INBC and Nestlé, I pledge our wholehearted support to achieve the objective of stopping discharge tins with the proviso of multilateral action as expressed above.

I would wholeheartedly welcome if this conference could at the same time, thoroughly review the list of utility items to make sure that none of these items could be construed as having a promotional effect.

This telex was read by Mr. Thompson prior to sending it.

At the same time, the European supporters of INBC, who had felt somewhat excluded from the process leading to the suspension of the boycott in January, were insisting that in addition to the original four points raised by INBC, Nestlé should also recognise the concept of universality of the Code. In effect this meant committing the Company to working for the application of the International Code in Europe as well as in the developing countries.

---

[1] The question was finally resolved only in May 1986, when the 39th World Health Assembly formally endorsed *Guidelines* on the subject which were to be addressed to member states [10] and thus provided the "definition" originally promised in January 1984. Nestlé then put into effect the process described in the *Statement of Understanding* (Appendix 2, attachment 2). However, as of the date of writing controversy on this subject is not fully resolved. The World Health Assembly Resolution also urges governments to ensure that maternity wards and hospitals obtain "the small amounts of breast milk substitutes needed", through "normal procurement channels", and not through free or subsidised supplies [11]. INBC claims that this resolution clarified Section 6.6 of the WHO Code, and that Nestlé should now implement "WHO policy on free supplies regardless of actions by competitors or governments" [12].

In response to this demand, a letter was written to the INBC European Coordinator [13], making it clear that the Company was in favour of "strong national codes which give practical effect to the principles and aims of the WHO Code, as required by Article 11.1". It went on to say that Nestlé would be willing to make this position public, and within the limits of its capabilities, to cooperate in the review of national codes where necessary.[1]

By way of recapitulation of the action taken by Nestlé since January 1984, NCCN issued an Addendum to the Nestlé *Statement of Understanding* on 25 September (Appendix 3 p. 161). The ball was now in the INBC court. On 1 October 1984, Douglas Johnson telexed the INBC decision to Dr. Angst:

Your commitments, together with the prior plans and progress Nestlé has made, enabled us as the INBC Steering Committee to pass the following resolution:

"Because of the progress made, and in process, in implementing the International Code and the joint agreement, and the written commitments from Nestlé for further progress, the INBC Steering Committee shall: adopt a strategy of compliance and accountability and act to resolve the remaining critical issues with the Nestlé Corporation, and recommend to its member organizations that the current International Boycott of Nestlé be terminated."

On 4 October the INBC decision was announced at a press conference held at the famous Mayflower Hotel in Washington, owned by Nestlé and run by the Company's Stouffer Hotels subsidiary (which had itself been a frequent target for boycott activity by INFACT over the previous 7 years). Once again the INBC leadership shared the platform with Nestlé representatives, including Dr. Angst (who had been unable to attend the previous joint press conference). Senator Muskie, whose Nestlé Infant Formula Audit Commission had played such a vital part in advising Nestlé on its Code implementation measures, was also on the platform.

While the INBC speakers did not give Nestlé a "clean bill of health", they recognised that the commitment of Nestlé management, personified by the presence of one of its most senior members "is visible not only here in the room, but is visible in the field." They referred to the need for further improvement and continued dialogue between the Company and INBC, but stressed that the termination of the international boycott permits the international movement to redirect its energies to other companies [14].

In reply, Dr. Angst acknowledged that the Company had learned much from the experience of the past years of conflict. Inappropriate preparation of infant formula was probably a greater problem than Nestlé had realised in the past, and there was now a clear commitment to avoid any practices which might discourage breast-feeding. On the other hand, there had never been any doubt in Nestlé's mind that breast milk substitutes filled a real need. He paid tribute to all concerned for being able to bridge their differences, to the help and advice given by WHO, and above all to the dedication of the members of the Muskie Commission, which had pioneered a new concept in corporate responsibility.

It is a matter of record that the Nestlé boycott ended on a positive note. The agreement reached after an international debate which had lasted over 10 years was almost beyond belief when viewed in the context of the bitter confrontations

---

[1] National Codes closely based on the International Code have been introduced in Denmark, Norway, Sweden and Portugal. A draft Directive on the approximation of the laws relating to infant formula and follow-up milks was submitted to the Council of European Communities by the European Commission in October 1986. It embodies most of the provisions relating to marketing practices contained in the International Code.

which preceded it. No doubt, the general satisfaction and good will which prevailed concealed a certain lassitude and a measure of scepticism, even bitterness. Yet at the same time there was a spirit of optimism. After all, it was the first time that concern over the fate of babies in impoverished communities, who have no voice of their own, had exercised the minds and energies of the scientific community, international agencies, the health authorities of 160 countries, churches, Industry, the media, and wide sections of public opinion. In spite of all the conflicting interests, attitudes, personalities and motivations, both declared and undeclared, common ground had been found. From beginning to end, the Nestlé boycott had been a paradox. Was it a precedent, showing the way to resolve major world issues like disease, hunger, poverty and all the other evils afflicting the developing world, through consensus reached after a period of confrontation? Or was it simply one of those skirmishes which end up by arming the adversaries for future economic or social conflict? These crucial questions must be answered elsewhere. On that day in Washington at least, there was real hope.

References

1   IBFAN News (1983) April IBFAN, Minneapolis
2   Church of the Brethren (1983) Letter to NCCN, 21 October 1983
3   International Code of Marketing of Breast Milk Substitutes, Art. 4.2 and 9.2
4   International Code of Marketing of Breast Milk Substitutes, Art. 4.2
5   Nestlé Infant Formula Audit Commission (1983) Quarterly Report No. 5, for the period ending 30 September 1983
6   WHO/UNICEF (1982) Notes on the international code of marketing of breast milk substitutes. WHO/UNICEF/IC/July 1982
7   Department of Health and Social Security (1983) Health Circular (HC(83)13) Health services development, international code of marketing of breast milk substitutes. July 1983
8   Johnson Douglas A (National Chairperson Infant Formula Action Coalition (INFACT)) (1984) Statement. INFACT, Washington DC, 26 January 1984
9   Wittet S, Zimmerman M (1987) Implementing the World Health Organization Code: improved information for mothers. J Nutr Ed 19: 73–76
10 WHO Guidelines (1986) Concerning the main health and socioeconomic circumstances in which infants have to be fed on breastmilk substitutes, WHO, A39/8 Add.1, 10 April 1986
11 World Health Assembly Resolution 39.28 (1986) Infant and young child feeding para 2(6), 16 May 1986
12 International Negotiators for Babyfood Code Compliance (INBC) (1986) Letter addressed to Mr. H Maucher, Managing Director, Nestlé SA, 13 October 1986
13 Angst CL (1984) Letter to Lisa Woodburn (on behalf of INBC Europe), 17 September 1984
14 Nestlé Coordination Center for Nutrition Inc. (1984) Minutes of press conference, Washington DC, 4 October 1984

Chapter 11

Epilogue

J. Dobbing

The story of this long controversy ends on an encouraging note, corresponding well with today's atmosphere. After so much noise and furor, the infant food industry, like its critics, is as pleased as it is surprised to have found some common understanding. It must be remembered that the great majority of the people who have taken part on both sides of this ethical, social and socio-economic debate have been men and women who have genuinely cared about the public interest and have wanted to behave responsibly.

However, for the spectator, for scientists and doctors, politicians and administrators, sociologists and journalists, it is too facile to conclude that "all's well that ends well". People need a more precise statement about a conflict which is in many ways unique, before deciding what has been learned for the future.

Thus, as my friend Professor Frank Falkner has said in his Foreword, there would be no Code today if there had not been such a confrontation. It remains to be seen, however, if the Code has been observed, whether it has been useful, and whether it serves as a good model in the future to help improve life on this earth.

At the time of writing, in late 1987, it has just been reported that the International Organisation of Consumers' Unions (IOCU), one of the big batallions in the campaign against the infant food industry, has explicitly renounced the idea of a similar Code for the pharmaceutical industry: "The WHO committee is on guidelines, not a code, because . . . a code in any case is unenforceable . . .", Dr. Andrew Herxheimer, chairman of the IOCU Health Working Group, is reported as saying in a press interview at the XII World Congress of the IOCU [1]. It is not difficult to see why. "There isn't anybody who could enforce a code . . .". It may therefore be that the Code which has been the subject of so much of our book will turn out to be a unique example of the species, produced by the exceptional circumstances we have described.

When the campaign against the infant food industry began, in the early 1970s, many factors played a part which have either disappeared, or are still with us, but in a very attenuated form. Firstly this was the era of large, highly political offensives against the "multinationals", in which the realities of economic and human problems played little part. The "Multinational Menace" was denounced with extravagant prophesies: "Today three hundred multinationals dominate the world; there will be only 200 in 1990, 50 at the turn of the century, and it may be we shall see only one Company controlling economics as well as politics in the twenty-first century" [2]. Such predictions are now very rarely heard. A Multinational Monster has not been discovered in the Loss Ness of Economics.

In addition, the industry was at first taken aback by the violence of the attacks against it. As lately as 1982, it was still being accused by one of the main French consumer groups of causing 10 million deaths each year [3]. Had this been true, it would have been by far the biggest case of genocide ever known, and it would have been surprising, to say the least, that health ministries around the world were unaware of it. Little by little Industry recovered from its stupor and decided to defend itself. Public opinion has also learned a hard lesson, which it had neglected at the time of post-war prosperity and of the ideological light-headedness which accompanied it: that the wealth of nations and of people is created by commercial enterprise. It is striking how much more moderate the international agencies have become over the practicalities as well as the legalities of Codes like that on infant feeding. Many distinguished experts, notably in these agencies, have come to accept that their rôle is not that of legislators in a world super-administration. They are coordinators, counsellors, guides, and, when the situation demands it, critics; but they are not "geo-bureaucrats" with directive powers over world affairs, a rôle which had little influence at the national level.

In short the controversy is an example to study, rather than a model to follow.

I would say that its dividends lie firstly in having helped to awaken a consciousness throughout industry, not only of the effects of its products on society, but also of the way the public sees them; and although industrialists have often taken this into account, they have not always understood the charges which can be laid at their door.

In another way, many a responsible political leader, especially in the Third World, feared, not entirely without reason, that Nestlé (for example) would get out of the infant food market in their countries and revert to the large, burgeoning markets of the industrialised world; and in this way the less-developed countries would find themselves in the inconsistency of taking the part of the critics of multinational industry, while at the same time trying to persuade that same industry to invest there.

Let us also note the decisive support that was given to the campaign by the Churches, by groups of well-meaning and well-concerned citizens, journalists and others. These people have come to understand that their quite reasonable feelings have sometimes been exploited, and today many of them have become much more circumspect. The tragic term "charity business" was coined in the 1980s to describe the abuse of people's generosity. This has certainly not diminished our awareness of our common, human brotherhood, which has never been more recognised; but people are now beginning to appreciate the need to understand the complex causes of world problems, so that they may be more effective in helping to solve them.

Experience in the field has led many activists to be better organised, as well as more realistic and more responsible than they have sometimes been in the last decade. With hindsight, it is astonishing how the originators of the conflict were so lacking in understanding and balance. Nowadays, however, we see citizen's organisations acting with a newly-found maturity; and this is important progress.

Although the expenditure in time, energy and resources may seem dispro-portionate to any concrete improvements achieved, the very least we can say about this long and drawn-out conflict is that it was a valuable experience. In the final analysis, all sides of the debate are united in their desire to solve the immense health problems which used to be accepted with resignation. If, as a result of the lessons learned, adversaries who were previously locked in confrontation can come to understand each other better and actually combine their energies in a common cause, then the experience will not have been in vain. It is with this hope that we have attempted to describe the anatomy of this controversy as completely and objectively as we know how.

References

1 Anonymous (1987) XII IOCU Congress: pharmaceutical update. International Barometer, Nov, p 14
2 de Bodinat H (1976) Summarising the statements made by Mumford, Vernon, Perlmutter and others, and the ONU Report 1973 "Les entreprises multinationales, mythes et réalités". Contrepoint Paris 1976, 21
3 Director of the Union Fédérale des Consommateurs (1982) Statement on French national television (Antenne 2), 3 December 1982

Appendix 1

The Nestlé Infant Formula Audit Commission — (NIFAC) Charter

As a result of the adoption by the 34th World Health Assembly of the International Code of Marketing of Breastmilk Substitutes recommended by the World Health Organization (WHO), Nestle has determined to:

1. continue to comply with National Codes for the marketing of infant formula; and

2. apply the internal Nestle Instructions, which have been developed to implement the WHO Code, except for those provisions that are inconsistent with national or local requirements or established governmental policy, as the government deems appropriate to their social and legislative framework and their overall development objectives.

In order to assure that this commitment is translated into practice, Nestle has issued precise instructions to its managers, employees, and agents and is reinforcing its internal monitoring procedures.

The health authorities in each country where the internal Nestle Instructions are to be applied have been duly informed. Nestle is responsible to the government in each country where it sells infant formula for the strict application of the Code in force—whether it be the National Code or the Nestle Instructions for implementing the WHO Code.

Prominent church leaders have proposed that Nestle invite a group, composed of prominent clergymen, medical authorities, civic leaders and experts on international policy issues to form the Nestle Infant Formula Audit Commission. The objective of this Commission is to examine complaints and allegations about Nestle's marketing practices and to satisfy itself that Nestle is honoring its publicly stated commitments in relation to the application of the WHO recommendations.

Article I. *Composition*

The Nestle Infant Formula Audit Commission (the Commission) shall be composed of a chairman and no more than eight members. Nestle (the Company) shall choose the Chairman of the Commission and consult with the Chairman, church leaders and other responsible entities in selecting the members of the Commission.

Article II. *Mission*

The mission of the Commission shall be to apprise the Company of any problems it discovers in the internal investigation and control systems of the company in its application of the WHO or National Codes. It shall answer inquiries from the public, as it deems necessary, regarding Nestle's implementation of the WHO Code or compliance with the applicable National Code.

Article III. *Procedures*

1. Nestle will provide the Commission with up-dated lists of those countries where National Codes apply and those where Nestle Instructions have been accepted by the authorities. It will place at the disposal of the Commission copies of the National Codes in operation, as well as the Nestle

Instructions. Where National Codes are still under development, Nestle will provide whatever information is available on the state of progress.

2. Any individual or organization wishing to query the conformity of specific Nestle activities with the Code applicable in any country may draw its concerns to the attention of the Commission, or to the Company directly. The company will inform the Commission of any such queries it receives directly.

3. The Commission will ascertain whether sufficient information is given to permit serious investigation. Should this not be the case the originator of the query will be requested to complete the standard Investigation Form (Nestle Instructions—attachment 6) and forward it to the Commission.

4. The Commission will forward the completed Investigation Form and any accompanying documentation to the Company.

5. On receipt of the Investigation Form, the Company will immediately conduct its own inquiries in the country concerned. The Company undertakes to report its findings to the Commission and details of any action taken, within 60 days of receiving the Investigation Form (or the original query if this was already adequately documented).

6. The Commission will examine the report provided by Nestle and will inform the company whether, in its opinion, Nestle comments, and handling of the query are in conformity with its publicly stated commitments.

7. Provided there is agreement between the Commission and the Company, the originator of the query will be informed.

8. In case of disagreement or doubt, the Commission may:
   • request further details (documentation, correspondence, etc.) relating to the matter;
   • independently seek the advice of the relevant government authority in the country concerned;
   • conduct an on-the-spot investigation.

9. It is understood that on-site visits will be resorted to only when considered necessary by the Commission. The company undertakes in these cases to provide all necessary cooperation in order for the Commission to determine the facts. The relevant government authorities may be consulted in any on-site investigation by the Commission.

Article IV. *Authority*

1. In accordance with Article 11.2 of the WHO Code, responsibility for monitoring its application lies with governments acting individually or collectively through the World Health Organization.

2. In the event of disagreement between the Commission and the Company on any matter relating to the marketing of infant formula in any country, the decision of the government concerned may be requested jointly by the Commission and Nestle and shall be binding.

Article V. *Budget*

1. The Commission shall have full and total control, under the Chairman, of the annual budget allocated to it by the Company and shall report quarterly on its management and expenditures under that budget to the Company.

2. The Commission shall have appropriate staff paid by the Commission who shall coordinate all affairs of the Commission and shall be chosen by the Chairman and the Company and report to the Chairman of the Commission. Logistical support for the Commission shall principally be provided by the Nestle Coordination Center for Nutrition, Inc. in Washington, D.C. but additional such support shall be available from the Company when required.

Article VI. *Scope*

The function of the Commission shall be strictly limited to Nestle's marketing practices as they apply to infant formula products only. Any and all proprietary information directly or indirectly acquired by the Commission, as concerns infant formula or any other Nestle product or service or practice shall be considered proprietary by the Commission and shall not be divulged during the life of the Commission or thereafter.

Article VII. *Meetings and Reports*

The Commission shall meet anytime at the call of the Chairman, with the Commission itself responsible for determining its own rules for calling such meetings and the nature of such call. In addition, it shall meet once each calendar quarter to review the status of Nestle's implementation of the WHO and National Codes, and review the conduct of Nestle's internal investigations and shall submit a comprehensive written report to the Company. Commission reports may be made available to the public after the company has had a reasonable time (e.g. one month) to respond and comment on said report.

Article VIII. *Liaison*

To facilitate communication on a day-to-day basis, the Commission will maintain continuing liaison with the Company through the Nestle Coordination Center for Nutrition, Inc. in Washington, D.C. The latter will provide such documents as required by the Commission and be responsible for communication with the Company.

Article IX. *Duration*

1. The Commission shall continue in existence for one quarter beyond the May 1983 meeting of the World Health Assembly at which time full reports on implementation of the WHO Code shall be reviewed and amendments to that Code considered.

2. The Commission may make recommendations to Nestle as to the need to extend the Commission's Charter, subject to any mutually agreed changes based on the experience gained.

Article X. *Familiarization*

The Commission shall be thoroughly briefed by the Company as early as convenient in the life of the Commission, regarding Nestle implementation plans, investigation procedures, internal controls, the WHO Code, and National Codes.

Article XI. *Commission Rules*

The Commission shall establish its own rules and procedures for the conduct of its business pursuant to this Charter.

MAY 1982

Appendix 2

Nestlé Statement of Understanding

The following paper delineates Nestlé's understanding of four areas of activity covered by the WHO Code and its policies regarding same.

January 24, 1984

Preamble

Nestlé made a commitment to support the aim and principles of the World Health Organization Code on May 21, 1981, the day it was passed. Throughout the past three years Nestlé has worked hard to keep that commitment, and seeks to effectively implement the Code, but finds itself in the position of having to determine, without being able to obtain official endorsement for its policies, exactly what that commitment to the Code entails.

Initially Nestlé hoped that the 118 nations which voted for the Code would quickly adopt national codes of their own that Nestlé could then follow. When it was pointed out that few developing countries were treating the matter with sufficient priority, Nestlé drew up comprehensive instructions to its markets in all developing countries as to exactly how to follow the WHO Code. Further, pursuant to Article 11.3 of the Code, it established an independent and objective body, the Nestlé Infant Formula Audit Commission (NIFAC), to review the company's application of the Code and to make suggestions as to how the company could better follow the WHO Code.

NIFAC consulted with UNICEF, the WHO and several church bodies and made several recommendations to the company as to changes it thought would make the Nestlé Instructions on the WHO Code more clearly in conformity with the Code. The company adopted those changes in October, 1982.

Since then NIFAC has made other suggestions, and the company, after consultations with WHO and others, has taken additional steps to ensure compliance with the Code.

In the meantime Nestlé has cooperated with NIFAC Chairman Senator Muskie and NIFAC in investigating more than 100 allegations that the company was in violation of the Code, and in remedying any deficiencies in the company's compliance procedures. In addition, the Commission has made several personal inspection trips to developing countries to observe the company's practices and to meet with local health authorities there and has released reports on their findings to the public.

The company has instituted an internal audit function to review and assess its marketing practices with the objective of ensuring that there is full compliance with the instructions relative to the Code in the field.

Now, several church leaders and some of the company's critics have asked Nestlé to review four areas of its compliance with the Code. Nestlé has agreed, and in doing so it is consulting with NIFAC, WHO and UNICEF.

Nestlé is encouraged to see that The International Nestlé Boycott Committee (INBC) and those churches and institutions represented therein have narrowed their concerns down to four points of the Code. Nestlé, with the help of the Commission, has been trying to develop acceptable procedures dealing with these four points.

Educational Materials

Nestlé will continue to seek professional advice from specialized consultants including those recommended by WHO and UNICEF, in the development and field testing of educational materials.

The objective of the field testing is to ensure that these materials help the mother make the best informed choice about the method she decides to use in feeding her baby, after serious consideration of all the consequences of her choice as implied by Article 4.2 of the WHO Code. An additional objective of information dealing with infant formula is to teach and remind the mother about its proper use.[1] As in the past, WHO and UNICEF have assured Nestlé that it can approach them for their advice. Nestlé is committed to this effort and to obtaining results as quickly as possible. Clear information will be included in all materials on all the points recommended by the WHO Code as listed below, (treatment, such as detail and means of presentation of the information, will vary according to the purpose and type of material):

A. Materials dealing with the feeding of infants will include information on:

1. The benefits and superiority of breastfeeding.
2. Maternal nutrition and the preparation for maintenance of breastfeeding.
3. The negative effect of introducing partial bottle feeding on breastfeeding.
4. The difficulty of reversing the decision not to breastfeed.

B. Materials dealing with infant formula will also include information on:

1. Possible health hazards of inappropriate foods or feeding methods; and in particular the health hazards of unnecessary or improper use of infant formula
2. Social and financial consequences of the decision to use infant formula.

Hazard Warning on Labels

The second area of concern is the hazard warning that Nestlé intended to print on its infant formula labels. This warning was developed in concert with NIFAC after consultations with WHO. Some concerned parties, nevertheless, pointed out differences of approach by different manufacturers and claimed that other companies had developed more effective warning statements. The matter was therefore rediscussed with WHO and UNICEF and efforts will be made to develop language that would be meaningful to Third World mothers most likely to need this information. No work has been done as yet to determine, in the field, which form of warning would be most appropriate. The decision was therefore made to test different statements in Third World countries, with the help of specialized consultants recommended by WHO and UNICEF. The purpose of the testing is to ensure that effective warnings are given on the consequences to the health of infants of inappropriate or incorrect use arising from:

1. unclean water
2. dirty utensils
3. improper dilution, and
4. storage of prepared feeds without refrigeration.

While the intended audience of this warning includes all purchasers of the product, this educational message is particularly targeted at low-income, urban and peri-urban mothers.

Nestlé is committed to obtaining results and implementing new warning statements expeditiously as part of an industry-wide solution.

Personal Gifts to Health Professionals

The third area of concern that we were asked to address was that of the provision of "personal gifts" to health professionals. The Code is not very clear on this point since it refers to "financial and material inducements."

Nestlé has already made it clear that it will not provide financial or material inducements to promote the sale of infant formula.

Personal gifts of a non-professional nature, such as chocolates, key-rings, and pens, although not considered inducements, will now be considered inappropriate, and will not be given to health professionals by Nestlé.

The provision of inexpensive materials of professional utility is in line with Article 6.8; it does

---

[1] Nestlé considers that the identification of the product referred to in specific product instructions is an essential element of information (see Attachment 1).

not fall under Article 7.3 of the code. Nestlé will not include proprietary information in such materials.[1]

The distribution of technical and scientific publications, such as the Nestlé Nutrition Workshop Series, is considered to be in accordance with Article 6.8. This distribution is an important service to health professionals and is not to be confused with the question of gifts. No proprietary information (such as product brand advertising) will be included in such publications.

Supplies

The final subject raised was the provision of free or low-cost supplies of infant formula to health institutions. Nestlé recognizes that the church leaders who have raised this subject, as well as NIFAC members and the INBC, have a legitimate reason for concern where these supplies are used as the routine, normative manner of feeding infants in health care institutions.

In the development of the section dealing with supplies in the WHO Code, the World Health Assembly relied heavily on the results of the 1979 WHO/UNICEF Joint Meetings on Infant Feeding where it stated:

Support through the health services

"Health service staff must play a critical role in the initiation, establishment and maintenance of breastfeeding and should ensure that the mother has a source of sustained support for as long as breastfeeding continues, and thus health workers should be well informed and provide consistent information.

A baby who is not breastfed should receive special attention from the health care system. Adequate instructions for the use of infant foods as well as warnings about its problems should be the responsibility of the health care system. Supplies of infant formula would thus be required for distribution only where necessary and not as a routine."

It is for this reason that Nestlé recognizes that the WHO Code is intended to discourage routine bottle feeding in hospitals and that it is important that industry policy be implemented in such a way that the provision of supplies does not bias the decision made by mothers and health professionals on how any infant is to be fed in the hospital.

Nestlé therefore recognizes and supports the aim and spirit of the provisions of the Code regarding limitations on the use of supplies to infants who have to be fed on breastmilk substitutes. It is recognized, however, that the definition of this term, "infants who have to be fed on breastmilk substitutes," requires further clarification in order to give practical guidelines to industry in its procedures for implementation, and to assist health professionals in reaching their decisions. The goal of Nestlé policy is to restrict the distribution of supplies to three areas of need: medical, economic and social.

Nestlé requests that these terms be further defined by WHO and UNICEF and that they then be communicated to health authorities and industry as the basis for government and company policies. Nestlé recognizes that industry has a responsibility together with the health care system in limiting the provision of supplies to these defined needs, once defined, and will ensure that hospital administrators are aware of Nestlé policy so that requests for free supplies will be formulated in the context of these needs only.

At the same time, Nestlé offers cooperation to WHO and UNICEF in ensuring that the limitation of supplies to meet real needs as specified by the Code is uniformly applied. Nestlé will therefore write to the health authorities in all Third World countries where Nestlé sells infant formula recommending that the WHO/UNICEF policy on supplies, once defined, be supported and implemented, and requesting precise government guidelines to health care institutions and industry.

This process could be facilitated by regional or national seminars involving all concerned, sponsored by WHO and UNICEF. Nestlé is ready to participate in such efforts.

The process should include, in addition to clarification and explanation of the term "infants who have to be fed on breastmilk substitutes":

— communication of the clarification and education of all concerned.

— implementation of the necessary procedures by health authorities and industry to limit supplies at the hospital and clinic level in accordance with that clarification.

Attachment 2 explains the procedure for adopting the Nestlé supply policy.

---

[1] Nestlé will establish a list of accepted items falling under this definition. This will be sent to the markets. A market which wants to distribute an item not covered by the list will be required to obtain specific clearance from Vevey. This list will also be made available to NIFAC for use in their auditing procedures.

Conclusion

Nestlé has acted in good faith to fulfill its commitment to the WHO Code. This commitment is firm. The WHO recommendations provide an agreed framework for the marketing of infant formula. In spite of its imperfections, inevitable in an international consensus of this nature, the Code helps to define the role of the infant food industry in ensuring safe and adequate nutrition for infants. We take this issue very seriously, and we will remain firm in our commitment.

Attachment 1

Pack Shots

Nestlé includes a product illustration (pack shot) on product instruction leaflets to be given to a mother by a health professional *after* a decision to use that product has been made. Nestlé considers this product identification to be an important element of information which helps to ensure that the mother purchases the product to which the instructions refer. If the mother purchases another product, to which the instructions *do not* apply, this could result in serious misuse of that product and be harmful to the health of the baby. The WHO Code seeks to minimize risks of misuse.

In consulting with the UNICEF staff on this issue, Nestlé was told that, in their opinion, such a product illustration is "promotional" in nature and therefore not in accord with Article 4.3 of the WHO Code. Nestlé would like further clarification from WHO and UNICEF as to how they define the difference between "promotion" and "information." Nestlé accepts that product instruction leaflets should not be given to mothers by health professionals after a decision to bottle feed has been made. Their purpose is therefore to ensure safe and correct use. They should not be used for promotional purposes.

These instruction leaflets will be developed in the future after consultation with WHO and UNICEF and as recommended and field tested by recognized Health Communications consultants to ensure that:
— they cannot be mistaken for promotional material.
— that the information on how *that* particular product is to be used will include effective warnings on the consequences to the health of infants of inappropriate or incorrect use.
— they contain all the information required by the WHO Code, Article 4.2.

Nestlé will make every effort to ensure that specific product instructions are not given to mothers who do not need them. Therefore, Nestlé personnel will give these materials only to health professionals and will strongly request that such product instructions not be displayed publicly in hospitals or other health care facilities.

Attachment 2

Summary of Procedure for Adopting the Nestlé Supply Policy

As company policy, Nestlé's goal is to have free or low-cost formula supplied to hospitals used only for infants who "have to be fed" on breastmilk substitutes within the health facility, except as provided for in Article 6.7 of the Code. This goal must apply to the entire industry.

In order to implement this policy, Nestlé believes that the following steps should be taken in the process of developing that policy by the entire industry and the health care system:
1. WHO/UNICEF define the term "have to be fed," to include consideration of the status of mothers who exercise their rights to free choice not to breastfeed. Nestlé will support the WHO/UNICEF definition with health care systems.
2. That definition will be transmitted to health authorities by WHO and UNICEF.
3. Nestlé will cooperate with WHO/UNICEF in the implementation of educational programs for the health community that clarify the term "have to be fed."
4. Nestlé will design its supply request forms reflecting only those uses intended by the Code, and will fill requests only for those uses.
5. Nestlé will keep careful account of amounts of formula being provided to hospitals.

6. If amounts of formula requested appear to be incongruent with reasonable needs for free supplies as outlined above, this will be taken into account in filling future requests for supplies.

It is obvious that this process of implementation, involving WHO, UNICEF, health ministers, health administrators and other concerned parties and industry requires adequate time to accomplish, and that each party must do its part if we are to succeed in our goal. Nestlé reiterates its commitment to implementation of the WHO Code in all its facets and hopes that all concerned parties can move forward expeditiously and without unnecessary delay, so as to facilitate the promotion of breastfeeding in hospitals and assure standard practices by all manufacturers and hospital administrators.

Appendix 3

ADDENDUM
To The
Nestle Statement of Understanding
September 25, 1984

On January 24, 1984 Nestle issued its *Statement of Understanding*, delineating the Company's understanding of four areas of activity covered by the World Health Organization Code of Marketing of Breastmilk Substitutes and Nestle's policies regarding those areas. The *Statement of Understanding* laid out specific steps that Nestle was taking in the continued implementation of the WHO Code. The statement was the result of clarifications of ambiguous sections of the WHO Code made by UNICEF and WHO at the request of Nestle and the International Nestle Boycott Committee, with participation of the Nestle Infant Formula Audit Commission (the Muskie Commission).

The *Statement of Understanding* included four areas of clarification: the information to be included in educational materials, the wording of hazard warnings on infant formula labels, the provision of free materials to health workers, and the provision of free or low-cost supplies to health facilities. Nestle indicated that it would move as expeditiously as possible in the implementation of specific steps in these four areas. During the eight months which have passed since the issuance of the *Statement of Understanding*, Nestle has done all within its power to put into action the steps it had outlined in the Statement. Described below are the steps which Nestle has taken in a very short period of time, moving as expeditiously as was humanly possible in implementing action within the four areas.

During the infant formula controversy, one of the most complex issues to deal with has been the provision and utilization of supplies provided to hospitals. Nestle has taken this question quite seriously and has consulted with church leaders, WHO, UNICEF, the Muskie Commission, and health experts in various countries.

Over one year ago, Nestle issued a clear policy that Nestle-provided supplies were not to be used in any way which would discourage breastfeeding, nor should they be provided as "discharge packs" to breastfeeding mothers leaving the hospital.

As a further major step, a letter is presently being sent by all Nestle affiliates in developing countries to health ministers where Nestle markets formula, strongly conveying that routinization of bottlefeeding and provision of "discharge packs" should be stopped, irrespective of method of feeding. For Nestle to apply such a policy, the governments must issue clear directives addressed to all health care facilities and to all infant formula manufacturers.

Nestle has offered its complete cooperation and support in the development of such directives, both in collaboration with national governments and together with plans developed by WHO/UNICEF. Such a plan is presently underway.

Once such directives are developed by governments, Nestle will move expeditiously to apply them since, as directives, they will be binding. Nestle is confident of their application by all parties concerned including all formula industries, hospitals, and clinics.

In summary, at present, Nestle is against the provision of "discharge tins" for breastfeeding mothers. We have notified hospitals of this policy. However, the company's goal is to seek an end to the provision of "discharge tins" by all health systems and industry in developing countries for all mothers, whether breastfeeding or not. This policy is to be developed by sovereign governments under the WHO Code and applied to all as soon as is practical.

Hazard Warnings on Labels
The development of new hazard warnings for labels has precipitated a redesign of the entire informational section of the label, including a new feeding table, new, full-colour pictorial instructions for preparation, new written instructions for preparation, and a complete redesign of the spatial

configuration of the label elements. The hazard warnings and other components went through extensive field testing with low-income periurban mothers in Mexico, the Philippines and Kenya, conducted by an independent research organization (Program for Appropriate Technology in Health, PATH) specializing in appropriate technology for developing countries.

The labels were repeatedly reviewed with WHO and UNICEF at various stages of development, and the International Nestle Boycott Committee was included in discussions concerning the development of hazard warnings and instructions.

The development process has been completed, and the new designs now move into the production phase, with the first labels being used in production lines by January, 1985.

Educational Materials

Nestle committed to field test the six points concerning breastfeeding and formula feeding of Article 4.2 of the WHO Code which will be included in all educational material over which Nestle has editorial control. The testing is being carried out with third-world mothers of varying socio-economic levels. The first stage of testing was completed in May, 1984, in conjunction with the testing of hazard warnings for labels. The second stage, to be completed by September 30, is presently being carried out by PATH in the Philippines. Over 70 pictures and alternative statements are being tested in the local language for development of the most effective means of conveying the six areas of concern in Article 4.2 of the Code.

PATH will prepare a report of its test findings concerning the development of statements and selection of pictures by October 15, 1984. Complete development of statements and of pictorial representations is targeted to be complete by the beginning of 1985.

The statements and/or pictures will be required material not only in educational materials for mothers, but will also be used in educational materials aimed at health professionals. Treatment, such as detail and means of presentation of the information will vary according to type of information and spatial restrictions. As with the design of labels, UNICEF and WHO will be consulted at every step of the process, and INBC is being included at critical steps of development.

Personal Gifts to Health Professionals

As of May, 1984, all personal gifts to health professionals have been eliminated. Instead, only items of professional utility of modest value may be given to health professionals. These items are restricted to an international list developed by Nestle which contains 16 items. The list has been shown to UNICEF and WHO for response, and their reactions will be taken into account in further refinement of the list.

Supplies to Health Facilities

In the January *Statement of Understanding*, Nestle made it clear that it supported the goal of discouraging routine bottle feeding in hospitals and that formula be provided to "infants who have to be fed breastmilk substitutes", as defined by medical, economic and social need.

If WHO/UNICEF were willing to issue a definition of the term "have to be fed" and would transmit that definition to health authorities, Nestle would redesign its supply request forms, and keep track of amounts of formula being provided. At the present time, if amounts of formula requested appeared to be incongruent with reasonable needs for free supplies, this would be taken into account in filling future requests for supplies.

Instead of a definition, WHO, through Dr. David Tejada-de-Rivero, has offered a process whereby WHO and UNICEF can give technical advice to governments, who will develop definitions based on that advice, with input from industry and consumer groups. WHO views this process as most appropriate, as it is the role of sovereign governments, acting individually and collectively in the World Health Assembly, to issue definitions. UNICEF has agreed to actively participate with WHO in this plan, and the first steps of implementation have begun. While this process is longer and more time-consuming than what was originally requested of WHO/UNICEF, it is the clear response of the world's highest health organizations, and Nestle will respect and support the process which has been suggested. Nestle will also encourage the active participation of the international infant formula consumer activists groups. In addition, Nestle will support whatever technical advice is offered by WHO/UNICEF and will encourage governments to develop strong enforceable definitions which apply to all sectors of the health system and to all members of industry.

Nestle also continues an active program encouraging the various religious denominations involved in the infant formula question to use their influence through health institutions operated by those churches and through local church bodies to see that the WHO Code is implemented as soon as possible.

New Steps Taken by Nestle After Consultation with WHO

In all advice received from WHO on the issue of use of supplies, both inside and outside the health facility it has been made clear that the implementation of Articles 6.6 and 6.7 of the Code involve the direct responsibilities of governments. Thus, Nestle is taking the additional unilateral step, independent of the plan suggested by Dr. Tejada, of making it clear to Nestle affiliates that "Nestle is committed to the objective of eliminating the use of free supplies as discharge packs." The following letter has been sent to managers of Nestle affiliates:

Letter to Markets

Infant Formula Supplies
WHO CODE

As you know, in 1983, after detailed consultation with the Muskie Commission, we advised hospitals everywhere that it is against our policy for free infant formula supplied under the terms of art. 6.6 WHO Code, to be given to breastfeeding mothers on their discharge from the maternity.

At that time, Nestle considered that if the hospital professional staff provided a discharge tin to a mother whose baby had been *bottle-fed* in the hospital, this filled a legitimate social need under the terms of the Code. This view was not shared by UNICEF staff. They considered that whether the mother was breastfeeding or not, the provision of a discharge tin must be regarded as "sampling" (art. 5.2 of the Code) and therefore should not be allowed. In the opinion of UNICEF, the only circumstances under which a mother should receive free infant formula on leaving the hospital, would be under the terms of article 6.7—i.e. the free supply should be continued for as long as bottlefeeding is necessary.

Under the terms of the January agreements between Nestle and INBC, it had been anticipated that this matter would be resolved once and for all by an official clarification of articles 6.6 and 6.7 to be provided by WHO and UNICEF. Unfortunately, such a clarification cannot be provided since the responsibility for interpreting and implementing the WHO Code lies with governments. However, after further consultation with WHO and UNICEF, as well as other parties concerned in the January 1984 agreement, it has now been decided to inform the health authorities in all developing countries that Nestle strongly supports the objective to eliminate the routine distribution of free discharge packs of infant formula.

At the same time, it must be made clear that this objective only makes sense if the same policy is accepted by the health services and is adopted by the entire industry, within the context of clear government directives. If this is not the case, Nestle infant formula will simply be replaced by competitive products, and distribution of infant formula discharge packs will continue to be routine practice in many third world hospitals. However, I believe that ultimately our competitors will co-operate notwithstanding the discouraging experience made to date.

In order to stimulate action, I am enclosing the text of a letter to be sent to the ministers of health as soon as possible (see Attachment). It is important to emphasize that Nestle does not wish to interfere in matters of government policy, but rather offers its cooperation in resolving one of the most difficult issues in the WHO Code. The reason for this difficulty resides in the fact that articles 6.6 and 6.7 involve the direct responsibility of governments. Nestle is committed to the objective of eliminating the use of free infant formula supplies as discharge packs, but cannot be placed in the position of having to "police" health care facilities. Therefore, I am asking you to request the authorities to issue directives concerning the WHO Code, articles 5.2, 6.6 and 6.7, addressed to all health care facilities and industry.

Please keep me informed of developments."

As is clear from the letter, Nestle has taken unusual action in strongly conveying to governments that routinization of bottlefeeding and provision of "discharge packs" should be stopped. Nestle has assumed, and will continue to assume, a leadership position in the development of policies and national guidelines that are truly effective in preventing the misuse of formula and in encouraging patterns of breastfeeding. Nestle offers its full collaboration to the World Health Organization, UNICEF, and national governments in this process.

Summary

On the basis of the extensive efforts which Nestle has undertaken in the past eight months, it is clear that all possible steps have been taken to implement the *Statement of Understanding* within the envisioned time frame. Nestle pledges itself to continue to cooperate with WHO, UNICEF, national governments, and concerned citizen groups in taking a leadership role in the implementation of the WHO Code. Our commitment is unchanged.

Attachment

"To the Minister of Health

Donation of Infant Formula

As you know, Nestle has expressed its total support for the WHO Code of Marketing of Breastmilk Substitutes and has issued strict implementation instructions to all its personnel.

Based on our experience in applying the Code, on the advice of WHO, UNICEF, the Nestle Infant Formula Audit Commission chaired by Senator E. Muskie, and other concerned parties, we have refined some of our implementation procedures since they were first announced in February 1982. One important problem area remains, however; the application of articles 6.6 and 6.7 concerning the donation of infant formula supplies to health care facilities. We have made it clear that Nestle will only consider donating infant formula on the basis of a written request by responsible health workers, and that use must be restricted to infants who have to be fed on breastmilk substitutes. Furthermore, Nestle stipulated in a letter to hospital administrators (date) that, if it is the hospital practice to give discharge packs of infant formula, it would conflict with the spirit of the WHO Code if these were given to breast feeding mothers.

We considered this policy to be consistent with the spirit and letter of the WHO Code, but unfortunately, we have enountered two problems.

- First, there are widely differing interpretations of the term "infants who have to be fed on breastmilk substitutes." UNICEF offered to work with WHO in providing an official clarification of the Code on this point, but have made it clear that the Code can only be interpreted by Member States individually, or collectively (at the World Health Assembly)

- The second problem is that we have been advised by UNICEF staff that it is a violation of art. 5.2 of the WHO Code for hospitals to give mothers, whether breastfeeding or bottlefeeding, tins of infant formula on their discharge from the maternity. Even if this is done without the knowledge or approval of Nestle, the company is considered in such cases to be providing samples to mothers indirectly. The UNICEF view is that Nestle should advise the hospital against this practice, and if it persists, refuse to donate further supplies of infant formula to that hospital, i.e. in effect, imposing sanctions.

Nestle is committed to protecting breastfeeding and recognizes that the routinization of bottlefeeding in maternity clinics is an important factor in discouraging mothers from breastfeeding. We are therefore committed to a policy of co-operation aimed at eliminating the routine distribution of free discharge tins of infant formula to mothers. On the other hand, we recognize that it would be an empty gesture for Nestle to apply such a policy unilaterally, since other manufacturers would simply fill the gap and the objective of encouraging mothers to breast feed would not be achieved. Even more important is the fact that for industry to apply such a policy would imply industry monitoring of hospital practices which we find unacceptable and, we believe, so would you.

We have therefore informed WHO and UNICEF that Nestle can only apply such a policy in the context of clear government directives addressed to all health care facilities and to all infant formula manufacturers. We have also stated that we will lend our entire co-operation to governments in formulating policies in this important area. It is for this reason that I take the liberty of writing to you today. I would respectfully request guidance of your Ministry in this matter, and are at your entire disposal to participate in joint consultations or any other measures you deem appropriate to resolve this question."

Subject Index